ROUTLEDGE LIBRARY EDITIONS:
TRANSPORT ECONOMICS

Volume 6

DEREGULATION AND TRANSPORT

DEREGULATION AND TRANSPORT

Market Forces in the Modern World

Edited by
PHILIP BELL AND PAUL CLOKE

Routledge
Taylor & Francis Group

LONDON AND NEW YORK

First published in 1990 by David Fulton Publishers

This edition first published in 2017
by Routledge
2 Park Square, Milton Park, Abingdon, Oxon OX14 4RN

and by Routledge
711 Third Avenue, New York, NY 10017

Routledge is an imprint of the Taylor & Francis Group, an informa business

British Library Cataloguing in Publication Data
A catalogue record for this book is available from the British Library

ISBN: 978-0-415-78484-9 (Set)
ISBN: 978-1-315-20175-7 (Set) (ebk)
ISBN: 978-0-415-79356-8 (Volume 6) (hbk)
ISBN: 978-1-315-21085-8 (Volume 6) (ebk)

Publisher's Note
The publisher has gone to great lengths to ensure the quality of this reprint but points out that some imperfections in the original copies may be apparent.

Disclaimer
The publisher has made every effort to trace copyright holders and would welcome correspondence from those they have been unable to trace.

Deregulation and Transport
Market Forces in the
Modern World

Edited by
Philip Bell and Paul Cloke

David Fulton Publishers
London

David Fulton Publishers Ltd
2 Barbon Close, London WC1N 3JX

First published in Great Britain by
David Fulton Publishers, 1990

British Library Cataloguing in Publication Data

Deregulation and transport : market forces in the modern world.
  1. Transport services. Deregulation
  I. Bell, Philip   II. Cloke, Paul J.
  388.068

  ISBN 1-85346-123-7

Typeset by Chapterhouse, Formby L37 3PX
Printed in Great Britain by BPCC Wheatons Ltd., Exeter

Contents

List of figures

List of tables

Preface

This book has two broad sets of objectives. The first relates to transport in the wider context of New Right governments and a policy agenda for state activity which clearly reflects a shifting relationship between the public and private sectors. The development of monetarism and its downstream policy impact on reducing public expenditure have been twinned with an innate desire to create a culture of decision-making in which the market place predominates. In practice, ideological pretexts have been variously transformed with political pragmatism shaping particular policy areas. The book's focus on deregulation and transport permits a multifaceted and international illustration of the implementation of policies often associated with the New Right, in one particular service sector. The book therefore offers evidence of how and why deregulation of transport has occurred in different parts of the world, and presents a detailed series of studies of the impact of deregulation in different types of locality in Britain.

The second of the book's objectives is to focus on transport *per se* and to provide evidence of the contexts, policies and practical outcomes of deregulatory measures. A series of international chapters presents a broad sweep of these issues. They are not restricted to analyses of bus transport services, offering rather a wider spread of evidence on deregulation in the transport sector. The section dealing with the British experience does focus in on bus transport, and offers an explicit evaluation of the economic, social and political impacts of bus deregulation in different locality types. In combination, these chapters present an informative fund of evidence on which to base broader conclusions at the end of the book.

The book is arranged in four sections. Part I provides a conceptual discussion – which draws together strands from theories of the state, public–private sector relationships and service delivery strategies – and an overview both of the regulatory history of transport in Britain, and of the experience of transport deregulation and privatisation in different parts of the world. Here, the framework is established for the series of detailed accounts of the economic, social and political impacts of bus deregulation in different locality types in Britain (Part II) and the series of wider accounts of the impacts of deregulation of transport on the international scene (Part III). The final part presents two essays which offer contrasting analyses of transport deregulation and of the policy directions required for the future of public transport services.

Our interest in transport, privatisation and deregulation came together in the undertaking of a research project on bus deregulation in rural Wales, funded by the Transport and Road Research Laboratory. We would like to thank: the various TRRL officials who were so helpful and patient during the research programme; David Fulton, whose faith in the idea of this book has in no small measure contributed to its completion; Caron Thomas who has translated our rough scribbles into manuscript form with professionalism and cheerful disposition; and Trevor Harris, king of Apple-Mac graphics. Phil dedicates this book to his family who have provided constant and loving support. Paul dedicates this book to the memory of Sadie, the much loved Welsh Border Collie of the Cloke family, who died on Easter Sunday, 1990.

PART I
Concepts and Overview

CHAPTER 1

Concepts of privatisation and deregulation

Philip Bell and Paul Cloke

1.1 Introduction

The 1985 Transport Act in Britain has prompted a vigorous debate in both the academic and public spheres. The measures to deregulate the nationalised bus industry, and to put out to competitive tender those services which although uncommercial are deemed 'socially necessary' and therefore require public subsidy, have been viewed as a radical policy package which has been expected to prompt considerable changes in the provision of public transport services. Local transport deregulation has been of interest *per se*, inviting important questions of cost, benefit and efficiency as well as of the special policies required in order to ameliorate conditions for those transport users who might suffer in the aftermath of the legislation, even if these 'sufferers' proved to be only a small minority. The 1985 Act and its various impacts should not, however, be examined in isolation. There were clear antecedents to the deregulation of buses (most notably in 1980 – see Chapter 2), and taking a wider view of the various other modes of transport, it is possible to trace wide variations in the degree of state control exerted over both the private and public sector activities over the years. The current trend towards privatisation and deregulation was mirrored in the past by national-isation and regulation, particularly in the immediate post-war period, and it is not improbable that the pendulum may swing back at least some way towards more control once again.

Transport deregulation should, however, be understood in a much wider setting. The changes in the bus industry are but a very small part of a surge towards privatisation in many sectors, affecting economy, society and the environment. In Britain, this trend has become inseparable from the

Thatcher government, and certainly the current administration has carried privatisation to lengths that even strong advocates of the concept would not have dreamed of ten years ago. Even here, however, it is possible to discern moves in this direction by the previous Labour government. In addition, although much has been made of Britain's pathbreaking role in this regard, many other countries have followed similar paths, if not travelling so fast or so far, and indeed not wishing to do so. The ideological push towards privatisation has been far stronger in this country than elsewhere, although it has not been absent outside Britain. Swann (1988) contrasts the UK and the USA in their approaches, with privatisation in the former being informed by a strong ideology within which actual evidence is seen as at best of marginal importance, and is disregarded if it fails to support the views already held. Such a heady mix of ideology, dogma and pragmatics will itself often trigger an instinctive reaction against the process from political opponents. In the USA, Swann suggests, there has been less heat and more light, with moves towards deregulation being based rather more on empirical evidence, being accordingly less partisan, and as a result being supported across a wider part of the political spectrum.

These wider debates have unsurprisingly been made more complex by problems of definition and semantics. The term 'privatisation' has appeared to mean different things to different commentators, some preferring a rather restricted definition concentrating mainly on the highly visible sales of major nationalised industries, whereas others would wish to include a range of areas where state involvement has been reduced, whether in direct provision of services, regulation, or the allocation of subsidy. This wider concept of privatisation raises the possibility of one particular sector of public activity being subjected to a range of initiatives under the privatisation banner, and this indeed has been the case with the public transport sector. As well as unpacking the *concept* of privatisation, however, the *practice* of transforming an ideology which has long lurked in the darkest shadows of right-wing thinking into an apparatus at the very centre of the policy process, both in theory and implementation, forms an interesting study in itself. A variety of justifications have been advanced for the privatisation programme, which has been variously characterized as, a carefully devised and meticulously prepared initiative, and as one informed largely by chance and short-term pragmatism, being far more worthy of labelling as 'muddling through' than as a clear, radical innovation. This opening chapter of the book traces the historical, conceptual and practical roots of privatisation, and examines the various forms it has taken, particularly in the British context, but also elsewhere. Only against this broad canvas can specific privatisation measures in the transport sector be adequately understood.

1.2 The growth of privatisation and its justifications

Within Britain, the initiatives which fall under the heading of privatisation have appeared to reverse a very long post-war process, during which the tendency has been for state involvement in both productive and consumptive sectors to increase. This has not been entirely a one-way process, as industries like steel have moved into and out of the public sector, and the balance in the 'user pays/subsidy' equation has also shifted (see section 1.3 below). In general terms, however, the post-war trend has been for increasing direct state involvement in industry, increased economic and social regulation and greater free or partly subsidized provision of services by central and local government. It should be restressed at this point that the experience of other nations was frequently quite different from this. For example, direct nationalisation never formed anything like as significant a force in the USA, where the emphasis was placed on increased regulation and where an 'anti-government interference' ideology, enshrined in the constitution, has ruled out many of the options pursued in Britain.

The Labour administration of 1974–79 in Britain can with hindsight be said to have cleared the way for privatisation policies, accepting the strictures of the International Monetary Fund in return for substantial loans, and increasing control over nationalised industry spending. During this period, therefore, certain commitments to social welfare spending were reduced or jettisoned. Despite this, Mrs Thatcher's Conservative government has been credited with developing the approach in a major way. Although previous Tory governments had made largely ritual noises about the need for greater efficiency and less subsidy for nationalised industries, and had returned a few industries to the private sector, the general bulk of the post-war reforms was not seriously challenged. The Heath government, for example, had by the end of its office compromised its early statements about a strict approach to public sector deficits. However, electoral defeat in 1974, coupled with the traumatizing effect of the miners' strike, led to a radical reappraisal. A prolonged period of rethinking ensued, assisted by the greater time and lack of pressure to respond to immediate events granted to a party in opposition. During this time, various New Right ideas were imported into central party thinking, drawing on the economic theories provided by the Austrian school and developed by Milton Friedman and others. These ideas were seen as having the potential to create a radical direction and identity with electoral appeal initially to displace 'wet' elements within the Conservative party and later to challenge the social democratic consensus style of the then Labour party. Long-time adherents of such views became respectable, rather than being regarded as embarrassments on the party fringe, while many ex-Heathites either underwent genuine conversion or at least muted their opposition, in the hope that it could lead to electoral success (and perhaps be modified later). In addition, newer MPs were generally more right wing than their predecessors.

This contextual background underlies the introduction of New Right ideas into the Tory party. Why it appeared to strike sufficient of a chord to give Margaret Thatcher power in 1979, and to allow her to retain it afterwards, is considered later. However, two points need to be stressed at this stage. First, New Right ideas cover a wide variety of elements, and although privatisation certainly sits neatly within the overall category, it was not pushed forward initially as the priority policy direction. Rather monetarism, the strict control of the money supply, formed the original keystone of the Thatcher approach, and was implemented fairly rigorously after 1979, with catastrophic initial effects on the manufacturing base and on unemployment levels. Advocates of the approach represented this as a necessary purge, stimulating efficiency and curbing trade union power, and generally backing the idea that the future for Britain lay in the service sector (especially higher level financial services). Critics have linked these policies with the massive balance of payments deficit of the mid to late 1980s, in that indigenous manufacturing capacity was decimated, making it inevitable that, as the economy recovered somewhat, rising demand would suck in imports at a substantial level. Only gradually did privatisation come to replace monetarism as the flagship of the Thatcherite project, often as the cost and failures of the latter became increasingly apparent (Keegan, 1984; Swann, 1988). Control of the economy, and especially the nationalised industries, had proved more difficult than initially thought, and the results in terms of the Public Sector Borrowing Requirement (PSBR), tax levels and so on, quite apart from unemployment, were disappointing. While hard-liners claimed that too many compromises has been made to the basic trends of monetarism, nervousness was growing amongst less committed party members. The search for a new 'Big Idea' developed out of this background, stimulated by the return of the Conservatives in 1983 in the aftermath of the Falklands conflict. A report prior to 1979 by Nicholas Ridley (later to become an important member of the Thatcher ministerial team) on the potential for privatisation has often been identified as an important seedbed for the later privatisation initiatives. However, the report made only limited suggestions for the disposal of public sector industries and services, and its main thrust was on the tightening of control over nationalised industries, based on increasingly strict productivity and profit measures. Privatisation was perhaps stumbled upon, therefore, and not promoted ideologically at the outset. It has, however, subsumed monetarism almost totally in practice, illustrated especially by the cheap sale of public sector assets (Abromeit, 1988).

The second point to note concerns an apparent tension between two distinct strands of New Right thinking, although the conflict therein has not yet sunk the project. This tension exists between what might be designated the liberal and conservative wings of the movement (King, 1987). Put crudely, the former see little justifiable role for the state in either economic or social spheres, and wishes to see any barriers to the free market swept away; no government interference is the driving aim. While the conservative element are also broadly sympathetic to such ideas, they are much more concerned with social values, and have been strongly connected with issues such as anti-abortion legislation and fundamental movements in religion. To some extent, policy prescriptions from the two wings coincide, with the conservatives also targeting the welfare state as a detrimental institution, not so much for its alleged effects in stifling enterprise and initiative, but in its weakening of the family as an important source of social support largely independent of the state. Private welfare and self-help are therefore on the agenda, but a fear seems to lurk in the back of many New Right minds of the possible social effects of such a policy. Mrs Thatcher's now-famous (or notorious) assertion that

> 'there is no such thing as society; there are individual men and women and there are families',

sits uneasily alongside the role that charity and private caring are supposed to take over from government, with little mention made of any extra resources to enable them to do this. A major concern over social regulation and the control of deviant behaviour also forms a powerful current in this brand of New Right thinking. Economic libertarianism combines with moral authoritarianism, with different compromises being made between the pure versions of either, a combination dubbed by Andrew Gamble, as 'the free economy and the strong state' (Gamble, 1988). Most commentations accept the need for some intervention to cover 'market failures', and for state spending in a few specific areas, such as the defence sector. These two strands of thinking are not totally contradictory, therefore, but prevent a simplistic view that New Right thinking is entirely coherent. Some form of regulation is envisaged, albeit often highly restricted.

The result of this complex history and identity of New Right ideas means that reasons for the privatisation drive vary widely, some being highly specific while others take on the role of universal, if often ill-defined, truths. The first is represented by goals such as the reduction of public sector borrowing and spending, a reduction of the tax burden, control of wage rates (especially in the public sector), and more generally, a reduction in trade union power. As noted earlier, attempts to achieve these goals by other means short of privatisation had frequently proved to be disappointing. Other arguments focused on such items as the general benefits of wider share ownership, and the greatly enhanced efficiency and responsiveness expected to attend increased competition and private sector management (Moore, 1986). This was compared to the lack of incentive inherent in public sector involvement which is often insulated from competition and free from concerns over takeover and bankruptcy. Such universal arguments lead to the conclusion that there are very few areas that should not be targeted for privatisation.

Privatisation is thus supposed to achieve a great many things. It has been argued, however, that the truth behind this array of benefits that may be expected to flow from the process:

> 'is not that the policy has a rather sophisticated rationale, but rather that it is lacking any clear analysis of purpose or effects, and hence any objective which seems achievable is seized as justification. The outcome is that no objectives are effectively attained, and in particular that economic efficiency – which is at once the most important of these and the most difficult to attain has systematically been subordinated to other goals' (Kay & Thompson, 1986: 19).

Kay and Thompson point particularly to the suppression of competition, and its associated global benefits, in favour of the immediate, tangible financial rewards to be gained from selling off monopolies intact (see section 1.6). Brittan (1986), in reply, while having reservations about some of the directions taken by the programme, believes that it is legitimate to embrace other goals beside straight economic efficiency and competition, and that if the measures are flawed, they still represent an overall improvement. There is always a certain advantage in leaving policy targets as loose and generalized as possible, to avoid any charges of eventual policy failure. The axiom, to use Brittan's analogy, is never to be specific about which examination is actually involved. As the privatisation programme has gathered pace, however, it has taken on many of the characteristics of an ideology (Heald & Thomas, 1986), with actual evidence as to the effects of the various initiatives being seen as irrelevant (the claims to universal benefits automatically and necessarily being correct, and alternatives being dismissed brusquely). Any merits attributed to the public sector, in particular, have been howled down. Various measures, including those in the bus industry, were claimed to be successful almost on implementation, and the substantial public interest in many sales has also been taken as an immediate and unquestionable indicator of policy success, regardless of the major discounts attendant on most of them. Detailed objective evidence is thus only one part of the picture; grand ideology and rather narrower electoral calculations form an inescapable backdrop against which privatisation must be assessed.

1.3 Categorizing privatisation and exploring its internal tensions

The blanket term 'privatisation' covers a variety of different trends and initiatives in various different sectors. It is, however, possible to disaggregate the idea into a number of conceptual schemes of varying degrees of complexity. The most immediate and simple version embraces a single category, that is the denationalisation of firms formerly in the public sector, with shares in varying degrees being directed towards managers and employees, and to private organizations and individuals. This has rarely been an entirely discrete process; some industries had less than 100% public ownership to start with, and sales have usually been composed of parts of the government holding rather than of the entire enterprise. These staged sell-offs have created problems of control, as more private involvement has complicated future government intervention (Steel, 1984; Heald, 1985). Government ambitions have increased, however, with sales getting larger; after an initial norm of reducing ownership to a controlling interest (commonly 51% of total holdings), the general trend has been for, firstly, the creation of a smaller, blocking 'golden' shareholding, and secondly, either the dispensing even with this weapon, or an indication that it will not be used in practice (as occurred in the sale of the Jaguar car company). The history and ramifications of this programme will be considered later, but it should be noted that other elements of privatisation can also be distinguished. Heald's (1984) fourfold classification is a useful attempt to display the innate variety of the measures while retaining some simplicity of categorization. He distinguishes:

(a) **Charging** – the partial or total replacement of subsidy provision with an intention to cover costs by making the user pay a more economic or 'market' rate. The rise in prescription charges and the removal of free eyesight tests are examples, and are illustrative of the tendency for sequential rather than discrete changes, with the proportion of costs recovered directly rising as an element of the whole. In the transport sector, the forced reduction of subsidy has affected local bus operations, particularly in urban areas, and is particularly controversial at present over railway funding.

(b) **Contracting out** – services here still being funded largely by the public sector, but now being provided under contract (usually after open competition) by private agencies and firms. Refuse collection, street cleaning, and school meal provision were the most notable examples of this approach originally, but many local goverment and other services are now affected. In the transport field, the expectation that deregulation will lead to many small private operators gaining contracts by providing cheaper services reflects this idea of contracting out most closely.

(c) **Denationalisation** – the most immediately identifiable element of privatisation, involving the transfer of state-owned industries into the private sector, with large sums of money usually being received in return. The sale of erstwhile National Bus Company subsidiaries, entailing the break-up of the overseeing body, is the case in point for the bus industry.

(d) **Deregulation or liberalization** – the removal or weakening of various legislative controls in differing industries, permitting a more free exercise of market forces. This can be accompanied by more positive measures to encourage competition, or it may be assumed that deregulation itself will be sufficient to allow effective challenges to existing monopolies or oligopolies. The relaxation of entry controls into the bus market is the public transport version of this process.

Other categorizations cover similar ground (Peacock, 1984), or introduce further refinements. For example, Young (1986) regards the last three of Heald's categories as the major tributaries flowing to a privatisation river, with user-pays charging constituting one of four smaller, if still significant, subsidiary streams. (The others being the full private provision of services formerly produced under the aegis of the public sector; the increasing leverage of private money into investment projects; and the subjecting of public sector organizations to management ideologies and practices derived from the private sector.) Privatisation is thus a highly complex process, which unpacks into a plethora of individual initiatives.

In some instances, these categories are mutually reinforcing, as might be expected if the movement is seen as a relatively coherent one. Subsidies have often been removed from industries before privatisation, forcing prices to rise, and making outside investment increasingly attractive. If this is done sufficiently in advance, it is hoped that the association between privatisation and higher prices will not develop in the public mind. Denationalisation measures can be accompanied by specific anti-monopoly initiatives to allow open competition. In other instances, however, tensions between the different strands of privatisation have become increasingly obvious, and by far the most significant of these is between denationalisation and deregulation. As the proceeds from the former have become very significant as an element in the government's revenue account, the temptation has often been to privatise public monopolies relatively intact, thereby gaining a higher price, but at the expense of reducing competition and its associated benefits, and perhaps suppressing them altogether. British Gas was an early example, and the government's refusal to break up the British Airways empire during privatisation allowed it to take over what had been its biggest national competitor, British Caledonian, shortly afterwards. With such cases in mind, the battle between the two elements of the privatisation programme has been characterized as no longer a 'conflict', but a 'rout' (Kay & Thompson, 1986). Criticisms along these lines have forced more competitive structures to be introduced in the sale of the electricity industry (and, to a lesser extent, the water industry). The interactions between the various initiatives are thus also complex. With these caveats in mind, the main elements of privatisation and their implications can be explored in greater detail.

1.4 Charging and subsidy reduction

A number of linked initiatives can be identified under this heading. A basic division is between direct user-pays policies, notably in health care, and a more general reduction in subsidies paid to various industries, although the latter may well lead to the former, or to the withdrawal of the service in question. Subsidy has long been unpopular with right wing commentators who tend to view it in particular as a distortion to the operation of the free market, but a growing crisis in funding welfare state services has been leading a wider body of councils and other organizations in this direction. In practice, charging for services according to usage rather than ability to pay has generally led to regressive impacts, with provision responding to demand rather than need. Increased prices are likely to depress demand particularly from poorer sections of society, in some cases raising the spectre of deteriorating health and other conditions as various services can no longer be afforded. This is not always so, however. Increased direct payments for, or reduced subsidy to, more luxury items may be seen as relatively progressive (Le Grand, 1983). The special tax relief given to company cars and high value mortgages can be represented in this way, and more controversially, higher education has been so labelled due to the under-representation of working class children within it. In the public transport field, cross-subsidy has also been criticized as tending to favour relatively richer areas (where demand is lower) by keeping fares on more profitable services (usually serving areas where people are poorer and car ownership consequently less) artificially high (Savage, 1985). Such a situation is very complex, and it should be stressed that area or location-specific measures are always likely to be imperfect in seeking to advance social goals. However, other cases at a personal level or household level, such as forcing the rents paid for council and other homes to rise from affordable to market levels are more blatantly regressive. The introduction of a poll tax has similar characteristics as, although not based on service usage in any direct sense, in replacing rates it has stripped away an (admittedly imperfect) system based on means rather than a simple flat-rate charge. The more equal resources are initially, the less regressive is a system like the poll tax, but in practice one means available to local government to redress a small element of the imbalance in society is removed.

A subsidiary justification for fuller costing and charging, and one that may become increasingly popular, is resource conservation. If the burdens of payment fall more directly on the consumer, wastage should reduce as the personal marginal cost of usage becomes much higher. To take water as an example, reduced demand could in turn mean less costly and controversial investment in new reservoirs and other extra capacity. Again, this idea may be more popular to a public service manager than a private entrepreneur seeking to generate profits on increased turnover. More tortuously, this same logic is being applied to public transport, though not to cars and lorries. Fares have been raised explicitly to drive people away and reduce overcrowding without calling forward extra investment. In both cases, however, the distributional implications are clear. Especially for water, this method of resource conservation will be bought at the expense of the poorest elements of society, in these cases in terms of health and mobility. In the transport case, too, any benefits that could be gained from a co-ordinated policy (reduced congestion, less environmental pollution and damage) are also sacrificed by a determination to treat public transport in isolation, using different rules to those used for private mobility.

Linked to the resource costing issue is the likelihood that, in the wake of denationalisation and liberalization, national systems of unitary charging and other forms of cross-subsidy will be removed in other services. Thus, charges for services to rural areas in particular could be expected to rise, especially where basic infrastructure is expensive to provide and may not have been modernized under public sector control. Relatively mobile facilities like the mail service would appear to be particularly at immediate risk, but even where withdrawal of services is more difficult (for example in the case of gas and electricity), the extra costs of provision may still be passed on to consumers. Again, in very general terms it could be argued that rural areas are generally richer than urban centres, but this is a very crude measure, and usually is least relevant to the most remote areas.

Charging, therefore, is likely to have essentially regressive impacts, although these can vary from case to case. Resource arguments can be advanced for it, although these can easily work against a case for equity if unsupported by other measures. Subsidy needs more careful analysis to assess its utility, but in many cases its removal or reduction will also have a negative effect.

1.5 Contracting out services

The scope of this particular initiative has expanded over the years, after an initial bridgehead was established over services like refuse collection and street cleaning (Evans, 1985), and in certain hospital services (Ascher, 1987). The flagship role played by certain New Right councils, such as Wandsworth, was significant (Scott & Benlow, 1983), akin to the missionaries on a global scale identified by Heald and Thomas (1986). The fortunes of private firms seeking to enter this market have fluctuated over the years, and the role of the zealot councils has not been emulated on a wide scale. Surveys by the *Local Government Chronicle* have revealed limited interest despite strong political pressures aimed at raising participation levels (Hardingham, 1984; Whitehead, 1987). The government response to this reluctance has been to push through further legislation requiring councils to put an increasing range of their services out to tender, and to prevent them from stipulating service standards in any great detail, bar a few strictly defined economic measures. Thus an increase in the use of outside contractors has been noted for the period 1987–88 (Fretwell, 1988), but even here interest was confined effectively to a few keen councils, and indeed a number have felt it necessary to take services back in-house, either on the basis of ideology or of bitter practical experience. In many cases, the private sector has also proved reluctant to get involved, and it appears that government desires for more contracting would require further strict legislation if implementation is to be successful.

Proponents of contracting out claim that costs will fall, partly due to the inherent improved efficiency achieved by a switch from public to private sector activity (Forsyth, 1983). Evidence on this point is conflicting, but the *Local Government Chronicle* survey revealed that, in general, local authorities got what they paid for in accepting cheaper private tenders (Fretwell, 1988). Savings have frequently come from either reducing the standard of service (central government has prevented local councils from stipulating 'unreasonably high' standards), or by paying lower wages and imposing poorer work conditions on staff. On the one hand, such moves can be hailed as beneficial, as managers are freed from previous constraints, restrictive practices are removed, union power is weakened or destroyed, and tax burdens reduced. Butler (1985) talks of growing public concern at the waning of official interest in this method of saving money. On the other hand, however, such measures impinge heavily on workers who are generally far from well paid already. While local authorities are prevented from intervening greatly in the tendering process (needing very good reasons to reject the lowest tender), there is little protection available against private loss-leading, where lower prices are charged just to get a foothold in the market, and perhaps forcing the dismembering of the authorities' own in-house staff, giving little alternative but to accept if prices charged are raised afterwards (Sonnet, 1985; Labour Research Department, 1983; 1985; 1987). Despite official disapproval of the award of many contracts to direct labour groups, evidence like the *Local Government Chronicle* survey show that in-house provision is still very significant. However, wages and conditions have often been lowered so that in-house labour teams can compete effectively, and for many councils and managers this may represent the ideal solution, retaining control over a service but paying less for it. The threat of privatisation is thus a powerful weapon to wield in negotiations.

A basic issue here is therefore the degree of commitment to decent job conditions, and the exact measurement of these. Depressing wages obviously allows savings elsewhere, although reduced purchasing power for employees itself has knock-on effects elsewhere in the economy. As with charging, the degree to which savings or extra revenue are directed to increased spending elsewhere (and if so, to which services) or just used to cut central and local government outlays, will affect the overall distribution equation. Contracting out has forced hard reassessments of service provision, and highlighted certain abuses, but the extent to which the actual efficiency of operations improves may be less dramatic.

Two final points may be made. First, it is hard to avoid the conclusion that, although great stress has been placed on the transfer of power from producers to consumers, much of the influence undoubtedly stripped from councils and unions has tended to move up the hierarchy to central government, rather than trickle down. Secondly, some services have gravitated into the self-help sector, a move also approved of by New Right commentators. Political evangelists may applaud the blossoming of enterprise and self-reliance that follows, but all too often such a transfer has been viewed pragmatically as a means of reducing financial commitment rather than being based on evidence that services will actually improve as a result.

Contracting out may extend its tentacles yet further in coming years, into areas like prison operation, traffic management and so on. Its main virtue, however, seems to have been in acting as a stimulus to greater thought about service delivery and management, rather than in any intrinsic merits of its own:

> 'Competitive tendering activity has confirmed that considerable scope for improvement in local services did indeed exist and that new approaches to service delivery were needed. But it has not served to demonstrate the virtues of the private sector over the public sector, as many Government supporters had hoped it would. Instead it has highlighted the need for more flexible and realistic approaches to service provision at local level, ones which take into account both the nature of the providing organisation and the needs of the community it serves' (Ascher, 1987: 270).

1.6 Denationalisation

Many general principles relating to denationalisation have already been discussed. The imposition of greater business controls, and the disillusionment with the prospect of these achieving the desired aims, has been noted. The programme has become more ambitious as it has progressed, with the selling off of fairly minor enterprises like Amersham International leading to the more recent sale of highly significant and basic industries like steel and water and electricity, and others (most symbolically, coal has been mentioned in this context) to follow. The privatisation of the whole of British Rail is now discussed, whereas initially it was more tangential components, of varying sizes, ranging from catering through hotels to the ferry services under the Sealink banner, which were hived off and sold to the private sector.

As with contracting out, a key question here is the degree to which greater efficiency in operation is attained in order to reduce costs and/or increase profits, or whether this effect is achieved largely via such methods as asset stripping, redundancies and worsening job conditions, and jettisoning unprofitable social commitments. The question of the inherent superiority of a private sector environment has been explored over the years by Pryke (1971; 1981). While initially commending public industries on their efficiency, he has more recently come to believe that their record is definitely worse than private enterprise. (Pryke, 1986; see also Swann, 1988). Nationalised industries often found themselves stretched over a number of objectives, and fulfilling none particularly well; for example coal and steel maintained loss-making capacity for social and employment reasons, without ever really giving the impression of being genuinely public industries. Political influence was another complicating factor, and one liable to violent fluctuations in its effect. The impossibility of preventing meddling by ministers and civil servants has indeed been advanced strongly by Conservative spokespersons as a basic justification for privatisation – a hint redolent with menace. It might even be supposed by public sector managers that some of this activity is a deliberate attempt to force them to embrace the private sector by making conditions within the public sector intolerable. Access to greater funds for investment is another advantage claimed for denationalisation, although again this can be somewhat illusory; deliberate restrictions have been imposed on borrowing by nationalised industries, when the latter may in fact get better borrowing terms through being seen as less of a risk due to their government backing. Critics might then put forward the 'crowding out' thesis, which would maintain that this unnatural advantage means money is not available for private enterprises, which are seen inevitably as more beneficial.

Various studies have been made of individual elements of the overall sales programme, in terms of mechanisms of disposal, the distribution of new ownership and the returns to government (Curwen, 1986). Some advocates of privatisation have also attempted to assess criteria which will indicate whether particular industries are strong candidates for action, based on their inherent demand prospects and the feasibility of multiple supplies. (Beesley & Littlechild, 1986). The question of post-privatisation economic performance is a key one, but other important issues surround the finances generated by sales and the distribution of benefits and electoral influence that they have generated, and these will now be considered.

The returns from sales of nationalised industries have formed a very significant part of government finances, and once again how the balance is struck between additional spending and the tax cuts that this makes possible can be resolved in a great diversity of ways, with different distributional implications. A common criticism, rising to a crescendo in certain cases such as the takeover by British Aerospace of the Rover Group, has been that sales have been made at values well below what a true assessment of the assets would suggest. Here, the new purchasers, whether individuals or organizations, gain significantly relative to other groups. In many cases, tougher management measures in the run-up to privatisation meant that companies were net contributors to the state economy or were at least paying off past debt rapidly. In these cases, sales may have produced an immediate short-term benefit, but at the expense of the permanent loss of an income source, whose surplus profits at least had potential for being used to finance other desirable services and schemes. The low prices set for shares in newly privatised companies have prevented all but a few schemes being failures in terms of public interest (the BP sale at the time of the stock market crash being an exception, when the underwriters of the offer were left with heavy liabilities), as many individuals have not wished to miss out on a bargain with likely quick returns. Sales of some industries may reduce the drain on public finance, but in practice either restructuring and/or price rises have been implemented in the approach to privatisation to make them more attractive propositions, or a variety of overt and hidden subsidies have been made available. In cases like the sale of Rover, this has occurred to such an extent that the government has been accused of paying to have the industries in question taken away. Again, if prices are sufficiently low (or negative), most things can be disposed of, although in the Rover case, EEC opposition to the scale of the benefits given to British Aerospace has forced an extra payment to be made by the purchasers. Quick asset stripping and works closures have occurred in this and other cases. These criticisms do not apply to privatisation *per se*, but relate to the way it has been implemented in practice. Certainly in the UK, such has been the ideological concern to 'prove' that this approach is desirable that the argument has been rigged from the start, so great care is needed before echoing the government's proclamation of the success of the privatisation programme. Equally the question of relative performance and other socio-economic goals achieved must also be considered as integral parts of this assessment.

A further benefit claimed for denationalisation has been in its creation of a 'shareowning democracy', with share ownership becoming both wider (more shareholders) and deeper (greater value for individual holdings). There is no doubt that this has been achieved, although the actual influence individuals possess over company decisions must still be regarded as highly constrained. In most cases, too, the number of small shareholders has reduced rapidly as many have taken short-term windfall gains after selling quickly (Buckland, 1987). Large corporate and financial interests have become ever more dominant, with problems of control aggravated by increased overseas ownership. While raising money for the industries concerned has undoubtedly been part of the overall aim of the privatisation project, it has taken a less prominent role than theory might suggest. Electorally despite the caveats made above, the presence of the sizable small shareholder sector is also seen to represent a major consideration, either to prevent the downfall of the current administration or at least to mitigate any risk of re-nationalisation should this occur. It was such considerations that were the deciding factor in the decision to sell the water industry at one go, rather than in stages; this would make policy reversal more difficult. It is less clear, however, to what extent the public approval of windfall gains or the underwriting of longer-term investment will translate into more general support for the whole political project. Again here it is apparent that the pure approach favoured by theorists has been heavily diluted by more pragmatic considerations. Taking the 'benefits of many small shareholders' argument to its logical conclusion, Brittan (1984) has argued for every adult to receive shares in nationalised industries, rather than a more restricted group, to ensure that everyone would be concerned with their performance. This would, however, dilute the targeting of benefits to groups seen as particularly significant in current political terms, and it is unsurprising that such suggestions have not been followed.

Denationalisation has penetrated far into the previously state-run sector, and now affects very basic utilities. The dice have been loaded heavily in its favour, but careful, complete accounting of the overall situation is needed (including other social goals which were previously followed, and the issue of hidden subsidy). Undoubtedly, the performance of the nationalised industries was often profoundly disappointing, and any 'public' aspect to them was almost invisible. Privatisation is thus one response, but others are possible. A key issue, however, is the extent of competition that exists alongside privatisation, and the new regulatory framework under which these industries will now operate (Veljanovski, 1987). Failure on this issue has become very sensitive politically, and accordingly this will now be considered.

1.7 Deregulation and competition

For economic liberals, few controls on privatised firms would be justified, and steps should not be taken which would hinder competition, which would be sufficient in itself to prevent undesirable behaviour. Nevertheless, the privatisation of all major infrastructural services in Britain (water, gas, electricity and telecommunications) has been accompanied by the establish-ment of regulatory agencies (National Rivers Authority, OFGAS, OFTEL, OFLEC) whose task is to oversee, and if necessary, restrain the activities of the newly privatised companies. A collection of essays edited by Veljanovski (1989) is predicated on the belief that the Government has:

> 'sacrificed the goal of greater competition and of introducing more market forces to the expediency of short-term considerations and that the programme relies to an excessive extent on the unproven ability of regulation to do what the market would have achieved costlessly.' (p. viii).

It is broadly accepted however that genuine monopolies (or monopoly elements) will require some degree of price and performance control. As an example, Littlechild (1986) advocated an RPI-X formula for the water industry, under which prices will be allowed to rise at a rate equal to the movement in the retail price index, minus a sum for notional improvements in efficiency. Significantly, however, this has been amended in favour of a more flexible formula, under which water companies will be able to pass some cost increases on to customers, due to the uncertain cost implications of stricter environmental protection. However,

> 'the challenge for policy-makers over the next decade or two will be to examine the mistakes which have been made in privatising the utility industries and how to foster more competition and less regulation.' (Veljanovski, 1989: ix).

It would seem, however, that deregulation has rarely been total, and that some controls are likely to remain for a considerable time at least. Thus, quality control remains in the bus industry even if quantity control has been abolished. Questions as to the regulatory framework devised, and the performance and power of the organizations concerned (such as the new National Rivers Authority for the water industry) are thus vital ones. Veljanovski (1987) believes that the regulation of the telecommunications industry by OFTEL is a good example of what could be achieved, despite his reservations about the overall process. A tightly regulated private sector would represent far less of a loss of control for the state than an unregulated system, especially if effective regulation extended between economic factors to encompass social and environmental matters. The tension between liberalism and conservatism also resurfaces over this issue. In the proposals for deregulating television broadcasting, for example, liberals would argue for almost total freedom over what is supplied, while conservatives have demanded stricter controls over the moral aspects of the output. Opponents of the measures have been concerned over selling the franchises to the highest bidders alone, risking the loss of the 'quality' element in programmes, and a possible concentration of ownership, power and influence. Regulations can thus apply to a variety of fields, and represent a spectrum of motivations ranging from the progressive to the authoritarian.

While it can be argued that the negative effects of a free market, such as externalities, justify action to prevent a totally unregulated sector coming into being, in other circumstances it has been felt that simply removing negative controls is insufficient, and that more proactive measures are required to stimulate competition. This would apply particularly where a public monopoly was previously in operation. After the sale of British Gas and British Airways as monopolies, the proposals for electricity have involved the creation of two private generation companies out of the existing Central Electricity Generating Board (with the possibility of other private suppliers entering the scene later) separate from the area distribution companies. It may still be doubted whether strong regulation of the monopoly might not still be better, if effective choice is hard to contrive. In the case of telecommunications Mercury have gained some of the market from the newly privatised British Telecom, cornering a section of the market without really challenging the core of BT business, in that the provision of a competing full independent network has been fraught with problems. Swann (1988) points out that there are arguments for regulation in the private as well as public interest, and he highlights the problems of regulatory capture, whereby a regulatory body is taken over by, and comes to represent the interests of, the industry it is meant to control at the expense of customers. The balance between just removing barriers and taking more positive action in either direction is thus difficult to strike and depends on the commentator's optimism or pessimism about free markets in action. In the bus sector, a range of options for the break-up of the National Bus Company network were canvassed, from taking little action and allowing existing companies to maintain economies of scale (if any) and power, to breaking up this framework to the level of individual garages (Mulley & Wright, 1986), again with ramifications for the price likely to be offered.

The most dramatic examples where deregulation has formed the major element within the privatisation process have been in the public transport sector and the financial markets, although the more radical proposals for an internal market within the health service fall along similar lines. Some of the more specific benefits and problems of a free market become particularly obvious in these instances. The transport example forms the subject of the rest of the book, but the financial experiment is of especial significance to this country's future. The Big Bang in the City of London in autumn 1986 aimed to preserve London's place among the leading world financial centres by sweeping away many of the restrictive practices characterizing the former system. Dramatic expansion took place at first, although a series of financial crises and retrenchments have occurred since, and there has been a growing tendency for amalgamations to take place to give added strength in the market. There have been secondary effects too, in the social character of the money markets and in commercial and residential development, both in the City itself and in Docklands. While London's position has been strengthened within an increasingly interconnected global financial framework, this has heightened the split between the City and manufacturing industry, and in spatial terms between north and south in Britain. Government now has even less control of a basic motor of the economy (a process replicated in the immediate abandonment of exchange controls by the incoming Conservative government) and there is increased pressure for short-term profits over long-term investment. The global angle tends to inspire a process of bidding down, with countries being forced to keep to the deregulatory levels offered in competitor countries, making the achievement of social regulatory goals highly problematic. The locus for debates about regulation therefore has tended to become the international level. From such a process arise the severe tensions between differing views of the future of institutions such as the EEC. On the one hand, the EEC is seen to preside over a totally free market, while on the other hand it also forms the source of much environmental regulation, and is likely to play a growing part with social measures as well.

Many of the questions surrounding regulation and competition can only be resolved definitely in the long term. As regards promoting competition, there seems to have been a growing, if grudging, acceptance that private monopolies need some action taken, in either or both of these areas. However, while the balance between denationalisation and competition is slightly less weighted towards the former in recent privatisations, there is still a heavy dose of short-term opportunism and electoral pragmatism in the proposals. The effectiveness of the new regulatory agencies will also be proven only in practice, when it becomes clear how strong their powers and finance will be, and to what extent they are permitted to intervene and force private interests to amend their activities. It is clear that their performance will be a key issue.

As a footnote to this discussion, it should be noted that the town and country planning system has also been incorporated within this deregulatory process. Planning has certainly been under attack as a bureaucratic, negative restriction on the operation of the free market, and particularly in the early years of the present government, it seemed that a major dismantling exercise would take place. In practice, though, certain aspects of planning have seemed to be in favour (Thornley, 1981), and many previous anti-planners, notably Michael Heseltine, have called more recently for a more planned approach both to areas like the South-East, facing rapidly escalating problems of congestion, and to areas in the north of the country, aimed both at a revitalizing of depressed locations, and at alleviating the 'overheating' in the south of England. The types of planning in existence now can vary widely, depending on the extent of private sector involvement and latent development interest (Brindley *et al.*, 1989). However, the predominantly private modes seem in the ascendancy, regardless of their actual achievements. What seems to have developed is a three-tier system, under which a fair degree of protection is still given to certain flagship areas (for example green belts), within a context where the rest of town and country operates under a weakened planning structure. As further insets to this pattern, there are areas where planning control has been almost entirely abolished (firstly through enterprise zones, under which gargantuan schemes like Canary Wharf are permitted with little scrutiny, and more recently using the so-called simplified planing zones in which private development can occur largely free of planning inspection). Other forms of privatisation have also affected planning, such as increased charges for planning applications, the use of private consultants particularly in plan preparation, and a general increase in private sector-led planning. This has involved the growth of phenomena like the tranche of Urban Development Corporations and the new City Grant scheme, both effectively bypassing local political and planning control.

If denationalisation is an undeniable and readily identifiable process, deregulation is rather more problematic; some regulations may remain, and it is unclear to what degree competition can or will be fostered. For disadvantaged people and areas, some regulation and direction will be essential, and much depends on the extent and form of the regulatory framework that comes into being. Without a commitment to preserve basic standards everywhere, or to prevent new competitors from 'skimming the cream' from a deregulated market, many locations and groups could suffer.

1.8 Reactions to the privatisation process

Broad mention has already been made of the popular response to the privatisation process. New Right advocates have claimed widespread support for their initiatives, and certainly the early stages of the process were eased by reaction against the failures of the previous regime. Now that privatisation is a tangible phenomenon in itself rather than a theoretical remedy for another system, some reaction against it is discernible, with growing criticism of the 'private affluence and public squalor', not to mention inequality, which has become increasingly evident. Virtually all privatisation sales can be described as a success when measured in terms of public interest, with the notable exception of BP which failed because it coincided with a stock market depression. As has been shown, the underpinning of the share offers has contributed greatly to this effect, allowing the potential for quick profits and creating a highly transitory generation of shareholders. However, more significant considerations arise in the long term, firstly as to whether there is a general support for, or at least tacit acceptance of, the overall ideology of privatisation, and secondly the more pragmatic consideration of the extent to which the new breed of shareholders will be swayed in their future voting by the fear of losing their benefits through renationalisation (a factor weakened by the transitory holding phenomenon). It is less clear whether the fear of extra regulations for environmental and other purposes will have the same effect.

Evidence on these points is limited, but a number of surveys have indicated that the public's attachment to the Thatcherist project is not particularly strong, and the almost unprecedented public support for issues such as the ambulance drivers' industrial action appears to point in the same direction. However, it would be foolish to ignore the fact that not only have a substantial minority of the population eagerly embraced the enterprise culture (and the social relations and lifestyles which accompany it), but that a steady procession of sweeteners may serve to retain sufficient support for the government to continue in office. The support of council tenants for the 'right to buy programme', again assisted by substantial discounts, is one pointer in this direction, regardless of longer term social considerations (Forrest & Murie, 1988) to the extent that reluctant councils, such as Norwich, were compelled to comply with this programme (Evans, 1985). It can at least be suggested, however, that very many have not been wholly converted to the fundamental tenets of the privatisation programme.

Two other interests should be noted in particular at this point. The managers of nationalised industries and other agencies affected by these initiatives might be expected to oppose the process as well as their employees, the effects upon whom have already been documented. Dunleavy (1986) notes that while the numbers of people controlled by them may have reduced, this has had little real effect on their influence over the key control functions which give real power and status. In addition, many of their salaries have been raised substantially, and they are revelling in new freedoms from governmental bureaucratic and financial control. The alternative indeed represented a barely veiled threat by Ministers to discourage resistance to privatisation. Under these circumstances, it becomes less surprising that opposition has been muted. In addition, it has been noted that the power of major managers has enabled them to bend the process to suit their own aims, usually to reduce the risk of outside competition. (Kay & Thompson, 1986). This has been notable in the cases of British Gas and British Airways. In addition, potential dissidents have been removed from key positions, and supporters of the privatisation drive installed well in advance of the beginning of implementation.

The final question concerns the reaction of the political left to the whole process. In some cases, this has taken the form of a basic defensive campaign, and advocating a return as soon as possible to Morrisonian style nationalisation of basic indistries. This could be associated with more moves to make such institutions truly public, and more responsive to customer concerns. Many others, however, while noting the deleterious effects of privatisation, advocate the selection of its positive points and their subsumption within a more progressive version of the phenomenon (Donnison, 1984). In particular, the concern with decentralisation, sensitivity to consumer needs and the breaking down of insensitive, remote bureaucracies chimes well with New Left interest in such directions (Murray, 1987), without, for example, making savings by imposing redundancies, lower wages and poorer working conditions. Privatisation, therefore, is not seen as the answer to the varied economic and social problems the country faces, but as a spur to a renewed, active search for such answers, forcing new and innovative responses from defenders of social provision.

Le Grand (1983) has argued for the need to make careful distinctions between different forms of state intervention, namely provision, regulation and subsidy. He sees state provision in certain areas as essential to any socialist government project, perhaps taking on board various initiatives in decentralization. Not only should existing provision be defended vigorously, but this sector should be extended via the abolition of private education and health care. However, he is less sure about the other two modes, highlighting the problems of regulatory capture and casting doubt on the potential for progressive social regulation. He reserves his most serious criticisms, however, for state subsidy, which often fails to reach particularly dis-advantaged groups, sometimes through lack of awareness, but often because it benefits better-off segments of society. Some are indeed directed specifically at such groups, while others benefit them indirectly; cross-subsidy from well used to marginal bus routes has been criticised on these grounds (Savage, 1985). If subsidy is to be provided, it therefore requires much more careful targeting if it is to be genuinely progressive in effect. The withdrawal of some subsidies may be beneficial *per se*; reduced support for company cars could at least enable public transport to compete on a more equal basis, although even here wider policy goals (such as those associated with congestion and pollution) could be better served by subsidy diversion into the latter sector. Higher education subsidies tend to benefit middle rather than working class families, though it would seem more useful to concentrate specifically on widening access rather more than just widening the range of excluded groups. Using these kinds of arguments, while the left would reject most of the ideologies underlying the privatisation programme, and many of the details, it is considered that responses should be carefully critical, rather than of the unthinking 'knee-jerk' variety. It is particularly important to have clear pictures of alternative systems and philosophies which could supplant current trends and initiatives, and a brief review of privatisation experience in other nations sets this in context.

1.9 Overseas experience

Although privatisation has become particularly associated with the Thatcher regime in this country, and devotees have tried to ascribe an instigating role to the initiatives carried out here, developments in the UK have been paralleled in other parts of the world. Indeed, as privatisation has been regarded almost as an automatic 'good thing', it is unsurprising that ideological adherents have suggested that the aim should be to 'privatise the world'. (Letwin, 1988). If in other countries the welfare state has never developed to the degree achieved in Britain, general reactions to bureaucratic interference and regulation have been similar. Powerful economic and political interests also favour the policy elsewhere, and have the resources and motivation to proselytize on its behalf. In the wake of the collapse of centralized East European regimes, British individuals and organizations such as the Adam Smith Institute have called for the extension of the free market to these countries and have arranged seminars and other gatherings to spread this message. It is less clear, however, that this is the inspiration for the movements themselves, even if the free market is at present presented as a touchstone for improved living standards and individual freedoms for all, rather than as an initiative which benefits certain groups rather than others, and which has given rise to major problems in implementation. The reduction in subsidies and industrial closures resulting in Eastern Europe is already generating significant disquiet. In many cases, the defence of place and individual identities entailed in the opposition movements has proved no less problematic for the globalizing tendencies of free market capitalism (Harvey, 1985). Again, it would appear that if market forces do come into greater play, there will be similar demands of stricter regulation of their operation.

Developments in North America have been well documented elsewhere, although the degree of state ownership has never approached the levels reached on this side of the Atlantic, and the ideological dimension has been less pronounced (Swann, 1988). Similar pro- and anti-privatisation arguments have been rehearsed in this context (Miller & Tufts, 1988; Hatry, 1988), and although some collections have broadly endorsed the process

(Hanke, 1987), questions have also been raised over the implementation of privatisation initiatives (Thackray, 1985; Kettl, 1988), particularly with regard to their possible impact on constitutional rights (Sullivan, 1987), and their impact on social welfare and basic measures of equality (Kamerman & Kahn, 1989; for a Canadian example, see Laws, 1988). Privatisation hardly initiates the development of inequality, but certainly undermines particular mechanisms that might be used to reduce it. There is also a European version of these viewpoints, with various initiatives going forward in countries such as West Germany (König, 1988), France (Bizaguet, 1988) and Italy (Del Casale, 1988). However, the free market obsession has seemed rather less influential in many of these countries, particularly in Scandinavia, and there has been growing interest in the potential of the EEC and its governing institutions in regulating the free market and setting minimum standards on such matters as wages, working conditions and environmental quality. These tendencies have indeed provoked alarm and anger among those who see the EEC as an entirely free market institution, and fear the reimposition at international level of many of the controls dismantled at the national.

Finally, privatisation has been advocated for, and extended into, many less developed countries (Cook & Kirkpatrick, 1988). This has often been at the instigation of first world financial institutions or governments as a condition for aid and other assistance. The role of the World Bank and the International Monetary Fund has been particularly influential in this, often with severe consequences for the poorest of the poor (Hayter & Watson, 1985). Free market successes have been claimed for cases such as Taiwan and South Korea, although it is doubtful whether their conditions could be replicated on a wider scale, and it should not be forgotten that their political structures are far from open and their ability to undercut competitors elsewhere is largely based on the breadline wages available. Chile has often been promoted as a free market success, though here too overall economic growth has been highly concentrated on specific groups, and maintained by political oppression and outside intervention. Behind these issues lie the basic questions as to whether poverty is the result of lack of enterprise within the countries themselves, in which case privatisation could make a considerable difference, or whether it can be ascribed to global trade relations and thus to global political and economic power – in which case opening up internal markets can easily make things worse. While stifling bureaucracy and corruption can certainly be identified in such countries, it is hard to see much growth occurring (and certainly equality occurring) without basic changes in the latter.

Privatisation has thus affected many more countries than just the UK, or even those in the Western World, as indeed the contributions to this book reflect. The specific conditions generating its development, and the form and degree of implementation, will vary from country to country, but broader tendencies can also be identified. Although the role of certain individuals and groups can be highlighted (and perhaps over-emphasized), the attempts of the free market capitalist system to break down political, economic and social barriers to continued accumulation, and thereby system regeneration, provides a strong unifying influence. While some adherents may claim that the benefits of individual freedom and capitalism are made widely available as a result, others recognize that there will be social casualties, and many of these advocate some form of modification to a total free market. From the left, while some would defend traditional versions of state intervention, others would argue for new initiatives, perhaps supplementing rather than supplanting other, older versions. These battles will be fought out on a world canvas.

1.10 Privatisation – a summary

This introductory chapter has established that the term privatisation, while acting as a useful summary of a drive towards a greater role for the market, encompasses a wide variety of individual initiatives, and contains within itself conflicting motivations and trends. Controls may be weakened and changed, but are rarely removed entirely. Neither is it a process confined within insular boundaries, although the subleties of the debate in other countries can only be hinted at here. At one very broad level, the basic workings of the capitalist market will always tend in this direction, although certain types of regulation and control have been defended by various market interests, and New Right conservatives have concerned themselves with the implications of a world where certain restrictions on individual and group behaviour have been lifted. Certainly in a British context, however, the process has seemed to arise almost by chance, after the failure of other market initiatives, and has been maintained by considerations of electoral pragmatism. This latter fact has in turn led to many amendments and distortions to the basic principles, further complicating processes of evaluation. Alternatives have also to confront specific local instances and the broader trends and motivations behind the overall programme.

Privatisation has also come to impinge upon a wide range of areas of economic and social life. In some areas, certain of its objectives (perhaps modified) could be accepted by those with other viewpoints, while in others the clash of basic ideologies would be too fundamental. What many could agree on is that privatisation has been an extra spur to the process of rethinking the role of state intervention to achieve a variety of aims, and encouraging greater responsiveness and sensitivity to the needs of those affected by it. There is a need to keep the actual achievements of intervention under constant scrutiny, and be aware that lessons from one sector of activity cannot readily be transferred into another.

Finally, there is the question of the actual achievements of the process, and of any disadvantages that arise from it. Both of these issues have been fiercely debated, but most commentators are agreed that it is a complex equation, and gainers and losers can be identified. Apart from the overall balance, the search must be for ways of retaining any advantages while obviating many problems, either by amending privatisation or devising and implementing an alternative. The division is not as simple as a pure economics versus social welfare dimension, although this is tempting at first sight. It is clear, however, that the ideology of privatisation is inclined to brush over these issues. It acts as a reminder, too, that underlying a technical analysis of initiatives in a single field, such as transport, there are political and ideological dimensions which cannot, and should not, be excluded from the account.

References

Abromeit, H. (1988) British privatisation policy *Parliamentary Affairs* **41(1)**, 68–85.

Ascher, K. (1987) *The politics of privatisation: contracting out public services* London: Macmillan.

Beesley, M.E. & Littlechild, S.C. (1986) Privatisation: principles, problems and priorities. In Kay, J.A., Mayer, C.P. & Thompson, D.J. (eds) *Privatisation and regulation: the UK experience*, Oxford: Clarendon Press, pp.35–57.

Bizaguet, A. (1988) The French public sector and the 1986 to 1988 privatizations. *International Review of Administrative Sciences* **54(4)**, 553–70.

Brindley, T., Rydin, Y. & Stoker, G. (1989) *Remaking planning: the politics of urban change in the Thatcher years* (London: Unwin Hyman.

Brittan, S. (1984) The politics and economics of privatisation *Political Quarterly* **55**, 109–28.

Brittan, S. (1986) Privatisation: a comment on Kay and Thompson *Economic Journal* **96(381)**, 33–8.

Buckland, R. (1987) The costs and returns of the privatisation of nationalized industries *Public Administration* **65(3)**, 241–57.

Butler, E. (1985) Contracting out municipal services: fading official interest, growing public concern *Local Goverment Studies* **11(6)**, 5–8.

Cook, P. & Kirkpatrick, G. (eds) (1988) *Privatisation in less developed countries* Hemel Hempstead: Harvester Wheatsheaf.

Curwen, P.J. (1986) *Public enterprise: a modern approach* Brighton: Harvester Wheatsheaf.

Del Casale, E. (1988) Privatization in Italy *International Review of Administrative Sciences* **54(4)**, 571–83.

Donnison, D. (1984) The progressive potential of privatisation. In Le Grand, J. & Robinson, R. (eds) *Privatisation and the welfare state* London: Allen & Unwin, pp. 45–57.

Dunleavy, P. (1986) Explaining the privatization boom: public choice versus radical approaches *Public Administration* **64(1)**, 13–34.

Evans, C. (1985) Privatization of local services *Local Government Studies* **11(6)**, 97–110.

Forrest, R. & Murie, A. (1988) *Selling the welfare state: the privatisation of public housing* London: Routledge.

Forsyth, M. (1983) *The myths of privatisation* London: Adam Smith Institute.

Fretwell, L. (1988) Contracting out gets a boost *Local Government Chronicle Supplement* **6314** (8/7/88), 3–33.

Gamble, A. (1988) *The free economy and the strong state: the politics of Thatcherism* Basingstoke: Macmillan.

Hanke, S.H. (ed) (1987) *Prospects for privatisation* New York: Academy of Political Science, vol. 36(3).

Hardingham, S. (1984) Privatisation gets close examination but interest fades *Local Government Chronicle* **6507** (22/6/84), 703–11.

Harvey, D.J. (1985) *Consciousness and the urban experience* Oxford: Basil Blackwell.

Hatry, H.P. (1988) Privatization presents problems *National Civic Review* **77(2)**, 112–17.

Hayter, T. & Watson, C. (1985) *Aid: rhetoric and reality* London: Pluto Press.

Heald, D.A. (1984) Privatisation: analysing its appeal and limitations *Fiscal Studies* **5(1)**, 36–46.

Heald, D.A. (1985) Will the privatization of public enterprises solve the problem of control? *Public Administration* **63(1)**, 7–22.

Heald, D.A. & Thomas, D. (1986) Privatization as theology *Public policy and administration* **1(2)**, 49–66.

Kamerman, S.B. & Kahn, A.J. (eds) (1989) *Privatization and the welfare state* New Jersey: Princeton University Press.

Kay, J.A. & Thompson, D.J. (1986) Privatisation: a policy in search of a rationale *Economic Journal* **96(381)**, 18–32.

Keegan, W. (1984) *Mrs Thatcher's economic experiment* Harmondsworth: Penguin.

Kettl, D.F. (1988) Government by proxy and the public service *International Review of Administrative Sciences* **54(4)**, 501–15.

King, D.S. (1987) *The New Right: politics, markets and citizenship* Basingstoke: Macmillan.

König, K. (1988) Developments in privatization in the Federal Republic of Germany: problems, status, outlook *International Review of Administrative Sciences* **54(4)**, 517–51.

Labour Research Department (1983) *Privatisation: who loses? who profits?* London: Labour Research Department.

Labour Research Department (1985) *Privatisation: the great sellout* London: Labour Research Department.

Labour Research Department (1987) *Privatisation: paying the price* London: Labour Research Department.

Laws, G. (1988) Privatisation and the local welfare state: the case of Toronto's social services *Transactions, Institute of British Geographers* NS **13(4)**, 433–48.

Le Grand, J. (1983) Is privatisation always such a bad thing? *New Society* **64(1064)** (7/4/83), 7–9.

Letwin, O. (1988) *Privatising the world: a study of international privatisation in theory and practice* London: Cassell.

Littlechild, S.C. (1986) *Economic regulation of privatised water authorities* Report submitted to the Department of the Environment. London: HMSO.

Miller, J.R. & Tufts, C.R. (1988) Privatization is a means to 'more with less' *National Civic Review* **77(2)**, 100–111.

Moore, J. (1986) Why privatise? In Kay, J.A., Mayer, C.P. & Thompson, D.J. (eds) *Privatisation and regulation* Oxford: Clarendon Press, pp.78–93.

Mulley, C. & Wright, M. (1986) Buy-outs and the privatisation of National Bus *Fiscal Studies* **7(3)**, 1–24.

Murray, R. (1987) *Breaking with bureaucracy: ownership, control and nationalisation* Manchester: Centre for Local Economic Strategies.

Peacock, A. (1984) Privatisation in perspective *Three Banks Review* **144** (December), 3–25.

Pryke, R. (1971) *Public enterprise in practice* London: MacGibbon & Kee.

Pryke, R. (1981) *The nationalised industries* Oxford: Martin Robertson.

Pryke, R. (1986) The comparative performance of public and private enterprise. In Kay, J.A., Mayer, C.P. & Thompson, D.J. (eds.) *Privatisation and regulation* Oxford: Clarendon Press, pp.100–18.

Savage, I.P. (1985) *The deregulation of bus services* Aldershot: Gower.

Scott, I. & Benlow, D. (1983) The struggle for Wandsworth. In Hastings, S. & Levie, H. (eds) *Privatisation?* Nottingham: Spokesman, pp.46–79.

Sonnet, K. (1985) Contracting local government *Local Government Studies* **11(6)**, 8–11.

Steel, D.R. (1984) Government and the new hybrids: a trail of unanswered questions *Fiscal Studies* **5(1)**, 87–97.

Sullivan, H.J. (1987) Privatisation of public services: a growing threat to constitutional rights *Public Administration Review* **47(6)**, 461–7.

Swann, D. (1988) *The Retreat of the state: deregulation and privatisation in the UK and US* Hemel Hempstead: Harvester Press.

Thackray, J. (1985) America's deregulation debacles *Management Today* (May), 70–3 & 128–36.

Thornley, A. (1981) *Thatcherism and town planning* Planning studies No. 12. School of Environment Planning Unit, Polytechnic of Central London.

Veljanovski, C. (1987) *Selling the state: privatisation in Britain* London: Weidenfeld & Nicolson.

Veljanovski, C. (ed) (1989) *Privatisation and competition: a market prospectus* Hobart paperback No 28. London: Institute of Economic Affairs.

Whitehead, M. (1987) Councils cool on contracting out *Local Government Chronicle* **6262** (3/7/87), Supplement, 4–11.

Young, S.C. (1986) The nature of privatisation in Britain, 1979–85 *West European Politics* **9(2)**, 235–52.

CHAPTER 2

Regulation and control of transport in Britain

Philip Bell and Paul Cloke

2.1 Introduction

In common with many other industries and services, transport has been subject to the ebb and flow of policy debates and decisions relating to competition, control and ownership within this country. At present, opponents of the measures of privatisation and deregulation are warning of a return to nineteenth century conditions, while defenders of the new initiatives herald such a reversion as a positive advantage, claiming that it is the system of control erected to restrict private enterprise which is largely responsible for the decline in public support. The arguments rehearsed in the bus industry have also affected other sectors, notably rail, while growing concern over the effects of road congestion may eventually force additional restrictions in the hitherto relatively little controlled road network. An added complication is the effect of hidden subsidies and other distortions, the removal of which is an integral part of the free market recipe for improvement. For others however, these subsidies are essential in a much more planned, co-ordinated and less openly competitive approach to provision.

This chapter documents the various stages both in the development of public transport in Britain, and in the control mechanisms that have arisen alongside. Inevitably, such an approach focuses at least partially on the various interest groups and lobbies who have been involved in the policy debate, and reiterates the point that, although more technical evidence on the performance of the various transport sectors can constitute part of the argument, developments seem to owe rather more to the political and economic power of the contending groups. Certainly, while the government is currently hoping to extend its privatisation initiatives into the rail sector, and to attract more private capital into roads, there seems to be growing public support for a greater measure of planning, including an enhanced priority for the provision of subsidies for public transport. What is less obvious is any great tide of support for restrictions on car ownership and usage, except perhaps where problems have become so serious that it is clear to almost everyone that newer, more radical measures must be tried. Central London is perhaps the exemplar of such a situation.

In order to show that the bus sector is not unique, and that the current debates are but a continuation of a longer-running argument over the need for, and extent of, control, developments will be traced first of all through the process of railway development during the last century, and the policy responses to the increasingly intense competition after the end of World War I. Attention is then turned to the debate on the need to regulate the emerging bus sector, which reached its apotheosis in the 1930 Road Traffic Act, and the proposals for nationalisation and integration in transport under the 1945 Labour government. Particular emphasis is placed on the strengthening and increasing support given to the bus industry up until 1980, and the reversal of previous policies under the 1980 and 1985 Transport Acts. The effects of the first measure were used as a justification for the subsequent legislation, and so are detailed here, while other chapters in this book examine the more detailed consequences of the 1985 Act.

2.2 Regulation and competition in the rail network

The growth of the national rail network provided perhaps the first occasion when a national overview of a transport sector was undertaken, although examples of various national and local planning provisions involving transport existed well before this time. In view of the transformative effect of railways on wider economic and social life, this is an important starting point for discussion of transport regulation. The rail network did not develop initially to any master plan, with separate companies just connecting towns and cities of importance (e.g. Liverpool–Manchester) or serving specific economic needs (Stockton–Darlington). The system developed rapidly, however, with the formation of larger groupings of amalgamated companies whereby small, local enterprises were swallowed by their larger neighbours. Longer distance through routes were pieced together, notably to Scotland, with the east coast line being developed rather later than the west, and shedding its dependence on the latter by the construction of new lines. Competition was fierce in the early days, with the promotion of many competing routes, and very complex patterns of shifting allegiances among the companies involved.

This free market approach had several consequences. Economic logic imposed a basic order on the railway system, but the lack of central direction gave rise to important anomalies. The progressive extension of the network to rural areas, often criticized as wasteful, at least provided wider travel opportunities to more of the countryside, whether as an incidental part of a large company's grand designs or as a result of a perhaps over-optimistic local venture. In urban areas, though, the problems of competition could greatly hinder co-ordination, and make interchange much more difficult. In some places, such as Carlisle, several companies managed to agree over a single central station, despite some territorial tensions between some of the partners, but in others basic disagreements proved fundamental. To secure its own routes, the Midland Railway in particular built competing routes to London (in two stages), Manchester and, finally and most spectacularly, from Settle to Carlisle to secure a share in the Scottish market. In Kent there was exceptionally strong competition between two companies, which left its legacy in the awkward rail arrangements still persisting in places like Maidstone and Canterbury, while similar problems in Ashford, Chatham and particularly the Isle of Thanet, had to be dealt with by the Southern Railway after it took over the contenders. Significantly, though, the two had already attempted to reach some form of *modus vivendi* over new lines and charges with the formation of a managing committee formed from both companies. Ironically, too, Kent has not suffered the closure of at least one network, as the rapid growth of population, unanticipated at the time of the construction of the lines, has preserved the viability of nearly all of the routes involved (White, 1970).

Competition therefore formed a strong influence over early development, and many towns were keen to avoid becoming the preserve of one company only, for fear of monopoly powers being used. In many cases, however, if competing lines were built, they provided a stimulus to the original company to improve their facilities and use their generally superior competitive position to marginalize the more recent competitor. Powerful interests in Hull even went to the lengths of promoting their own railway to Barnsley in order to break the monopoly enjoyed by the North Eastern Railway. Some competitive practices survived into later days, with the coal-based wealth of the South Wales valleys supporting the construction of an expensive new competitive dock and railway system based on Barry, which was for a time highly profitable, and the London extension of the Great Central Railway, which was not, owing a lot to the chairman's dream of services to Paris.

The attitude of Parliament was generally to attempt to foster competition, with a general fear of monopoly permeating many of their decisions. This meant not only that it was relatively rare for lines to be refused on the grounds that competition would be excessive, but that many merger schemes were rejected, even where they could have done little to reduce effective choice (for example, the proposal for an end-on merger between the Midland and its Scottish partner in through services). However, although state regulation was on a lesser scale than that achieved in countries such as Belgium, where the basic network was planned to a much greater degree, certain regulatory measures were taken during this period. Indeed, there were early arguments for nationalisation of virtually the entire system, with an Act introduced by Gladstone in 1844 giving an option to purchase all railways built between then and 1865, although these provisions were never exercised. Parliament also intervened to compel companies to provide at least one train a day for cheap fares, while the Board of Trade fought a long and often bitter battle with mostly recalcitrant companies over a number of basic safety measures. Financial scandals also gave cause for considerable concern. Willingness to intervene was restricted, however, as the direct and indirect railway interest in Parliament was considerable (Hamilton & Potter, 1985).

In many instances, the companies themselves were coming to the conclusion that open competition was not proving to be in their best interests. Increasingly, cartels replaced competition, with working arrangements, alliances and agreed standard rates developing (Salveson, 1989). The Great Central Railway's London extension, built around the turn of the century, developed few links with other railways at first, as it was cutting across interests and services that were hardening into a fixed pattern. Indeed, the companies often seemed to be moving faster than government towards this conclusion, so that by the end of the nineteenth century, there was little effective competition in the network. The view of the period up to 1914 as the 'Golden Age' of railways is not therefore to be correlated with open competition, and as Salveson (1989) shows, this perceived utopia was flawed from the viewpoints of both passenger and railway worker, and based on a general lack of innovation and investment. The position of the railways deteriorated as road competition for passengers and freight began, tramway networks developed in towns, basic traffic began to decline, and as the strain of the war years took its toll. Although complete nationalisation was resisted, by 1923 virtually all existing companies were enfolded by four major amalgamated bodies, a process anticipated by a couple of years with a number of significant mergers.

The broad economic details of the rail (and other) networks have been commented on elsewhere (Barker & Savage, 1974; Dyos & Aldcroft, 1974), but it seems clear that the rail network did expand rather more than could be expected on economic grounds, although social benefits (particularly at the local level) should not be discounted. Excess competition may have had less beneficial effects in reducing other types of investment elsewhere (for example to improve safety), and competitive attitudes became softened over the years as local monopolies formed. Competition also was insufficient to provide services to areas deemed needy, but which were too poor to support services. Mainline companies often displayed considerable reluctance to provide such lines unless a competitive principle was involved, and in the later years of the nineteenth century the government was driven to intervene more directly. Under the legislation for light railways, it became permissible to construct (usually rural) railways under less stringent engineering criteria, in return for slower speeds. In the remotest districts, particularly the west of Ireland, even such provisions proved insufficient, and direct central and local government financial aid was given to encourage the extension of rail transport into these areas.

This brief account of the early development of the railways shows, therefore, some benefits of competition in terms of increasing coverage and providing more choice, but also illustrates some less welcome features, such as inconvenient networks in places and dubious safety practices. It has been claimed that a far more state-directed process would have produced better results (Foreman–Peck, 1987). The system also headed away from an openly competitive pattern towards that of controlled oligopoly, again increasing co-ordination but also diminishing effective choice. Social issues were also little considered, especially in deep rural areas, and required state intervention before rail services extended into these locations.

2.3   The growth of road transport

Initially, the grouping of road transport interests was relatively coherent in the face of their main rail competitor, and both road passenger and freight traffic grew dramatically in the years after 1918. Apart from the obvious importance of growth in private motoring, there was an expansion in road freight haulage, often as a consequence of the release of men and vehicles from the services, while buses and (in urban areas) trams, began directly to attract passengers from the railways. Indeed, buses were able to expand into areas still left largely untouched by railways. These developments spurred the rail interests into action, with, for example, the new Southern Railway engaging in a vigorous programme of electrification in an attempt to ward off the loss of traffic. Inevitably, however, significant inroads were made. The road lobby developed significantly over this period, developing usually from the efforts of the cycling interests to achieve better roads, and soon being able to challenge the railway voice in Parliamentary decision-making (Plowden, 1973; Hamer, 1987). The Ministry of Transport was created in 1919, and once proposals for it to control the (to be nationalised) railways as well had been defeated it assumed its present position largely as a ministry for roads.

Within this overall mushrooming in the importance of road transport, bus services were also expanding dramatically. This growth was subject to little regulation or effective control, and in some urban areas there was very fierce, and potentially dangerous, competition (Glaister & Mulley, 1983). Throughout the twenties, there was a growing undercurrent of pressure for a greater degree of control over the industry, culminating in the 1930 Road Traffic Act. Although the impression is commonly given that pressure by railway and tramway interests against the bus industry was the prime mover for legislation, representing one of the last gasps of the once all-powerful rail lobby, Mulley (1983) has concluded from the written evidence of the time that this was secondary to considerations of road safety. The designers of the Act were particularly concerned over the numbers of accidents caused by free-for-all competition, and wished to enact measures to regulate vehicle quality and driving practices. In recognition of the additional burden likely to be placed on operators as a result, it was decided to afford them some compensatory protection from competition on their own routes. This specific purpose led on to a consideration of wider aspects of the industry, and at this secondary stage complaints by rail and tram operators over unfair competition and other matters certainly added to the pressure for regulation. Thus set in place the legislative framework which was to dominate the bus industry until the 1980s, for some perceived as stifling the spirit of competition and responsiveness evident up to 1930, while for others as increasing safety and certainty and putting an end to the 'bad old days' of excess competition.

The initial development of the industry under the framework provided by the 1930 Act will not be considered in any detail here. It suffices to note the establishment of the Traffic Commissioners, working on a regional level throughout the country. They had jurisdiction both over quality licensing (each vehicle having to possess a certificate of fitness), and over quantity of service (each route had to carry its own licence, approved by the Commissioners). A distinction was made in this process between express and local stage carriage services. The Commissioners were permitted to consider several aspects of local services, such as whether the roads involved were adequate, the nature of the public interest and the degree to which the needs of the area were already met by other services, with particular weight being given to the frequent objections of railways and other operators. Glaister and Mulley (1983) provide a useful summary of the early years of the Commissioners' operations, and their attitudes to particular issues. Behind the barriers of this regulated and protected environment, amalgamations and takeovers reduced the numbers and increased the size of the operators involved over the years, while the network expanded to reach the more remote corners of rural areas and started to place heavy pressure on much of the then extensive rural rail system, continuing a process begun before 1930.

2.4 Postwar approaches to transport regulation

The strain of dealing with the pressures of the war years proved very great for the transport sector, particularly for the railways. As part of the approach of the new Labour government to the economy and social welfare, it was proposed to nationalise virtually all transport interests, and this was done under the 1947 Transport Act. Among the services transferred to the newly created British Transport Commission were those belonging to the railways (including their ancillary businesses), canals, and some road haulage and passenger undertakings. Executives were created for London Transport (in this case, a body had existed since 1933), railways, docks and inland waterways, hotels and road transport. The formation of the latter proved the most fraught, and this executive, significantly, was rapidly split into haulage and passenger wings (Hamilton & Potter, 1985).

Even among its supporters the Act was not considered to be perfect, with one of the most common complaints being the relative independence of the individual executives, which inhibited co-ordinated planning. Even so, it was expected that some of the advantages of a single system as seen on the continent would be replicated, and that the basic tenets of nationalisation of transport would be accepted. The railway companies themselves were violently opposed to such measures, but their influence in Parliament had by this time been greatly diminished, and the main attack from the Conservatives came over the proposals for road transport. Hamilton and Potter (1985: 39) believe that despite its shortcomings:

> 'given time and good faith (the 1947 Act) could have become the basis of fully co-ordinated and integrated transport planning in Britain'.

The return of a Conservative government in 1951, however, heralded the return of competition and the removal of government mechanisms to co-ordinate activity across different transport sectors. The executives were abolished, with government taking direct control of the services with the exception of road haulage, which was returned to the private sector. A small unsaleable element was retained in public ownership as British Road Haulage, but this was itself sold off in the early 1970s. This process meant that operators received compensation for their old vehicles, and then shortly afterwards also became owners of the new vehicles bought by the Executive to replace them, at beneficial rates. Hamilton and Potter's (1985, 42–3) verdict is that:

> 'With the 1953 Transport Act, transport planning at a national level effectively ceased and has never returned. Under the Act, the British Transport Commission took on a totally different form. It became little more than an umbrella organisation to run the transport services that were in too bad a state to have private buyers.'

The potential for a nationalised, planned transport system was therefore never fully exploited and instead the term has come to be synonymous with a failing, declining sector, for a long time hampered by other restrictions not applying to the favoured road sector. This period also saw the beginnings of the growth of the motorway network, again a great boon for private car owners and road haulage firms (Starkie, 1982; Charlesworth, 1984).

Meanwhile, so far as the bus sector was concerned, the post-1945 re-strictions on private travel maintained the position of the industry for some while into peacetime, a factor also visible on the railways. Hibbs (1986) indeed has identified this period up to the end of the 1950s as the golden age of the rural bus. As on the railways, however, some selective contraction had already taken place, and as the growth of car ownership accelerated during the late 1950s and early 1960s, public transport was seriously undermined. The growing divide between the bus transport interests and those of the private car and haulage concerns becomes increasingly apparent from this period. Many rural railways were already condemned by the time of the 1963 Beeching Report, but despite their demise, the bus sector experienced little stimulus as potential passengers tended to transfer instead to the private car. Under the protected framework laid down by the 1930 Act, operators had been able to cross-subsidize their least profitable, usually deep rural routes from more profitable urban and inter-urban operations. They were perhaps more willing to do so if imperatives of public service were then relatively stronger when compared to strict commercial considerations. As the move from public to private transport continued, however, reduced profits on the more viable routes restricted the operators' ability to maintain loss-making services; indeed, some of the former moved into deficit themselves. Rural services in particular were, as a consequence, subject to service reductions and indeed complete abandonment. Government investigations into the impact of these losses began as early as 1961 with the Jack Committee's report on rural bus services in England, which advocated the use of subsidies to maintain adequate transport opportunities. This was followed in the following year by the Aaron Committee's report on Wales.

Towards the close of the 1960s, therefore, public transport appeared to be under increasing pressure, and it was obvious that outside finance would be necessary if the systems were not to shrink rapidly. All vestiges of the Attlee government's attempts at co-ordination were swept away, the British Transport Commission itself being abolished in 1962, and road transport interests were given consistent priority. This period of time dovetailed with the tenure of Ernest Marples at the Ministry of Transport, and saw both the Beeching Report on the rail network – narrowly focused but devastating for the railways – and the Buchanan Report on traffic in towns – not co-ordinated with the former despite their obvious overlap. The latter saw public transport as the long-term solution to problems of traffic congestion and environmental damage, particularly in the urban areas, but devoted most of its recommendations to a shorter view, illustrating the implications of designing the cities to cope with expected levels of car use. Again, some observers claimed that the public transport system had ossified behind its protective framework, making it unable or unwilling to respond to changing conditions. Others pointed to the breakdown of an overall vision implied in the 1947 Act, and saw greater planning, support and co-ordination as the way forward. At this stage, however, little thought was given to privatisation and deregulation, and policy initiatives followed an almost totally different direction.

2.5 Innovations in transport planning from the 1968 Act

In response to these increasing pressures, greater state involvement was seen as desirable, and under the 1968 Transport Act, the National Bus Company was created, incorporating the largest operators in England and Wales. The Scottish Bus Group performed a similar function in Scotland. The major conurbations also received new Passenger Transport Authorities (PTAs) under this legislation, whose function was to co-ordinate all public transport in their areas. The daily handling of these responsibilities was to be carried out by Passenger Transport Executives (PTEs) under the direction of the PTAs. The four original PTEs in Merseyside, Tyneside, West Midlands and Greater Manchester, were added to after local government reorganisation by counterparts in West and South Yorkshire and Glasgow. The Act was perhaps the first to give real priority to people's travel needs, and aimed to create sizable, efficient units to derive economies of scale and operating strength. Notwithstanding this, the bias towards road interests was still very strong, with major projects under construction or in the pipeline, and the Act could hope to do little more than plug the gaps and engage in 'firefighting' (Hamilton & Potter, 1985). Capital and revenue grants were made available, and particularly after local government reorganisation, a more integrated approach to transport planning became possible, particularly in the major conurbations where the county councils had control of both roads and public transport. Even in more rural areas, county councils had many of the same responsibilities. Here, the regional subsidiaries of the NBC were still important, together with a number of municipal operations and a dwindling number of independent operators.

The latent potential for integration continued to be developed, although this was never made compulsory. The county councils were required to submit an annual document covering all forms of transport, the Transport Policy and Programme (TPP). This would provide an overview of problems, set out short-term spending programmes and provide a benchmark against which to judge longer term progress towards wider goals. This document was used by central government to decide on an appropriate level of finance for transport purposes, paid partly through a specific Transport Supplementary Grant (TSG) and partly via general rate support. A further refinement followed under the 1978 Transport Act, when shire counties were also required to produce a Passenger Transport Plan, a document aiming to sharpen the focus on public transport by taking a five-year view of problems and priorities. Certain deficiencies in these strategies as positive planning instruments have been detected (Rigby, 1980), but at least they gave a promise of a greater priority for public transport. The 1978 Act also strengthened the counties and PTAs in their duties to co-ordinate transport in their areas. It required the Traffic Commissioners to pay particular attention to their comments in making decisions on applications for services, prompting suggestions that the latter bodies might be dispensed with altogether. In the seventies, too, environmental resistance to further road development was growing, with the abandonment of ringway proposals for London (Hamer, 1987), and with some commentators anticipating an imminent end of the motorway age (Starkie, 1982).

Local government had been taking an increasing stake in public transport via subsidies provided, and by 1982 these had risen thirteenfold in real terms in the period since 1972. In monetary figures, the rise was from £10 million to £520 million expenditure in attempting to counteract the increasing financial difficulties of the industry and to preserve services. However, even this rising expenditure did not prove sufficient to turn around the fortunes of the bus industry. Fares had risen by 30% above the rate of inflation over the same period (DoT, 1984), which naturally depressed patronage further and usually resulted in additional fares increases in an attempt to compensate for lost revenue. Although the overall market for transport was expanding quite rapidly, the share captured by buses and coaches had fallen from 42% to 8% over the 30 years from 1953 to 1982, representing a halving in absolute terms. However, while richer people had increasingly abandoned public transport for their own private car, many other social groups still relied on public buses. These were almost inevitably the poorer elements of society, as well as those without the effective use of a family car (those unable or ineligible to drive and those, often housewives, whose partner took the car for work). Such social differentials must always be remembered in discussions of declining patronage as should the massive sums paid out for road improvements and the increase in tax-subsidised company cars. The effects of a diversion of finance from such sectors, and perhaps even a cessation of payments to them, could have very beneficial effects for bus users, but the latter are generally poorly represented in the corridors (and on the backstairs) of power, when key decisions are made.

Local authorities and operators were not purely passive recipients of these trends, and made a variety of attempts to break the vicious circle of declining patronage, rising fares, and ultimately route and service losses. The urban authorities were often the most radical, aiming for a major boost in the number of passengers carried with a consequent reduction of city congestion, and improvements in transport opportunities for disadvantaged groups and in environmental conditions. Various traffic management measures, such as bus lanes and park-and-ride schemes had already been tried, but more interventionist approaches were also implemented. In some cases, major network improvements were instigated to this end, notably Newcastle's metro system based on suburban railways (some of them closed), but with new construction in the city centre and integrated bus services acting as feeders, often with improved interchanges (Morris, 1985; Robinson, 1985). This investment route to improvement is currently being followed by the plethora of schemes for urban rapid transport systems, in places such as Manchester, the West Midlands and Southampton (Williams, 1985; Hurdle, 1988). Other authorities made drastic fare cuts the main platform of their approach, particularly South Yorkshire (Goodwin *et al.*, 1983; Hill, 1986; Blunkett & Jackson, 1987) and the Greater London Council with the Fares Fair policy (Banister, 1984; Morriss, 1983; Garbutt, 1985). Passengers were certainly attracted and congestion elsewhere declined, but the subsidies involved were large and this flew directly in the face of central government policy, as did initiatives these metropolitan county councils were taking in other sectors. A number of fiercely contested confrontations with central government therefore developed, culminating in the abolition of the councils themselves. Particularly in London, these clashes entailed dramatic fluctuations in services, fares and subsidies, and therefore considerable uncertainty for the passenger. Although the replacement transport authorities have striven to maintain the basic character of these approaches, it has inevitably proved impossible to maintain previous service conditions. In these cases, too, congestion could become a problem, requiring some complementary major investment to increase capacity. This has been a particular problem on the London Underground, when combined with recent economic growth there. Again, this route has not been followed wholeheartedly. The Docklands Light Railway, for example, was built very much to minimal cost standards, and although this decision allowed a rapid construction and a flagship role, it has given rise to capacity problems, fewer and more basic stations than was desirable, and a poor connection to the City, which is only now being corrected. It has also been accepted, belatedly, that a more standard Underground connection will be needed in the Isle of Dogs (Church, 1990).

In contrast to these initiatives the responses in rural areas were generally less dramatic and controversial, although practice could still vary widely. Most rural authorities have been conservative in action if not Conservative in politics, so solutions involving high expenditure have found less favour than in the urban arena. Contrasts between the minimalist approach of, for example, Oxfordshire (Barrow, 1978) and the more positive attitude displayed, for example, by Bedfordshire (Blowers, 1978), have still been quite striking, however. Rural areas have also seen the development and promotion of a variety of unconventional services as supplements or replacements for the standard bus services. Even at this time, some deregulation was taking place in an attempt to encourage such initiatives, which could have been stifled by having to meet the strict requirements of a full service. Examples of such schemes are car sharing, community minibuses, post buses, social car schemes and greater public use of school transport services (Glassborow, 1978; Nutley, 1988). This process culminated in the series of Rural Transport Experiments in the mid to late 1970s (Milefanti, 1978; TRRL, 1980; Nutley, 1983), which provided useful information about the relative worth of different unconventional approaches. However, none of these methods has proved to be a panacea for rural transport. Attempts to fine tune services tend to run into financial restrictions, and an uneasy compromise between social and financial goals has to be reached. It is also unclear whether such self-help and community initiatives are seen as a way of genuinely increasing travel opportunities, just maintaining existing service levels, providing a 'least worst' gap filler, or as a legitimation of a gradual process of service withdrawal (Banister and Norton, 1988).

2.6 The 1980 Transport Act

Prior to the accession of the Conservative administration in 1979, therefore, an increasingly planned, co-ordinated and regulated system of public transport had developed. Linkages between modes were weak, and roads still had high priority; the dreams incorporated into the 1947 Transport Act of integrating this sector properly had long since faded. Local government had become increasingly involved both administratively and financially in directing the network, and had attempted to reverse the long process of decline in the bus market. While in opposition, however, the Conservatives had been applying their free market, monetarist principles to thinking about the future direction of transport policy, and indeed transport was one of the few areas earmarked for denationalization and deregulation in the original Conservative manifesto. They saw the answer to the transport problem as lying in the removal of the regulatory framework deriving from the 1930 Act, so as to produce an environment in which far more direct competition could occur. For some advocates, the injection of free market ideas was an end in itself, while others concentrated on more tangible objectives such as the reduction, and ultimate removal where possible, of subsidies. Given the background of transport planning in metropolitan counties, as described above, it was predictable that this would lead inevitably to battles with left wing local government. Indeed, it can be argued that a desire to increase control over urban town halls was the driving force behind the whole package of transport measures, and its fallout in more rural areas was little considered – an accidental by-product of an urban battleground.

These free market ideas first found expression in the 1980 Transport Act. Here attention was focused particularly on the express coach market which was freed from all quantity and fares control, inaugurating a spell of fierce, headline-catching competition. The legislation also made provision for local authorities if they so wished to designate trial areas, where restrictions on local stage services could also be lifted on an experimental basis. Despite the potential political affinity between a Conservative central government and the conservative shire counties, interest was muted, with only three areas (Devon, Norfolk and Hereford) being nominated as trial areas. These developments are now considered in turn, as their results have been used to justify the more widespread changes introduced by subsequent legislation.

Deregulation of the express coach market

A tremendous surge in interest and competitive activity followed in the express coach market immediately upon the 1980 Act. A number of operators expanded their involvement in this side of the bus and coach industry, although very few totally new firms felt it worthwhile to participate. Most operators tended to concentrate on routes to and from London, and on the commuter market in competition with the railways. The response of National Express, the erstwhile express service subsidiary of the nationalised National Bus Company (NBC), was equally dramatic, as they intensified and expanded their existing measures to counter falling patronage. The fares charged by new entrants, usually significantly lower than pre-existing levels, were swiftly matched, and extra services were introduced. Coupled with the advantages to public perception of already being significant operators, and having visible and usually well-placed terminals to which access was denied to competitors, this enabled National Express to retain its dominant position in the market.

The 1980 Act illustrates the need for a long-term view to be taken in evaluative analysis of deregulation, as over time the apparent success of deregulation has been diluted, though not dissipated. In addition, the results have been somewhat different to those apparently expected by the original proponents of the legislation. Fuller descriptions of the process have been provided elsewhere (Kilvington & Cross, 1986; Douglas, 1987), so only the main points are mentioned here. Over time, competition has been reduced, as several of the new competitors have withdrawn, some going out of business altogether. Others have managed to survive, although in several instances full-blown competition has been replaced by co-operation, as these firms now combine with National Express to provide services (e.g. Devon to London). British Coachways, a network set up by the leading independents as a potential rival to National Express, collapsed as it proved impossible to sustain the competitive potential available in the immediate aftermath of the legislation. Some competitors survived by identifying particular niches in the market, often involving higher quality services rather than the minimal, low cost approach of the British Coachways system. Even here, though, National

Express hit back by introducing its Rapide services on particular routes, offering extra facilities in return for a slightly higher fare.

Away from the main routes, however, service gains have been far more modest. Particular settlements experienced a varied pattern of gains and losses, with some new journeys being provided while other existing ones were severed. In particular, the drive to compete led to the elimination of calls at many smaller settlements so as to speed journeys between major centres (Dean, 1983; Kilvington & Cross, 1986), although some of these changes are also attributable to the construction of new bypasses. Fare reductions were much less apparent on those cross-country routes where no challenger emerged, and there has been a tendency for all fares to rise since the initial ferocious competition for passengers. British Rail, initially hit by competition, also responded by cutting fares, running some extra trains, and increasingly engaging in differential pricing (Bleasdale, 1983; Douglas, 1987). This case acts as a reminder that apparent savings and benefits in one area may be counterbalanced by more detrimental changes elsewhere, as rail subsidies might have to rise or cuts are made to services or the overall network. Based purely on results from the first year, an overall welfare evaluation of this competition concluded that the reduction of coach fares to uneconomic levels and loss of rail passengers initially produced a negative result, as gains to coach users were offset by losses to operators (Douglas, 1987). The British Rail response, however, turned this into a large positive balance, as cheaper fares boosted rail patronage without affecting the revitalised coach market, although it was unclear whether this could be sustained indefinitely.

Overall, while most commentators have concluded that there have been some benefits from express coach deregulation, their verdict has been a heavily qualified one (Davis, 1984; Jaffer & Thompson, 1986; Kilvington & Cross, 1986). In the light of the success of National Express in maintaining its dominant position largely unchallenged, in spite of few obvious economies of scale, Davis points to its advantages of longer establishment (therefore being more easily known and recognised by potential customers) and of its control of access to key coach terminals. From this, he concluded that liberalisation can be beneficial even in the absence of asset sales (indeed, the latter may be largely irrelevant), but also that market incumbents may begin competition with a significant advantage over their rivals, and that if any action is to be taken over issues such as access to terminals, such action is far better carried out *before* asset sales proceed. The image of great innovation and substantial initial success for the 1980 Act may well be what lingers in the public mind, but a more balanced view has taken longer to emerge. The stage and express bus markets are undeniably different in detail, but the lessons derived from one may be of some relevance to predictions of future trends in the other under deregulation (Cross & Kilvington, 1985). Obviously, however, it is not in the interests of proponents of these changes to see the initial impressions of uncomplicated success become modified in the light of more recent evidence.

Lessons from the trial areas

In parallel to the express coach changes, some far more tentative measures were enacted in the stage bus sector. Local authorities were encouraged to apply for licensing requirements to be abolished in all or part of their areas, while the Traffic Commissioners were advised to be more receptive to suggestions for new services. In fact, the level of interest in this opportunity was very low, with all three applications for such status accepted, none being in a major urban area. This makes the links between trial area results and the 1985 Act proposals as they affect urban areas particularly tenuous. The three areas were West Norfolk and Hereford (both designated in 1981) and East Devon (1982). Once again, conflicting views on their success have arisen, again depending on ideological standpoint and the length of time analysed. Detailed histories of events in the trial areas have been provided elsewhere (Fairhead & Balcombe, 1984; Jones, 1986; Evans, 1988), so again only the main relevant points will be highlighted here.

Of the three areas, Hereford has attracted most attention, as the changes in Devon and Norfolk proved to be very restricted. In the latter, the county council took little positive action, and the area proved unable to sustain competition on any services. This can be interpreted either as meaning that controls can be lifted without adverse effects in such deep rural areas (Jones, 1986), or that a deregulated system cannot fulfil the claims of its proponents to improve services, and that therefore the existing system should be retained. Norfolk County Council also privatised many routes in the whole county, after Eastern Counties, the local NBC subsidiary, submitted a list to them in November 1983 of five alternative levels of service and the costs associated with each. These options ranged from maintenance of the current network (costing £1.3 million) to a no-subsidy version involving only town services in Norwich and King's Lynn, and a very few inter-urban services. The eventual option chosen was still relatively draconian, with many services then being taken up by private operators. Although large savings have been claimed, Guiver (1985) calculated that these were in fact quite limited, and in some ways the new network was significantly worse for passengers, due to factors such as uncertainty and loss of connections. Additional money had to be spent on administering the new system, and despite the county council's apparent preference for private operators, there were suggestions that their much-vaunted cost advantages relative to NBC companies tended to disappear when they began to operate on a similar scale. Devon county council took a slightly more active role in their area, but again innovations proved to be very limited, due both to the lack of a substantial market, and the need for private operators to keep the goodwill of the NBC companies over subcontracted work and access to bus stations (Evans, 1985).

More striking changes were observed in Hereford, but here an important division occurred between the city and its suburbs, and the rural areas surrounding it. In the urban areas, several firms competed over profitable services, while outside these the county awarded contracts to run unremunerative routes to the operator submitting the lowest tender. The driving force behind the application for trial area status seemed to be a wish to break the monopoly of Midland Red, the local NBC company whose reputation was often poor. Although this pressure came primarily from the Conservative contingent based around Worcester, the area actually designated was in the old county of Hereford, which would have been unlikely to adopt the idea if it had still been an independent county (Dunbar, 1984). This meant also that the area was atypical in that it contained a large freestanding urban settlement and already had a significant presence of private operators, conditions not satisfied in many rural areas. Dunbar speculates that a better test of the general efficacy of the legislation would have been provided by Worcester, where the NBC monopoly was stronger.

In a parallel fashion to the early days of express coach deregulation, competition was at first intense in Hereford itself. In terms of benefits there was an increase in services, some reduction in revenue support and a lowering of fares; on the debit side there were examples of dangerous driving practices, poor vehicle safety standards (the earliest main competitor had his licence revoked by the Traffic Commissioners for this reason), congestion in the city centre, and ignoring of some passenger needs (not running to timetable, and missing minor bus stops even if passengers were waiting). More generally, the network proved unstable, as competition occurred at uneconomic levels (including the use of free buses), and services changed hands frequently. This proved unsettling for some consumers, who preferred a regular and reliable service to one liable to violent fluctuations over short periods of time. There was also a tendency over time for competition to decrease and fares to rise, although not back to former levels. Midland Red initially stood aloof from tendered services, but later competed vigorously all round and retightened their grip on the area, even buying the profitable Credenhill service from the independent firm who operated it prior to the designation of the trial area. The rural areas, by contrast, saw little change in services or fares, as most routes were just retained under the county's tendering system. Here, the situation was very reminiscent of the conditions in Norfolk and Devon. Services did deteriorate on certain routes, however, when their operators were also engaged in competition in Hereford.

In summary, therefore, many of the features of express coach competition were replicated; after dramatic initial changes, the network returned towards the situation that had existed previously. Most of the administrators involved (Jones, 1986; Hartman, 1986) and some commentators (Higginson, 1984; Evans, 1985), despite some reservations believe the changes to have been beneficial overall, while others are positively hostile (Dunbar, 1984). Hereford was particularly well fitted for the experiment to be successful, and even here the verdict is far from clear, as many changes were due to decisions and actions internal to Midland Red rather than truly being caused by the Trial Area itself. There was an obvious need for either or both the Traffic Commissioners and the county council to intervene over problems concerning congestion and vehicle safety, which could be repeated on a larger scale where competition arises elsewhere. The increasing involvement of private operators will also tend to lead to lower overall safety standards, although this will not be a uniform process. The county's involvement managed to preserve most of the rural network, at least initially, but certain of the powers they used have not been made available to future legislators. In particular, they were able and willing to withhold contracts from any operator who began competition against a subsidized service (or the most profitable part of one), an issue of particular concern to many worried over the government's subsequent legislation.

2.7 The Transport Act 1985

After their return to office in 1983, the Conservative government was emboldened to extend the approaches described above to cover the whole country. This took the form of compulsory deregulation for all stage services throughout the country (except in London, although the intention is still to extend it to the capital), and the initiation of measures to privatise the NBC. The deregulation of the express market, the experience of the Trial Areas, and some other instances of competition that had arisen under the looser provisions of the 1980 Act (Savage, 1985) were promoted as major successes, despite the limitations and qualifications most analysts had expressed. Such a massive extrapolation from a few, restricted experiments to a full blown application of a deregulated system provides an illustration of the tendency of the government to regard privatisation as an act of faith, a magic touchstone which will resolve all problems, as was the readiness with which any evidence which might point in an alternative direction was instantly dismissed (Heald & Thomas, 1986). Their basic approach was set out in a 1984 White Paper (DoT, 1984); no Green Paper had been issued, so the basic ideas were already fixed before any attempt was made at consultation, which therefore could only consider the small print of the proposals (Higginson, 1984). Four main provisions can be identified (Banister, 1985):

(a) The abolition of road service licensing – any operator wishing to run a service commercially was to be free to do so, just needing to notify the Traffic Commissioners. The function of the latter was reduced to that of intervening over bus safety, dangerous driving and congestion, and ensuring compliance with the details submitted.

(b) Any services felt to be socially necessary, but not registered commercially, were to be tendered by the county council, with the lowest price being chosen unless very good reasons could be advocated why this should not be done. Comprehensive planning of profitable services was therefore to be abolished, but some elements of this would survive in the subsidized network. Grants were made available to support rural services over the transition period, and to support new innovatory services.

(c) Quality licensing was to be retained, and possibly strengthened in view of the likely changes in the market, introducing many new operators.

(d) The National Bus Company was to be split into its constituent companies, which would then be sold off to the private sector.

Passenger Transport Executives and municipal bus operations were also to be split formally into companies separate from their parent bodies.

The basic contention underlying these proposals was that the industry would become much more efficient and competitve, offering better services at lower fares for much less revenue support. The power of a free market to achieve all these aims was propounded strongly. The privatisation measures were felt essential to prevent monopolies persisting, either encouraging services to pass to lower cost private operators, or to improve efficiency within ex-NBC firms where they continue to run a route. It was also suggested that such efficiency improvements would be sufficient to counteract the loss of cross-subsidy. There was a widespread recognition that some form of action in the industry was required, and few would quibble with the stated aims, although conflicts could still arise over the payment of large subsidies in urban areas to encourage greater travel and reduce car usage. What was in much greater dispute was whether these broad aims could be achieved with the instruments provided under the 1985 Act, and proponents of the new system (Beesley & Glaister, 1985; Hibbs, 1985) debated fiercely with advocates of a more centrally planned and co-ordinated system (Gwilliam et al, 1985). Other commentators saw some merit in the proposals, but felt that too much was being left to the market (Higginson, 1984).

The proposals in the Bill were subject to intense parliamentary scrutiny by the House of Commons Transport Committee (1985). The response was largely critical, calling for the abandonment of, or at least major modifications to, the proposals in the White Paper. Alternatives were canvassed, such as a mere relaxation of the old system to make it easier for competition to emerge, by weakening the power of veto wielded by the incumbent operator. Two major alternatives emerged, however, which aimed to retain perceived benefits of the changes while controlling less desirable features. One such was *franchising* which would involve creating parcels of routes covering a particular area, with operators to offer either the greatest return to the county council if the area was generally profitable, or seeking the smallest subsidy if it was not. The idea has been particularly associated with the Leeds transport group (Gwilliam, 1985). The Transport Committee, while feeling that this system had some merit, preferred the second alternative of *comprehensive competitive tendering*. This mirrors the government's proposals more closely, but diverges in proposing that all routes should be awarded on tender, inclusing those considered to be commercial. This would circumvent the problem that, under franchising, only the larger (usually ex-NBC) companies would have the resources to sustain a worthwhile sized network, and it would be easier to see any competition off and create a stronger position when the franchise came to be renewed. (Advantages of franchising would be the easier retention of network effects, such as connections and joint ticketing, and of supportive cross-subsidy, although the government are clearly against the latter.) Comprehensive competitive tendering would also achieve the main effect sought by franchising, that is the creation of competition for the market (and thereby stimulating efficiency of various types) while preventing competition in the market, with the possibly wasteful and potentially dangerous effects of running buses in opposition along the same route. The spectre of increased numbers of accidents was beginning to hover, reawakening memories of the events which had triggered the 1930 legislation. The network could then be planned in total (again something not favoured by the government), but would give smaller operators greater opportunities to enter the market, and it would assure the county councils of profits from commercial services. These could then be used to support subsidised routes and journeys, so cross-subsidy of a sort would persist, but this would now be made explicit (as the government wanted) and be administered by the counties rather than the operators.

Despite the fact that few unbiased commentators could be found to speak in favour of the White Paper proposals, these alternatives were rejected, and the Transport Act of 1985 enshrined the original scheme almost unchanged. The debates during the passage of the Bill highlighted the opposing views of what deregulation would achieve (Bell & Cloke, 1990), though this issue thereafter passed from the realm of theory into practice. All operators were required to give notice of any commercial services they wished to run by the end of February 1986, and the intervening time up to deregulation day itself (26 October of that year) was allowed to local councils to analyse the gaps left by these registrations, and to decide what services should be tendered to compensate for any identified shortfall. Subsidised services were not supposed to compete with and abstract from commercial services, in contrast to the Hereford example, although it was likely to be difficult to eliminate this completely. The network then had to operate unchanged for three months, with operators being liable to penalties for failing to fulfil their registrations, but from 26 January 1987, full deregulation would begin. Thereafter services could be altered at 42 days' notice, with local authorities not only having to publicize any changes, but also being ready to extend (or reduce) their subsidized network in response. Dramatic early changes were quite likely, as had happened in the express coach industry, but a full assessment of gains and losses was not likely to be possible in the short term.

2.8   Conclusion – the scope for privatisation in British transport

Following chapters illustrate the effects of this legislation in practice, and provide some indication of its success in achieving such goals as creating competition, reducing the need for subsidy, and stimulating extra services. The crucial indicator, however, should perhaps be patronage levels. The causes of the decline of public transport must be considered, as many supporters and critics of the legislation have failed to do, as this will have a key bearing on what deregulation can achieve:

'If the cause is simply that regulation has ossified the industry, then deregulation will work as a cure. If the cause is solely the inefficiency of public enterprise then privatisation by itself may be a sufficient cure. If, however, the cause is simply lack of demand, it is unclear whether the changes proposed will do much to cure the problem' (Keasey & Mulley, 1986: 174).

Privatisation has highly diverse effects on particular social groups, and if the problems do prove to be associated primarily with a market too small to support services, at least at current levels and standards, future responses to such a situation could be even more diverse. One reaction could be to cut services to save money, regardless of the real needs of those still with no realistic alternative to public transport. In contrast, an altogether more promotional role could be taken, seeking to boost public transport not just for reasons of equity, but also for environmental and (ultimately) economic purposes. Positive promotion of public services could attract some of the overwhelming majority who have alternative private transport available, thereby reducing congestion and environmental damage in both urban and rural areas. Other traffic management and pricing schemes would reinforce such a direction. The government clearly believes that the deregulated bus market is capable of achieving this goal, through such means as greater attentiveness to passenger demands and lower fares, while the former metropolitan county council approaches are available, at least in the memory, as competing models for future public transport. Most of these alternatives do require much greater co-ordination and restriction than the fragmentary competitive approach applied at present. If and when the focus of government pronouncements turns from the revitalizing effect of deregulation to claiming that, in the face of a declining market, it could not realistically be expected to reverse the situation, these alternatives should be remembered. It is clear that public opinion is now turning towards a far more planned approach to transport.

Although all of the main aspects of privatisation are present in the bus industry, deregulation was the most striking component of the 1985 legislation, and the extent to which this removal of restrictions will itself alter conditions is of great significance. One view is that the trial areas illustrate that the previous system could be dismantled in rural areas without creating apparent harm, a conclusion extended to the whole system by Glaister and Mulley (1983). The extent to which competition is generated and maintained under this system is critical. The privatisation of the NBC was designed to facilitate such competition, although inevitably there was a tension between maximizing competition and making a hived-off unit attractive to any buyer, not to mention profitable for the seller, the government (Mulley & Wright, 1986). It is not surprising in view of the earlier discussion that the second element has often appeared dominant, and where break-up is contemplated, this will now make companies vulnerable to immediate takeover by one of the emerging major conglomerates. Both elements are designed to increase efficiency, though the balance between more efficient operation and asset usage, and a straight reduction of employee numbers and conditions, is another imponderable issue. The legislation was predicated on the basis that savings will offset any loss of cross-subsidy, especially in rural areas when transitional monies have been withdrawn; the likely response of central and local government if these expectations remained unfulfilled is another question for the future.

The procedure of contracting out was integral to the expectation that work would be transferred to private operators, quite apart from privatisation of the NBC in any case. One view is that economies of scale in the industry are limited, so small private operators could take over unprofitable workings leaving the larger companies with a more even and profitable business (Foster, 1985). Under deregulation, this may be difficult to achieve, as not only would some economies be lost (for example with regard to information), but certain advantages smaller operators possess (such as more flexible use of labour as well as lower wages) may be whittled away if they operate at a higher level of output. Such flexibility in dividing services between firms also requires a degree of co-ordination, thereby again opposing other more general trends in the legislation. As in other servicing areas now open to tendering, lower level employees could be major losers from the legislation. Finally, it should not be forgotten that within these changes social transport provision has been increasingly contracted out to voluntary groups, thus rendering self-help an integral part of privatisation.

Behind all these considerations is the question of subsidy, which provides a link to the issue of full cost charging. It is clear that the Conservative government holds most subsidies to be undesirable, seeking their rapid abolition or at very least a far more selective targeting. As already discussed, the relatively high spending urban authorities, who have placed great stress on increasing opportunities for low income groups, have been particularly singled out for attack. The 1985 Act certainly makes the allocation of subsidy more transparent, and there could be advantages for more heavily used urban routes if their cross-subsidization of rural services is reduced. Again, the actual response to this situation is critical. The extent to which local councils prove willing and able to provide support for unprofitable services when the financial implications of this action are so starkly apparent must be a source of great concern, particularly when those making the decisions are unlikely to suffer the consequences directly. It has been argued that providing subsidies directly to those unable to pay a market price for transport, perhaps via tokens, is far more effective than subventions to operators (Hibbs, 1987). This will not help where no service is provided at all, however, and without a far more equitable distribution of basic resources, such needy consumers are unlikely to have their requirements adequately considered. Unless such apparently utopian goals are realized, the provision of transport with due regard to equity goals is likely to entail subsidies in some form.

The first two chapters of this book have therefore demonstrated that the regulatory history of transport has fluctuated over the years, with controls gradually increasing, particularly as part of the post-war welfare state settlement, but never really achieving the degree of co-ordination and control across sectors that would have allowed a truly comprehensive approach. The rebirth of privatisation and private enterprise has often merely revived many longstanding debates in the transport field, and these have rarely been resolved by technical argument. What is important to note is the shifting balance of interests behind the various policies. For any progressive transport policy, it will now be essential to place some shackles on the unrestrained influence of the road lobby, and there are signs that this is being done reluctantly. Paul Channon, the former Transport Secretary, declared in 1989, that it was likely that some formal controls on road usage would have to be introduced, but hoped that this initiative would not have to be taken by himself, while his replacement, Cecil Parkinson, was compelled, in early 1990, to abandon some of the grandiose suggestions for a renewed major road construction programme in London. However, the basic priority given to car transport is still strong. Apart from increased interest in securing private sector finance in whole or in part for new roadbuilding, major national construction programmes are still planned, new road schemes are evaluated for their benefits far more benignly than the equivalent for public transport, and road restrictions (e.g. lorry weights) are still in political disfavour.

Privatisation initiatives have spread into other sectors aside from that of buses. Deregulation of the airways has aimed to provide more service at lower fares, and some restrictions on airport usage have been removed; for example Prestwick is to lose its protected status as Scotland's international airport. The terminal issue has been as significant here as in the express coach example, while the government's unwillingness to reduce the power of newly privatised British Airways led rapidly to its ability to force British Caledonian, its main national rival, into a takeover. Privatisation proposals have also begun to surface for British Rail, already having divested itself of several subsidiaries, and under heavy pressure to reduce subsidies drastically, in contrast to the approach adopted in most other European countries. Current British Rail management would favour privatisation en bloc, but it is unlikely to be supported by the government. The alternatives which have been canvassed have been to sell off current sectors of activity individually, the most profitable going first, (e.g. Inter-City) and raising major questions over the future of the least attractive rail networks. Accounting procedures which are already complex would become even more convoluted and arbitrary, and further substantial fare rises would be likely on privatisation as subsidy is removed from others, especially the commuter division of Network South East. Other possibilities are the creation of a central track authority, maintaining the infrastructure and selling railspace to competing companies (Irvine, 1987; 1988), or reconstituting the pre-1923 system of regional companies (Gritten, 1988). Critics have argued against these possibilities, feeling that progressive revisions to British Rail operations are best conducted within the present framework, albeit with increased local government involvement and control (Salveson, 1989). The bus sector story may be about to be repeated for rail, especially if the Conservatives win further periods of office. As evidence from the former will undoubtedly be used as part of the propaganda surrounding schemes for the latter, it is important that careful analysis is evident in discussions of the effects of the 1985 Act. Foster (1985), for example, claims success for the deregulation of freight haulage, while wider accounting might stress the problems caused for the railways.

Aims and functions for the transport sector thus vary widely. Some aims prioritize maximum choice, at least for those who can afford it, and are against regulatory restrictions; other modes can compete with road if they can do so profitably. Others would argue for a more planned system, not leaving basic decisions about transport infrastructure and mode usage to the market, but operating by state dictat or encouragement. This could be centralized or decentralized, remote or local, bureaucratic or popular democratic, but by this process there is at least the possibility of a policy that strives for equity and emphasizes environmental and energy saving goals. Some form of regulation and planning survives in the current bus system, and the task in the short term will be to utilize this effectively to preserve some elements of social welfare. In the long term, the new system may need to be modified or replaced to achieve these goals, and much will depend on the future political ideologies and interest group power, whether being powerful, incorporated and secretive or attempting to break into a closed decision-making framework and introduce more radical alternatives.

References

Banister, D.J. (1984) Central-local relations in Britain: the case of the Fares Fair policy in London *Transport Policy and Decision Making* **2(3)**, 275–89.

Banister, D.J. (1985) Deregulating the bus industry in Britain – the proposals *Transport Reviews* **5(2)**, 99–103.

Banister, D.J. & Norton, P.F. (1988) The role of the voluntary sector in the provision of rural services – the case of transport *Journal of Rural Studies* **4(1)**, 57–71.

Barker, T.C. & Savage, C.I. (1974) *An economic history of transport in Britain* 3rd ed, London: Hutchinson.

Barrow, J.F. (1978) Public transport – a key issue in county plan making? In Cresswell, R.W. (ed) *Rural transport and country planning* Glasgow: Leonard Hill, pp. 8–16.

Beesley, M.E. & Glaister, S. (1985) Deregulating the bus industry in Britain – a response *Transport Reviews* **5(2)**, 133–42.

Bell, P.J.P. & Cloke, P.J. (1990) Deregulation and rural bus services: a study in rural Wales *Environment and Planning* A, **22**.

Bleasdale, C. (1983) Coaches: a case of wasteful competition? *Modern Railways* **40(421)**, 513–8.

Blowers, A.T. (1978) Future rural transport and development policy. In Cresswell, R.W. (ed) *Rural transport and country planning* Glasgow: Leonard Hill, pp.45–60.

Blunkett, D. & Jackson, K. (1987) *Democracy in crisis: the town halls respond* London: Hogarth.

Carr, J.D. (ed.) (1986) *Passenger transport: planning for radical change* Aldershot: Gower.

Charlesworth, G. (1984) *A history of British motorways* London: Thomas Telford.

Church, A. (1990) Waterfront regeneration and transport problems in the London Docklands. Paper to session 'Port cities in context: the impact of waterfront regeneration', IBG annual conference, University of Glasgow, 4 January 1990.

Cross, A.K. & Kilvington, R.P. (1985) Deregulation of inner-city coach services in Britain *Transport Reviews* **5**(3), 225–45.

Davis, E.H. (1984) Express coaching since 1980: liberalisation in practice *Fiscal Studies* **5**(1), 76–86.

Dean, C. (1983) Winners and losers in the recent coaching revolution *Area*, **15**(1), 1–6.

DoT (Department of Transport) (1984) *Buses* London: HMSO, Cmnd 9300.

Douglas, N.J. (1987) *A welfare assessment of transport deregulation: the case of the express coach market in 1980* Aldershot: Gower.

Dunbar, C.S. (1984) Hereford and Worcester: a model for the future? *Buses* **36**(355), 444–6.

Dyos, H.J. & Aldcroft, D.H. (1974) *British transport: an economic survey from the seventeenth century to the twentieth* Harmondsworth: Penguin.

Evans, A. (1985) Deregulating buses: the three trial areas *Public Money* **5**(2), 48–52.

Evans, A. (1988) Hereford: a case study of bus deregulation *Journal of Transport Economics and Policy* **22**(3), 283–306.

Fairhead, R.D. & Balcombe, R.J. (1984) *Deregulation of bus services in the trial areas 1981–84* Crowthorne: Transport and Road Research Laboratory, TRRL Report 1131.

Foreman-Peck, J.S. (1987) National monopoly and railway policy in the nineteenth century *Oxford Economic Papers* **39**(4), 699–718.

Foster, C.D. (1985) The economics of bus deregulation in Britain *Transport Reviews* **5**(3), 207–14.

Garbutt, P.E. (1985) *London Transport and the politicians* London: Ian Allen.

Glaister, S. & Mulley, C. (1983) *Public control of the British bus industry* Aldershot: Gower.

Glassborow, D.W. (1978) Rural bus services – an assessment of current experiments. In Cresswell, R.W. (ed) *Rural transport and country planning*, Glasgow: Leonard Hill, pp.161–8.

Goodwin, P.B., Bailey, J.M., Brisbourne, R.H., Clarke, M.I., *et al.* (1983) *Subsidised public transport and the demand for travel: the South Yorkshire example* Aldershot: Gower.

Gritten, A. (1988) *Reviving the railways: a Victorian future?* London: Centre for Policy Studies. Policy Study No. 97.

Guiver, J. (1985) Passengers lose out in the bus subsidy game *Surveyor* **165**(4845), 10–13.

Gwilliam, K.M. (1985) New policy directions in bus transport. In Knowles, R. (ed) *Implications of the 1985 Transport Bill*, Department of Geography, University of Salford: IBG Transport Geography Study Group, pp.5–19.

Gwilliam, K.M., Nash, C.A. & Mackie, P.J. (1985) Deregulating the bus industry in Britain: the case against *Transport Reviews* **5**(2), 105–32.

Hamer, M. (1987) *Wheels within wheels: a study of the road lobby* London: Routledge & Kegan Paul.

Hamilton, K. & Potter, S. (1985) *Losing track* London: Routledge & Kegan Paul.

Hartman, M.D.T. (1986) Deregulation of local bus services against the background of the Hereford and Worcester trial area *Municipal Engineer* **3(3)**, 167-70.

Heald, D.A. & Thomas, D. (1986) Privatisation as theology *Public Policy and Administration* **1(2)**, 49-66.

Hibbs, J. (1985) *The debate on bus deregulation* London: Adam Smith Institute.

Hibbs, J. (1986) *The country bus* Newton Abbot: David & Charles.

Hibbs, J. (1987) How to help people who need transport *Town and Country Planning* **56(4)**, 113.

Higginson, M.P. (1984) *Buses after 'Buses': possible implications of the 1984 White Paper* University of London: Department of Extra Mural Studies.

Hill, R. (1986) Urban transport: from technical process to social policy. In Lawless, P. & Raban, C. (eds) *The contemporary British city*, London: Harper & Row, pp.85-106.

House of Commons Transport Committee (1985) *Financing of public transport services: the Buses White Paper* 3 vols, London: HMSO.

Hurdle, D. (1988) Guiding the light *Planning* **794**, 14-15.

Irvine, K. (1987) *The right lines* London: Adam Smith Institute.

Irvine, K. (1988) *Track to the future* London: Adam Smith Institute.

Jaffer, S.M. & Thompson, D.J. (1986) Deregulating express coaches: a reassessment *Fiscal Studies* **7(4)**, 45-68.

Jones, V. (1986) Trial areas – the lessons of experience. In Carr, J.D. (ed) *Passenger transport: planning for radical change*, Aldershot: Gower, pp.69-88.

Keasey, K. & Mulley, C. (1986) Deregulation and privatisation of local buses in the United Kingdom *International Journal of Transport Economics* **13(2)**, 153-75.

Kilvington, R.P. & Cross, A.K. (1986) *Deregulation of express coach services in Britian* Aldershot: Gower.

Milefanti, D.C. (1978) Government rural transport experiments 1977. In Cresswell, R.W. (ed) *Rural transport and country planning*, Glasgow: Leonard Hill, pp.169-78.

Morris, S. (1985) Towards integration *Buses* **37(363)**, 246-9.

Morriss, P. (1983) Should we subsidise public transport? *Political Quarterly* **54**, 392-8.

Mulley, C. (1983) The background to bus regulation in the 1930 Road Traffic Act: economic, political and personal influences in the 1920s *Journal of Transport History*, NS **4(2)**, 1-19.

Mulley, C. & Wright, M. (1986) Buy-outs and the privatisation of National Bus *Fiscal Studies* **7(3)**, 1-24.

Nutley, S.D. (1983) *Transport policy appraisal and personal accessibility in rural Wales* Norwich: Geo Books.

Nutley, S.D. (1988) 'Unconventional modes' of transport in rural Britain: progress to 1985 *Journal of Rural Studies* **4(1)**, 73–86.

Plowden, W. (1973) *The motor car and politics in Britain* Harmondsworth: Penguin.

Rigby, J.P. (1980) *Public planning in shire counties: an evaluation of the public transport plan as an aid to transport policy making* Oxford Polytechnic: Department of Town Planning, Working Paper, No. 46.

Robinson, S.E. (1985) Tyne and Wear metro: the development of an integrated public transport system in an urban area. In Williams, A.F. (ed) *Rapid Transit Systems in the U.K.*, Department of Geography, University of Birmingham, IBG Transport Geography Study Group, pp.4–26.

Salveson, P. (1989) *British Rail: the radical alternative to privatisation* Manchester: Centre for Local Economic Strategies.

Savage, I.P. (1985) *The deregulation of bus services* Aldershot: Gower.

Starkie, D.N.M. (1982) *The motorway age: road and traffic policies in post-war Britain* Oxford: Pergamon Press.

TRRL (Transport and Road Research Laboratory) (1980) *The rural transport experiments* Crowthorne: TRRL Supplementary Report 584.

White, H.P. (1970) *A regional history of the railways of Great Britain: Vol.2: Southern England* 3rd edn, Newton Abbot: David & Charles.

Williams, A.F. (ed) (1985) *Rapid transit systems in the U.K.: problems and prospects* Department of Geography, University of Birmingham: IBG Transport Geography Study Group.

CHAPTER 3

Introduction to international transport deregulation

Martin Higginson

3.1 Why regulate?

Before considering why and how governments reduce their regulatory influence over transport industries, it is instructive to assess why transport became a highly regulated industry. The origins of transport regulation are found in the desires on the part of governments to ensure safety of operation and to facilitate the provision of comprehensive transport networks, including services which are not individually remunerative. Thus, the United States' Motor Carrier Act of 1935 and Transportation Act 1940 set out to

> 'ensure sound operating conditions, adequate sevices at reasonable rates, cooperation among state and federal regulatory agencies, prevention of unjust discrimination among shippers, preservation of services considered to be in the public interest, and maintenance of sufficient profits to enable industry development and expansion'

in the interstate bus and truck industries (Phillips, 1988).

The origins of regulation in the desire of governments and the general public to create order out of 'chaos' are exemplified by British and Hong Kong legislation. The British system of road passenger transport regulation, introduced in 1930 sought, inter alia, to reduce on-the-road competition and the Hong Kong government acted to reduce congestion and improve the on-the-road behaviour of minibus drivers when the system of licensed Public Light Buses was introduced in 1969 (Hibbs, 1985: 120).

As in the Hong Kong example, quality and quantity controls may be combined in the same licensing system. Quality licensing is clearly intended to improve safety directly. Quantity licensing may also be considered by governments to be justified on safety grounds, firstly as a means of reducing congestion and, more contentiously, in order to reduce extreme financial pressures, which might tempt operators to make unsafe economies in order to reduce costs of operation.

Governments have adopted different approaches to fulfilling their objectives for regulation which typically relate to the countries' systems of commercial law. Countries whose commercial law is based on a civil code tend towards a franchise system of road passenger transport quality control, as exemplified by most mainland European countries. In countries such as the United Kingdom and many former British colonies, an arbitrational system of regulation was typically adopted (Hibbs, 1985: vii).

Both arbitrational and franchise systems of quality control have given rise to monopolies in the supply of transport. In most Western and many Third World cities, public transport is dominated by a single, usually municipally or government owned, undertaking. Most railway networks are government monopolies, which in many countries are protected against competition from road passenger and freight operators. The European mainland provides numerous examples of this phenomenon; the most strictly controlled regime has been that of West Germany. European transport regulation is now under considerable pressure from the liberalization policies of the European Community.

In addition to the justifications for regulation already mentioned, the desire on grounds of national security to protect networks and infrastructure is also present in respect of certain elements of the transport system. This may apply to railways, roads and air and seaports. The link between air transport and military requirements, for example in the control of airports and navigational control systems, is of importance in many countries.

3.2 Failures of quantity regulation

The regulation of transport often follows a period of intense and controversial competition. While designed to instil 'order' where there was perceived to be 'chaos', regulation soon begins to have an adverse effect on companies' willingness to innovate and ability to compete, a shortcoming identified by Chester as early as 1936. This stifling of the competitive urge may affect the industry the regulation seeks to protect as well as the new competitor. For example, many railway administrations became lethargic, bureaucratic and slow to respond to new market opportunities, while bus and road haulage operators developed anti-competitive characteristics such as the tendency to amalgamate into monopolistic groupings, high rates and a market in licences.

Thus, while initially protecting investment and allowing monopoly profits to be earned, these benefits are susceptible to erosion as the attractions of the 'quiet life' set in. Eventually, services may become expensive, of poor quality and uncompetitive. Either inertia, or the conditions of their licences or franchises, may inhibit firms from rationalizing loss-making activities or diversifying into more profitable areas, as for example with respect to United

States' railroads, prior to their partial deregulation under the Staggers Act of 1980 (Moore, 1988). It was the pressure of increased deficits, amounting to more than a trillion (million million) yen per annum between 1980 and 1986 that led to the corporatization, in preparation for eventual privatisation, of Japanese National Railways in 1987 (Suga, 1988).

Management of incumbent firms tends to favour the status quo and considers itself to be performing satisfactorily, as is evidenced by the scepticism from within regulated industries when deregulation is proposed. The Bus and Coach Council was critical of the UK government's White Paper proposing the deregulation of bus services (DoT, 1984):

> 'The White Paper fails to recognise the benefits of the road service licensing system, still . . . based on meeting public need – however that changes – with due economy of resources. No system works perfectly, but the high level of public transport provision . . . and the diversity of destinations served are undoubtedly due to road service licensing. The system is not designed to further the interests of the operator' (Bus and Coach Council, 1984, para. 4.2).

Management does not, however, appreciate regulation in the form of 'interference' by politicians, as shown by Garbutt (1985), writing about the impact of local authority control on London Transport:

> 'This book has been written to show the effects of increased political interference in the affairs of London Transport in the past twenty years or so, particularly while the undertaking was under the control of the Greater London Council. A public transport system needs a measure of political control to ensure that its business is conducted on the broad lines of policy for which the electorate has voted. But it does not need political involvement in its professional management to the degree that we have witnessed in London in recent years, nor should it be subjected to radical changes of direction immediately the complexion of its political masters alters.'

Not only does regulation fail to provide the incentive for incumbent operators to perform efficiently, it may also prevent entry by more efficient operators seeking a share of the market. In Britain, before the deregulation of road haulage in 1968, for example, licensing authorities were required to consider the interests of providers of transport facilities, as well as those of users (Gwilliam & Mackie, 1975: 261). A similar situation prevailed in respect of road service licence for the operation of bus services. Incumbent operators were thus able to object to the award of licences to potential competitors. Numbers of road hauliers and bus operators increased following deregulation, although most of the new entrants were small and many did not survive the initial period of deregulatory fervour. From a figure of 120,000 goods vehicle operator licences immediately after deregulation (1968), the number quickly rose to 143,000 by 1975, but fell again to 125,000 in 1977. There has subsequently been a slower, but more steady increase to the 1988 total of 130,000 (DoT, 1989). In Norway, where domestic goods transport was deregulated in 1986, road gained at the expense of rail freight, subsidies decreased by 5% in the first year and permits issued to market entrants rose by 41% (Gildestad, 1988).

In countries where franchises are awarded, these may be of long duration, such as an initial period of up to ten years, renewable for up to a further seven, in the case of Hong Kong bus operators (Hibbs, 1985: 121). The incumbent operator may, in normal circumstances, expect the contract to be renewed, or rolled forward, in his favour, as has happened, for example in West Germany. Such awards are too long to provide adequate incentives to good performance.

In Australia, private bus operators wishing to increase their share of urban markets struggle to wrest monopoly franchises from state and city transport undertakings with higher costs. Rather than being allowed to prove their ability to operate as good or better services by entry to the market, the operators have to resort to campaigning, in order to convince the legislators of their case (Bus and Coach Association of New South Wales, undated; Higginson, 1989).

3.3 Moves towards deregulation

Prior to, or instead of, embarking on the complete deregulation of a whole industry, governments may start in a small way. This may take either of two forms; the deregulation of a specific market sector; or liberalization that stops short of full deregulation. Sometimes these approaches may be combined. For example, bilateral air traffic agreements may be negotiated between pairs of countries, such as that liberalizing air transport between Britain and the Netherlands, which abolished controls on market entry and on tariffs. Britain, which is a stronger advocate of deregulation than are many of its partners in air services, adopts an incremental, gradualist approach towards the negotiation of more liberal international air service agreements, such as those negotiated with Hong Kong, Japan and Malaysia and agreements for the introduction of lower fares on some routes to France and Germany in 1988–89 (Civil Aviation Authority, 1989: 19).

In a number of countries, including Britain, Australia and the United States, express or long distance and interstate coach services were deregulated separately from the consideration of local bus service deregulation. In Britain, local bus services were deregulated six years after express service deregulation. In Australia, while local deregulation is not formally on the political agenda at present, the subject has received extensive attention from political, industry and academic interests and may still be considered to be a live issue. In the USA, despite initial interest in British bus deregulation by the Urban Mass Transportation Administration, which received regular monitoring reports on progress in the UK during 1986–87, the preference remains for urban public transport services to be operated on a planned basis, with efficiency encouraged by the greater use of competitive tendering, rather than through deregulation.

Pressure for deregulation is not universal. In particular, it is commonly perceived to be unsuited to urban public transport operations which are heavily subsidized and offer higher levels of service at lower fares then would be justified in conventional economic terms, as an element of social, planning and environmental policy. This approach to urban public transport has predominated in mainland Europe, including both Western and Eastern bloc states and in North American cities.

An unresolved issue in the United Kingdom is whether local bus deregulation will be extended to London, the sole area not to be deregulated in 1986. Currently, almost a third of London Transport bus services have been tendered, with the proportion due to rise to 45% by 1993. Cost savings averaging 17.5% have been achieved compared with previous non-tendered operations, reliability improved and bus mileage and ridership increased, without sacrificing network planning and ticketing. While the government maintains that it will deregulate in London, perhaps around 1993, there is some doubt that this will actually take place. The success of network ticketing, which the government itself has encouraged, and fears over the possibility of increased road congestion combine with a preference among independent operators for the lower risks associated with LT contracts (which are full cost contracts) to fuel this doubt. The extension of deregulation to London's local bus services is also dependent on the Conservatives winning the next general election, as no other political party supports this policy.

3.4 The experience of deregulation

It is of the essence of a deregulated environment that no stable, 'final' outcome should be reached, as operators who are free to compete will always have the opportunity to innovate in order to exploit new market opportunities. The rate of change may, however, be expected to become slower after an initial burst of activity in the years immediately following deregulation, as the most pressing adjustments to the new environment will have been made.

In Great Britain, the rapid exploitation of the expanding motorway network by deregulated road hauliers in the 1970s contrasts starkly with the failure of the regulated bus industry to take similar action. Although the data includes journeys on all types of road, the different rates of change in road freight tonne kilometres (up 24%) and express coach passenger kilometres (down 16%) between 1968 and 1978 reflect the relative buoyancy of each industry over a decade when the length of motorways available tripled (DoT, 1989). Travel by express coach only began to increase after deregulation in 1980, one of the principal effects of which was the rapid replacement of slow and infrequent services based on traditional routes with a comprehensive motorway-based, high-frequency national network (Robbins & White, 1985).

In the United States, the deregulation of interstate bus services under the Bus Regulatory Reform Act of 1982 has resulted in an almost threefold increase in the number of operators and a small increase in revenue, but a decline in the operating ratio, as competition has squeezed profit margins (Phillips, 1988).

In Australia, following the earlier deregulation of interstate bus operations (Bureau of Transport Economics, 1985), individual states began to deregulate intrastate services. The deregulation of the Canberra–Sydney coach route in 1986 resulted in a reduction of 25% in fares, an increase from one to four operators and significant frequency improvements. The previous monopoly operator retained 65% of the market share, while running only 40% of the total number of departures, and achieved higher load factors (71%) than the competing companies (33–50%). An analysis of the first year's competitive operation showed all four operators to be making surpluses over direct costs (Carnahan, 1989). The New South Wales state government considered this experimental deregulation to have been a success and in 1987 announced that the complete intrastate coach network would be deregulated.

The impact of deregulation extends beyond the industry which is deregulated. In Britain, express coach deregulation resulted in British Rail introducing a package of discounted 'Saver' return tickets, aimed at the leisure market, on longer distance trains. In Australia, the Sydney–Canberra train service is to be reduced from four to one train per day.

The impact of deregulation on route structures is best known with respect to the development of hub and spoke operation by US airlines. While airlines had traditionally operated out of hubs, they had tended to concentrate on long haul routes. After the deregulation of domestic air services, under the Airline Deregulation Act of 1978, increased long-haul competition resulted in low returns for such services, causing airlines to seek alternative markets. The development of local hubs became easier, as it was now possible to expand on to new routes, to which entry had previously been barred. Instead of attempting to gain the maximum revenue per passenger on long-haul routes, airlines reoriented their operations and concentrated on providing a comprehensive range of services in the area they knew best.

Exploitation of the hub and spoke philosophy is exemplified by Piedmont Airlines, which adopted this route structure as a means of feeding its own services, and expanded to operate from three hubs as a means of spreading the commercial risk and of strengthening market penetration (Gialloreto, 1988). While a popular competitive strategy in the wake of deregulation, it is possible that hub and spoke operation may become diluted as consumers seek to avoid the inconvenience of interchange associated with this route structure. The next phase of competition may take the form of direct services, which may successfully woo passengers from interchange journeys via a hub.

The United States has also experienced the partial deregulation of road freight transport. The 1980 Motor Carrier Act, which only affected interstate haulage, removed entry and distance-related operating restrictions and facilitated commercial rate-making. A decline of up to 25% in freight rates in the first two years of deregulation was claimed and many new carriers have been granted authority to operate interstate transport services, with others increasing the scope of their operations.

The continued restriction of intrastate haulage has, however, reduced the impact of US road freight deregulation. It is also possible that some of the benefits claimed to stem from deregulation should more correctly be attributed to technological developments. These include improved efficiency resulting from computerization of management information and inventory management systems and the success of road *vis à vis* rail haulage due to the greater security and door to door service offered by road transport (Canny & Rastatter, 1988).

Road freight transport has also been deregulated in New Zealand, where the 40-mile protection limit in favour of rail transport was first extended to 150 kilometres and then phased out altogether during the 1980s. In order to equalise road–rail competition on a fair basis, road freight deregulation was accompanied by the restructuring of goods vehicle taxation, which is now related to the vehicle's weight, axle configuration and distance travelled. At the same time, New Zealand Railways (NZR) was reconstituted as a government owned corporation, in place of its former status as a department of state, to enable it to operate more commercially. Subsequently, NZR has reorganized into business sectors and become more market-oriented, developments in which parallels with British Rail may be observed (Taylor, 1989).

In the Irish Republic the process of deregulating road freight transport, which began in 1970 with the deregulation of some agricultural sectors, was completed in September 1988 (Barrett, 1988). In Ireland, as in the United Kingdom when road haulage was deregulated in 1968, deregulation is accompanied by strengthened quality regulation. The award of an operator's licence is dependent upon satisfying European Community criteria relating to good repute, professional competence and financial standing.

Where a loss-making industry is deregulated, deregulation forces operators to separate profitable from unremunerative services. The very similar British and New Zealand legislation deregulating bus services takes account of this aspect of bus operation by requiring services to be separated into commercial and non-commercial routes. Commercial services are those which bus companies register on their own initiative. Non-commercial routes are devised by county or regional councils to run services considered necessary on social grounds, but which operators would be unable to run commercially. Tenders are let by the local authorities for the operation of the subsidized services. While the discipline of improved service costing is advantageous, the separation of commercial from unremunerative services is an essentially artificial one, which has led to difficulties in areas such as profitable and unprofitable sections of route (by time and by geography), fare levels, frequencies and the total amount of resources required to run the services.

Under its Transport Law Reform Act of 1989, the New Zealand government has sought to emulate and expand upon the model of British bus deregulation. Commencing on 1 July 1991, route protection for the provision of scheduled passenger services will be abolished and operators allowed to compete on any route. Operators will be required to register details of routes, timetables and, unlike the British system, fares. New Zealand deregulation extends to all scheduled passenger services, including taxis and rail services, and is not limited to bus services as in Britain.

A further parallel with the British legislation is the requirement for publicly owned public transport undertakings to be established as independent companies by December 1990. Thus, as in the United Kingdom, the selection of subsidized routes and the letting of tenders will be separated from the preparation of bids and operation of the services. Only a minority of the directors of the new companies may be members or employees of any local authority, but, unlike in Britain, it is intended that the companies should continue to be owned by the local authorities (Ministry of Transport, New Zealand, 1989).

3.5 Deregulation in developing countries

The experience of developing countries with respect to public transport deregulation is often overshadowed by shortages of vehicles (which are attributable to import restrictions imposed to constrain foreign exchange requirements) and an excess of demand. These constraints may cause governments to restrict private bus operations, in order that they may control service levels and networks according to considerations of equity. Thus, in Tanzania, bus transport was brought into public ownership following the Arusha Declaration of 1967 as part of a wider policy for public ownership and control of the 'commanding heights' of the economy (Mwase, 1989). The same author criticizes the 1986 Advisory Committe on Transport Services' proposed programme of bus deregulation in the emerging Namibia as unlikely to result in lower fares or adequate coverage of all areas of the country, which he considers would be prejudiced by private bus operators' commercial considerations.

There are, however, many examples of deregulation in developing countries. In Sri Lanka in 1978, import restrictions were eased and tax incentives provided to encourage the purchase of new vehicles (Armstrong–Wright & Thiriez, 1987). The following year, the state monopoly on the provision of bus services was broken and private undertakings permitted to compete on all routes. The presence of competitive pressures is observed in the admission by 10% of private bus operators to running off permitted routes and the stated opinion of the operators that too many buses operate on certain routes, as a result of which 'decent profits' cannot be earned (Ramasinghe, 1988). In Sri Lanka, an important constraint on competition is the need for the private operators to keep their fares down to match the subsidized fare levels of the government buses.

Perhaps a surprising example is the partial deregulation of long distance coach services in China. Here, entry restrictions have been lifted, leaving only a quality requirement. Fares are no longer fixed, but are allowed to vary by up to 10% (15% in remote or mountainous areas) from the standard level. In order not to bias the system against potential privately owned entrants, the depreciation level for state coach enterprises has been increased from

5.2% to 10%. Since the introduction of the first privately run coach service in 1980, the revised regulatory regime has resulted in the private sector owning 28% of the coaches and carrying 12% of the coach passengers in 1986. Rather than taking passengers away from the state corporations, entry of the private sector has facilitated more rapid market growth (44% more passenger kilometres run by all operators in 1986 than in 1981) than would otherwise have been possible, and at lower fares (Song *et al.*, 1989).

A feature of many developing countries is paratransit operations. In some countries, paratransit operates in an environment of controlled competition, such as Hong Kong's two styles of public light buses (shared taxi and line haul operations). Elsewhere, paratransit is subject to less, or ineffectual, regulation and may be considered by the authorities as an unsatisfactory form of public transport, operating unsafe and unreliable services at unregulated fares.

Where such situations prevail, as for example in some African and South American countries, this may be due to governmental inability to enforce controls, rather than through an overt preference for deregulation. Thus, in Lima, Peru in 1989, three weeks after all bus routes had been re-registered, only the state owned buses (20% of the total) were found to be running on their correct routes (Tyler, 1989). In Chile, where the deregulation of bus services was undertaken between 1973 and 1980 (Hibbs, 1985), an element of route control has subsequently been introduced. Route associations, controlled by consortia of owner-drivers, restrict the operation of routes to member drivers. In Brazil, while bus operations are licensed, a small, illegal paratransit operation also exists.

3.6 Future prospects

The deregulation of transport services has spread across all continents over the past decade and embraces parts of all modes of transport. The future is likely to see a combination of complete deregulation in certain markets and more gradual liberalization in others.

One of the largest opportunities for liberalizing transport regulations comes with the introduction of the Single European Market on 1 January 1993. Operators from countries with liberalized regimes are expected to be more readily able to adapt to the competitive environment than those accustomed to operating under strict regulatory controls. Large undertakings will be better placed to exploit pan-European markets than will small firms. However, the value of small, low-cost businesses, especially those from low-wage countries, should not be underestimated in industries such as road haulage (Violland, 1988).

In European aviation too, the pressure for further liberalisation grows as 1993 approaches. This is expected to result in additional liberalized bilateral agreements; further fares liberalization, perhaps embracing business fares; and more fifth freedom rights (Bass, 1989). Airlines will become increasingly commercial, which may lead to further politico-economic merger and takeover battles, possibly involving national flag carriers.

If present political philosophies prevail, changes from public to private ownership of transport undertakings will increasingly influence the regulatory scene. While many government and municipally owned organizations are willing adherents to strict regulation, private companies, and even corporatized concerns still in public ownership, are obliged to earn profits for their shareholders. Their competitive motivation is therefore stronger than that of their public sector ancestors, and may prove an important influence for deregulation. Chilean bus deregulation was introduced at the instigation of the bus industry and the eleven subsidiaries of London Buses Ltd were expressly created as a prelude to their privatisation and the deregulation of London's local bus services.

Following the changes of political control in east European countries such as Hungary and Poland since 1989, the economies of these countries have shifted towards the private sector. It is therefore likely that moves towards the commercialization of transport, including the relaxation or removal of state monopolies and the introduction of competition from a newly formed private sector will take place within the next few years. In Asia, deregulation is under consideration by the government of Benazir Bhutto in Pakistan.

Pressure for further deregulation is also expected to be strong in countries where some deregulation has already occurred. This pressure will arise on two accounts. First, the management of still-regulated industries will press for opportunities to participate in wider markets. Secondly, governments will be obliged to release industries remaining under their control from constraints which prevent them from competing effectively with newly deregulated competitors. Thus, pressure for deregulation may come hand-in-hand with that for the privatisation of organizations such as state-owned airlines, railways and urban transit operators. The role of governmental and regulatory bodies will move away from ownership and control of the operation of transport to assuring the continued regard for safety in all branches of the industry and the provision of adequate public transport services to all sections of the community.

References

Armstrong-Wright, A. & Thiriez, S. (1987) Bus services: reducing costs, raising standards. World Bank Technical Papers No. 68, Urban Transport Series. Washington.

Barrett, S. D. (1988) Freedom for Irish road freight *Transport*, **9**, No. 9 (September).

Bass, T. (1989) Air deregulation *Transport Economist* **16**, No. 4, (Summer).

Bureau of Transport Economics, (1985) Australian long distance coach industry review. Occasional Paper No. 74, AGPS, Canberra.

Bus & Coach Association of New South Wales, (undated) Towards efficient urban bus services: role of the private sector, Sydney.

Bus & Coach Council, (1984) Bus and Coach Council responses to the 'Buses' White Paper, London.

Bass, T. (1989) Air deregulation *Transport Economist* **16**, No. 4, (Summer).

Bureau of Transport Economics, (1985) Australian long distance coach industry review. Occasional Paper No. 74, AGPS, Canberra.

Bus & Coach Association of New South Wales, (undated) Towards efficient urban bus services: role of the private sector, Sydney.

Bus & Coach Council, (1984) Bus and Coach Council responses to the 'Buses' White Paper, London.

Canny, J. & Rastatter, E. (1988) United States trucking deregulation since 1980. Paper to OECD/INRETS Conference 'Road Transport Deregulation: Experience, Evaluation, Research'. Paris.

Carnahan, M. (1989) An economic analysis of the Canberra–Sydney coach route following deregulation. Paper to International Conference 'Competition and Ownership of Bus Services', Macquarie University.

Chester, D. N. (1936) *Public control of road passenger transport*. Manchester: Manchester University Press.

Civil Aviation Authority (1989) *Annual report and accounts 1988-9*, London.

DoT (Department of Transport) (1984) White Paper *Buses*, London: HMSO cmnd 9300.

DoT (Department of Transport) (1989) *Transport statistics Great Britain 1978-1988*. London: HMSO.

Garbutt, P. (1985) *London Transport and the politicians*, London: Ian Allan.

Gildestad, B. (1988) The Norwegian approach to road freight transport deregulation policies. Paper to OECD/INRETS Conference 'Road Transport Deregulation: Experience, Evaluation, Research'. Paris.

Gialloreto, L. (1988) *Strategic airline management*. London: Pitman.

Gwilliam, K. & Mackie, P. (1975) *Economics and transport policy*. London: George Allen & Unwin.

Hibbs, J. A. B. (1985) Regulation: an international study of bus and coach licensing, Cardiff: Transport Publishing Projects.

Higginson, M. P. (1989) Future provision of Brisbane's bus services: options for change. Canberra: Resolution Pty Ltd, for Bus and Coach Association of Queensland.

Ministry of Transport, New Zealand, (1989) Transport law reform fact sheets. Wellington.

Moore, T. (1988) Regulation and deregulation of road transport (in the USA). Paper to OECD/INRETS Conference 'Road Transport Deregulation: Experience, Evaluation, Research'. Paris.

Mwase, N. R. L. (1989) Public and private sector competition in bus transport in Africa with special reference to Tanzania: lessons for independent Namibia. Paper presented to International Conference 'Competition and Ownership of Bus and Coach Services'. Macquarie University.

Palmer, J. (1988) Deregulation in Great Britain: road haulage, express coaches and the railways. Paper to OECD/INRETS Conference 'Road Transport Deregulation: Experience, Evaluation, Research'. Paris.

Phillips, K.B. (1988) Intercity bus deregulation: origins and effects (USA). Paper to OECD/INRETS Conference 'Road Transport Deregulation: Experience, Evaluation, Research'. Paris.

Ramasinghe, P. C. H. (1988) *Private bus transport in Sri Lanka*, Colombo: Friedrich Ebert Stiftung.

Robbins, D. K. & White, P. R. (1985) The experience of express coach deregulation in Britain *Transportation* 13, No. 4.

Song, L., Wang, M. and Shi, B. (1989) Competition in socialist China's coach industry. Paper to International Conference 'Competition and Ownership of Bus and Coach Services'. Macquarie University.

Suga, T. (1988) The privatisation of Japanese National Railways. Paper to OECD/INRETS Conference 'Road Transport Deregulation: Experience, Evaluation, Research'. Paris.

Taylor, M. (1989) New directions in New Zealand transport *Transport* 10, No. 5, (September).

Tyler, N. (1989) Transport Study Group, University College London, Personal communication.

Violland, M. (1988) The lessons to be drawn for European transport policy from the experience acquired in the process of regulatory reform. Paper to OECD/INRETS Conference 'Road Transport Deregulation: Experience, Evaluation, Research'. Paris.

PART II
The British Experience

CHAPTER 4

Bus transport in the
Metropolitan Areas and London

David Banister and Laurie Pickup

4.1 Introduction

Deregulation of bus services in Metropolitan Areas and London was introduced in the 1985 Transport Act and tendering of bus services in London in the 1984 London Regional Transport Act. To cover all the issues would require a book in itself and the interested reader is referred to the reviews of the theory of contestable markets and predatory practices produced by Dodgson and Katsoulacos (1989), and the early experience in Metropolitan Areas produced for the Association of Metropolitan Authorities (Tyson, 1988; 1989; Pickup *et al.*, forthcoming) and by the Transport and Road Research Laboratory (Balcombe *et al.*, 1988), and on London (Higginson, 1988; 1989; Bayliss, 1987). In this chapter we focus on one issue in detail, namely the processes by which services are provided in the Metropolitan Areas and London, highlighting the differences between the two systems and commenting on the advantages and disadvantages of each.

Under the 1985 Transport Act the whole of the country except London became a trial area. This meant that all operators had the opportunity to register commercial services which they were prepared to run without any subsidy. Operators register their intention to commence, change or withdraw a bus service with the area traffic commissioner giving details at least 42 days in advance. Competition would take place on the road. Additionally, local authorities could supplement these services with others which had been put out to competitive tender. Competition would take place off the road and the operator who won the tender would have limited monopoly rights to run that service as specified by the local authority.

Two basic forms of tender document have been used. With the 'minimum cost contract' the operator is required to provide a specified level of service and to collect the fares which are then passed on to the local authority. In return the operator receives an agreed payment from the local authority. The risk here is with the contracting authority. The 'minimum subsidy contract' allows the operator to tender a price after making allowance for the revenue from the service, and the operator keeps the fares. The risk here lies with the operator and there is an incentive for him to maximize revenue through marketing and providing a high quality service. Details of both systems are presented in Table 4.1.

Table 4.1 *Comparison of cost and subsidy-based tenders.*

Cost contracts also called Fixed cost contracts or minimum cost contracts	Subsidy contracts also called Bottom line contracts or minimum subsidy contracts
Advantages	
1. Reduced risk for operator	1. Greater incentive for operator
2. Greater stability may result	2. Reduced risk for authority
3. Attractive to small operators	3. Maximum commercial freedom
4. Simpler administration of network ticketing schemes	4. Simpler administration of operator based ticketing schemes
5. Greater control for authority	5. Minimum 'interference' with commercial market
6. Easier to retain authority marketing schemes, return fares	6. Easier marketing of network
Disadvantages	
1. Increased monitoring costs and manpower for authority	1. Difficulty in retaining authority based ticketing schemes
2. Need for detailed audit	2. High risks for operators may result in high tender prices.
3. Reduced incentive for operator	3. Potential conflict of operator and authority fare objectives
4. Authority must budget to cope with trading risks	4. Risk may deter competition

Source: Huntley (1989).

Metropolitan Areas have almost exclusively adopted the minimum subsidy contract as it reduces their risk, and they have accepted the problems it can create when fares are increased and the complications it can cause with payments for concessionary fares. London on the other hand has made extensive use of the minimum cost contracts with London Regional Transport providing the ticketing equipment and in some cases even the vehicles to run the service as part of the contract. In this way London Regional Transport has maintained much closer control of the services operated in London through the conditions stated in the contract and this has in turn maintained an integrated service in terms of the routes operated, timetabling, marketing and ticketing.

In addition to the basic differences in the type of contract used for tendered services, there are basic differences in the process of tendering used in London and in the Metropolitan Areas. In London all competition takes place off the road with no direct competition on the road – *competitive regulation*. This means that the contract gives the operator exclusive rights to run the services and more control is maintained over the system through full integration and publicity for services. More important it has permitted a smoother process of change and allowed more stability within the system. As we shall argue in this chapter the advantages of stability in London contrast with the volatility of service provision in the Metropolitan Areas under a regime of *full deregulation*.

4.2 Deregulation in the Metropolitan Areas

Figure 4.1 identifies the seven Metropolitan Areas in Great Britain together with Greater London. Until 1986 these Metropolitan counties were responsible for all transport planning functions including the provision of an integrated and efficient system of public transport to meet the needs of that area. The 1985 Local Government Act (effective from April 1986) abolished the Metropolitan County Councils and the Greater London Council. The responsibility for public transport in the Metropolitan Areas (excluding London) remained with the Passenger Transport Authorities, but these PTAs are now composed of Joint Boards of Councillors from the district councils making up the old metropolitan counties. These changes in the organizational structure of the Metropolitan Areas, together with strict financial controls exerted on local authority expenditure and the secular changes that have taken place with the decentralization and spreading of cities provide a dynamic background against which bus deregulation should be set.

The impact of bus deregulation has been very varied between the Metropolitan Areas. The changes relate to the differences in existing public transport policies in each Metropolitan Area, the differences in the urban structure and the different attitudes of operators towards competition. For example, in 1985, while 96% of passenger journeys in the West Midlands travelled on PTE operated buses, only 37% did so in Strathclyde. Details of the population, size and travel characteristics of each Metropolitan Area are given in Table 4.2.

The debate prior to deregulation concentrated on the scale of competition which might emerge after October 1986. Actual levels of competition are difficult to measure and compare in the bus industry. However, it is clear that from the outset of deregulation, competition did exist in the Metropolitan Areas, both on the road and for tendered services. In some cities, the extent of competition was considerable, and in others it was piecemeal. One reason for this variation in response is the wide differences in urban structure and the opportunities for competition. Differences in levels of competition can be partly explained by geography. By the end of 1988, the short-term effects of bus deregulation were emerging from the more immediate consequences of

Figure 4.1 The seven Metropolitan Areas and London.

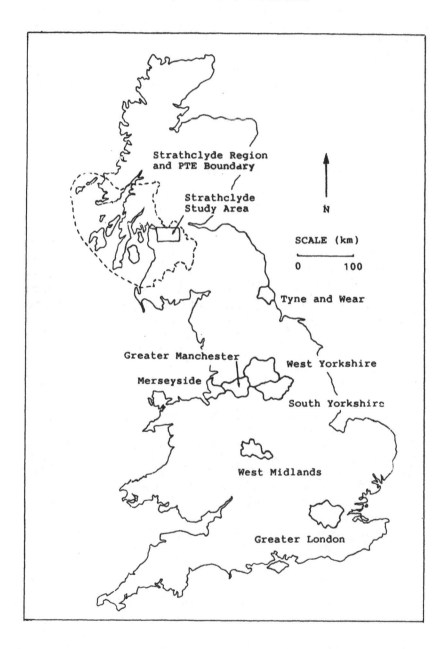

Table 4.2 *Characteristics of the Metropolitan Areas (1981 census).*

	Population 000's	Area sq. km. 000's	% households with car (urban)	Mode of travel work journeys (%)				Employment characteristics		
				bus	rail	car	walk	% males unemployed	% manufacturing employed	% children with mother full-time working
Greater Manchester	2596	1284	52.6	22.3	2.4	50.0	16.3	14.1	32.7	16.7
Merseyside	1512	646	49.9	25.5	4.9	45.9	14.0	19.9	27.2	11.7
South Yorkshire	1304	1560	50.4	33.5	0.6	43.3	15.1	13.4	30.2	11.8
Strathclyde	2405	13727	44.1	28.0	5.7	42.6	17.9	18.4	27.2	14.8
Tyne and Wear	1143	540	45.5	32.7	1.9	41.9	16.6	18.5	27.8	12.1
West Midlands	2649	899	55.7	26.3	2.1	49.1	14.7	17.2	41.2	13.6
West Yorkshire	2037	2039	52.6	24.1	1.0	49.6	16.9	12.6	32.8	14.1

the transition itself. Tyson (1989) summarizes these developments:

(a) The increase in competition has come largely from existing operators competing more actively rather than from new entry into the market which characterized the first year.
(b) There has been a small but steady flow of new entrants into the market which has been more than sufficient to offset withdrawals from it.
(c) The number and scale of withdrawals from the market have been relatively small.
(d) Competition for tendered services has increased to the point where three bids per contract have become the norm.
(e) On commercial services, competition has continued to be on the main corridors and against one of the pre-deregulation established operators. There have been relatively few examples of new operators just competing against each other.
(f) In general, established operators, including some of the PTCs, have lost ground to newer operators.
(g) Although there have been instances of operators closing 'out stations' in the Metropolitan Counties, there are many more examples of operations of this nature being consolidated into a well-established operation. For example, East Midland and North Western services in Greater Manchester.

Commercial competition

The deregulated bus market in the UK Metropolitan Areas has thus emerged to be more contestable than many opponents of the legislation predicted. However, the growth in 'occurrences' of competition and new operators masks what has generally been only a marginal change in market share. Deregulation has produced new operators. However increases in 'number of companies' operating bus services includes operators who previously ran similar services on contract prior to deregulation. In Strathclyde for example, analysis of route and service data (Pickup *et al.*, forthcoming) shows that the number of operators nearly doubled between November 1985 and June 1986. However, the number of larger operators only increased from 12 to 14, the market share of the five largest operators only declining from 84 to 81%. The significant amount of on-the-road competition which did occur largely on the main radial routes in Strathclyde after October 1986 was between previously established operators.

The initial competitive positions were the first registrations of operators' commercial networks during 1986. The larger bus operators in the Metropolitan Areas registered between 80 and 90% of their mileage (mainly cutting evening and Sunday services) in a bid to retain territory. Only in Strathclyde was more mileage registered as commercial than had operated in total before deregulation. Competition has mainly occurred on route patterns rather than on fares or ticketing. However, the fiercest competitive moves on busy radial routes have involved frequent minor retimings to services to 'leapfrog' competitors' operating times.

A growth in minibus use accompanied deregulation, and was to a large extent stimulated by it. Minibus fleets have been used by many larger operators either aggressively to establish patronage in previously badly served suburbs or defensively to consolidate territory and deter entry from competitors using cheaper labour.

While larger companies have competed with each other on commercial services, smaller companies have found it difficult to gain the scale of operation needed and have tended to compete mainly on tendered services where they will be left alone. Where smaller operators have tried to increase their market share on profitable routes, lower cash fares have sometimes been used. Other entries to the market have followed the price of the major operator in an attempt not to provoke fares competition.

The reaction of large operators to competition by smaller companies has been mixed, dependent largely on the perceived threat on specific routes. In general, competition from small operators is tolerated provided that small operators do not attempt to provoke the large operators too much.

Competition for tenders

On tendered services previous research (reviewed in Pickup *et al.*, forthcoming) suggests that competitive tendering is most successful where the number of bidders is sufficiently large; there is no collusion; 'sunk' costs are low enough to allow easy exit from the market; new entrants have access to information; services can be clearly and appropriately specified and contracts are easy to monitor and enforce.

The numbers of operators bidding for contracts and the bids per tender are shown for each Metropolitan Area during the first two years of deregulation in Table 4.3 (Tyson, 1989). Prior to deregulation, it was envisaged that commercial and tendered networks would operate as separate entities. In practice, the two closely interact and effect the formation of overall operator strategies and PTE practice. Labour costs outside normal working hours have had a significant influence on the competitive position of operators for tenders. Table 4.3 shows a general pattern of increasing competition for

Table 4.3 *Operators and bids per tender in the Metropolitan Areas 1986/88.*

Area	Operators		Bids per tender		
	1987	1988	Initial	1987	1988
Greater Manchester	40	63	2.55	2.45	4.00
Merseyside	29	46	1.70	2.77	3.10
South Yorkshire	47	48	1.32	2.43	2.87
Strathclyde	124	128	2.36	3.20	3.40
Tyne and Wear	26	39	1.30	2.75	3.16
West Midlands	38	41	1.49	3.22	3.01
West Yorkshire	36	34	1.36	2.00	3.01

Note: the 1988 West Midlands bids per tender figure is for February 1989.
Source: Tyson (1989)

tenders in all Metropolitan Areas. A more detailed analysis of 422 contracts awarded for tendering services between October 1986 and May 1988 (Pickup *et al.*, forthcoming), showed that uncontested bids over the period fell from 58% to 28%. The share of tendered vehicle mileage operated by the PTC fell from 77% to 67% mainly due to the success of the ex-NBC subsidiary in winning contracts. By May 1988, other small operators still only ran 7% of total tendered vehicle kilometres in the area.

Competition and service levels

Since deregulation, service levels, measured by vehicle kilometres operated have continued to increase. By 1988, vehicle kilometres operated in the Metropolitan Areas had risen by 12% above the pre-deregulation level (DoT, 1989). Other general developments in service levels have been:

(a) Increasing kilometres as a result of more minibuses. While vehicle kilometres in Greater Manchester increased by nearly 30% between November 1985 and June 1988, the increase in seat kilometres was only 2%. Differences in other areas have been less significant (summarized from Pickup *et al.*, forthcoming).

(b) Large variation in service level increases between areas. From November 1985 to May 1988 increases ranged from 1.7% in West Yorkshire to 28.6% in Greater Manchester. Within Metropolitan Areas, further differences have emerged between districts and suburbs. Increased kilometres are mainly on major radial routes. In some areas kilometres actually fell.

(c) Vehicle kilometres have increased in most time periods. Important exceptions are reductions in the early mornings and in some areas on Sundays. While peak services have increased, the largest percentage rises in kilometres have been during weekday inter-peak periods and on Saturdays.

(d) Evidence from studies in selected Metropolitan Areas indicate increased network penetration and a reduction in the distance to the nearest bus stop. Attempts to improve speeds led to increased unreliability. The need to change buses for a given sample of origins and destinations had been reduced. Early problems of reliability existed but available data is patchy. While kilometres have increased, competing services tend to bunch so that passengers experience little improvements in service headways.

(e) The changes in service levels have not been evenly spread across areas and there have been gainers and losers. In Strathclyde, analysis suggests the largest service increases are to areas of low/medium car availability and lower rates of owner occupation.

(f) In November 1986, tendered services accounted for just over 15% of vehicle kilometres in the Metropolitan Areas although the figure varied from 7.8% in Strathclyde to 24.2% in Tyne and Wear. The trend up to May 1988 was for the proportion of tendered kilometres to fall to 11.5%. However tendered services have helped to maintain the overall level of vehicle kilometres. In four areas, commercial kilometres fell by May 1988 to below the pre-deregulation level. Tendered kilometres have 'topped up' the commercial provision so that all areas except the West Midlands show an overall increase in vehicle kilometres.

(g) Tendered services have played an important role filling gaps in the commercial network due to a redistribution of vehicle kilometres after deregulation with frequency enhancements and evening services, so that an 'accessible' network can be maintained.

Competition and fare levels

A detailed analysis of fare level changes in the Metropolitan Areas is given in Pickup *et al.* (forthcoming) and Tyson (1989). Significant fare increases occurred during 1986 as a result of expenditure limits, particularly in South Yorkshire and Merseyside.

Relatively little large scale price competition has occurred since deregulation. Standard fare scales have been retained across operators although the number of exceptions is increasing. In the period 1985/86 to 1987/88, fares rose by 27.5% in real terms (DoT, 1989), most of which occurred at the onset of deregulation. Deregulation has had a one-off effect on fares with few bus users experiencing lower fares. Experience in individual areas has again varied considerably as shown in Table 4.4 for cash fares.

Table 4.4 *Changes in standard cash fares (%).*

Area	Month or months in which increases occurred	1988 % increases on each occasion	1986–88 % increases
Greater Manchester	July	10	36.7
Merseyside		5–13	100.1
South Yorkshire	June/October	14–20 + 8	300.0
Strathclyde	April/May	5	11.0
Tyne and Wear	April/November	6 + 3	41.9
West Midlands	March	3.5	14.5
West Yorkshire	October	6.0	11.6
Increase in RPI		6.8	15.0

Note: these figures are not comparable.
Source: Tyson (1989)

Deregulation – the effects on passengers

Department of Transport figures for the period 1985/86 to 1987/88 indicate a fall in patronage following deregulation of 16.2%. The reductions were far greater in some areas where the effects of expenditure limits have had an added effect on the transition to commercial fare levels and instances of hardship have occurred (Donald & Pickup, 1989). In a period of increasing general mobility, the inability of deregulation to halt the decline in bus use and the reduction in bus use identified among certain low income groups is disturbing.

To judge the performance of deregulation in terms of patronage depends on expectations. On the one hand it can be argued that previous patronage levels were artificially high becuase of subsidized fares, and that the effect of deregulation has had (in general) little effect on patronage (or in some cases has increased patronage over what it would have been with the higher fares). On the other hand one can argue that the deregulated system does not give the scope for effective subsidy (in terms of lower fares), and that the whole package together has (in all but two cases) led to a decline in patronage.

If one looks at bus patronage trends in the country as a whole, the late 1970s and early 1980s saw a departure from the trend of increasing car use and decreasing bus use in the Metropolitan Areas, due to the subsidy of bus services by local government. The abolition of the Metropolitan County Councils and deregulation meant that this level of subsidy was no longer possible, and bus services were set on a course towards their 'natural market role', topped up by subsidized services regarded as 'socially necessary'.

When deregulation is separated from the abolition of the County Councils the effects of deregulation on patronage have not in general been very great, leading to a small loss in patronage. Previous patronage could have been regarded as being 'unnaturally high', because of the high subsidy level.

When one analyses the situation from a non-market perspective, viewing the changes in terms of what could have occurred given a continuation of the policies being carried out by the Metropolitan Areas a very different view emerges. The fares rises can be seen as a direct result of the 'package' of deregulation and abolition, and the situation in most areas has resulted in a large fall in patronage, where the alternative might have been a continuing growth and resurgence in public transport.

4.3 Deregulation in London

London is different. Apart from being the largest city in Great Britain, the capital city and the major international centre for finance and communications, when tendering is discussed it comes under different legislation from the rest of the country. It will be argued here that the form of liberalization in London is preferable to that implemented elsewhere in Britain as services are contracted out wherever possible and the market is now open to all operators. All competition is controlled and takes place off the road. The operator winning the contract has exclusive rights to provide the service over the contract period. On the road competition is not permitted.

In 1984, the London Regional Transport Act transferred control of the London Transport Executive from the Greater London Council to the Secretary of State for Transport and renamed it London Regional Transport (LRT). It was effectively a nationalisation of London Transport and went against the general trend towards privatisation. The background to the conflict between the Conservative central government and the Labour local government is well known (Banister, 1984), leading eventually to the abolition of the Greater London Council and the Metropolitan County Councils. The subsidy to LRT is funded by central government (one third) and the London ratepayer (two thirds), and LRT has to provide or secure public passenger transport services for Greater London taking account of the transport needs of Greater London. LRT had to establish subsidiary companies to run the bus and underground services (this has been done with the formation of London Underground Ltd (LUL) and London Buses Ltd (LBL)), and private capital can be used to run these services, either through tenders and contracting out of services, or through selling shares in the subsidiary companies. Other bus operators can run services under agreements with LRT or independently with road service licences from the traffic commissioners. Since 1984 there has been a remarkable upturn in the demand for transport in London as the economy has grown, unemployment has fallen and income levels have increased at unprecedented rates, particularly if the rise in private capital assets (principally house prices) are taken into consideration (Table 4.5). In 1989 more people have travelled on London Underground and British Rail's Network South East than at any time in the past.

In London there is no competitive network and the market is still regulated through 'competitive regulation'. The monopoly control exerted by London Buses is gradually being reduced as services are put out to competitive tender (Table 4.6). According to the Annual Business Plan (LRT, 1988), some 72

Table 4.5 *Transport in London: the facts – 1987.*

Population	6,771,000	
Employment	3,503,000	
Central London commuting	1,125,000	+9% since 1980
Private cars	2,195,000	+14% since 1980
Car ownership (1985/6)	58%	15% of these households have more than one car
Taxis	14,800	Licensed taxi drivers 19,700 Real increase in fares of 27% since 1980
Bus journeys	1,286 million	+9% since 1980
Passenger km	4,656 million	Real increase in fares of 6% since 1980
Underground journeys	798 million	+47% since 1980
Passenger km	6257 million	Real decrease in fares of 11% since 1980
Network South East (British Rail)		
Passenger km	14,200 million	+9% since 1980 Real increase in fares of 17% since 1980

Source: DoT, (1988)

Table 4.6 *Tendering in London.*

(a) Routes

Description	Tenders invited	Bids	Bids per route	Services started
12 peripheral routes 4.0 million bus km	October 1984	47	3.92	July/August 1985
12 discrete suburban routes 4.2 million bus km	July 1985	46	3.83	Spring 1986
Cross-boundary routes Surrey, Essex, Hertfordshire 9.8 million bus km	1985	66	3.47	1986
10 routes including Central London 4.0 million bus km	July 1986	37	3.70	Early 1987

(b) Networks

Description	Bids per route	Percentage of contract value won by LBL
Surrey	3.50	36
Orpington	2.25	83
Kingston	2.43	87
Harrow	2.09	100
Bexley Heath	3.20	87
Hornchurch	6.33	12
Wimbledon	4.50	100
Surrey Docks	2.40	47
Average	3.85	57

Note: In Bexley Heath LBL offered any combination of routes plus 20 specific combination tenders.
Source: Higginson (1989) and Beesley & Glaister (1989)

million bus kilometres will be operated under contract by the end of 1988, some 18% of the network and an increase of 50% in one year. The actual figure achieved was 64 million bus kilometres with London Buses Ltd operating about 57% of the 135 tendered routes. The financial savings from tendering have been £13 million (17.5%) with individual savings on groups of routes ranging between 22% and 3% (Higginson, 1989). Plans for 1990/91 involve a further 29 million bus kilometres including networks in Barnet and Wandsworth and 29 other bus routes. By 1993 it is anticipated that 45% of the network will be contracted out.

As noted in section 4.1 LRT adopted cost contracts so that small operators could effectively bid against the established large operators. However, by using minimum cost contracts, operators would also have been encouraged to use old vehicles where the depreciation was low or zero. Even here the market for secondhand vehicles was limited as it is not in one operator's interests to sell vehicles to a direct competitor. LRT has therefore pioneered the possibility of leasing appropriate vehicles to the operator as part of the contract procedure. This allows LRT to provide modern vehicles that meet their own requirements for accessible transport and can ensure that stringent safety standards are met. For example, Optare Citypacers have been leased as part of the Camden Hoppa midibus operation. This option seems increasingly popular in getting smaller operators to tender for services and will be a feature of the new city centre midibus services such as the Golden Arrow service. This service will be the first major substitution of midibuses for big buses in Central London and involves an investment of £3 million with frequencies being increased by 60%.

The first signs of on the road competition in London have been seen in Docklands where Harry Blundred has set up a network of 98 minibuses operating a hail and ride service in a part of London that is undergoing rapid change. London Buses only operate a limited service in Docklands. A holding company (Transit Holdings) has invested £4 million in vehicles, but as with some on the road competition in the Metropolitan Areas these new services have not been fully integrated with London Buses as different tickets are required.

4.4 Deregulation or competitive regulation?

In this chapter two types of competitive regimes in bus operations have been outlined. One is based on the identification of a commercial network by the operators which is supplemented by a tendered network of socially necessary services, usually based on a minimum subsidy contract – *deregulation*. The other is based on the authority maintaining control over the whole network and gradually contracting out particular routes and area networks, usually based on a minimum cost contract – *competitive regulation* (Table 4.1). It seems that it is still the Conservative government's intention to move to full deregulation in London in the 'early 1990s' despite the apparent advantages of competitive regulation.

The three most important conclusions on the differences between the regimes will be highlighted here. The competitive regulation in London still allows fares co-ordination and ticketing, and the maintenance of a full network of services together with the possibility of a corporate management strategy. It has allowed London Regional Transport to maintain full control over the quantity and quality of services being operated, as well as maintaining a stable environment for the passengers. The disadvantages are relatively minor. First, there is the time taken in the contracting process between the call for tenders and the actual commencement of the services. This process has taken over nine months, but it has gradually been reduced to six months. Even in the Metropolitan Areas, over 110,000 tender documents have been sent out, and some 11,000 tenders have been considered for the 3577 services tendered in 1988 (Tyson, 1989). The other main disadvantage in London has been the anomalous position of London Buses Ltd which is part of London Regional Transport, the contracting authority. This 'cosy' relationship could be to LBL's advantage or as some commentators have suggested to their disadvantage (e.g. Higginson, 1989). However, despite these limitations it seems that there are clear advantages in having a system of competitive regulation that allows the implementation of a co-ordinated public transport policy which in turn permits a smooth transition from a heavily regulated system to a competitive system.

The deregulation of bus services under both regimes has led to significant cost savings amounting to some 20% in the Metropolitan Areas, and some 20% in the peripheral services in London and some 10% in Central London. These savings include reductions in wage levels as well as improvements in productivity. Wage levels do not seem to have been reduced significantly in London as salaries in the capital are traditionally at higher levels than elsewhere and there have always been recruitment problems. Much of the savings in London can be attributed to increases in productivity and the introduction of minibuses (Banister et al., 1989).

In the Metropolitan Areas savings have been achieved through both productivity improvements and reductions in wage levels. Recruitment of staff has been easier in the Metropolitan Areas and when deregulation took place unemployment levels were higher than those in London. Savings have been achieved through direct reductions in basic wages, lower wage rates for new and promoted staff, and lower wage rates for minibus drivers. The local authorities also provided generous voluntary redundancy schemes which enabled the Passenger Transport Companies to trim staff levels between 1985/86 and 1987/88, particularly in engineering and maintenance staff (-41%), but also for platform staff (-17%). However, the tendency for wage demands to rise with inflationary pressures will limit the ability of metropolitan bus operators to maintain such cost savings. Pressure may again be placed on fares levels and services unless productivity gains can be increased. It seems that in London most savings have come through reductions in the contract costs and increases in productivity with costs per operated kilometre being reduced by over 10% (1985–87). In the Metropolitan Areas there have been some improvements in productivity and through the introduction of minibuses, but a much greater saving seems to have been made in labour costs than has been the case in London. The crucial question here is whether these savings in wage costs can be maintained.

The third conclusion concerns the contestability of the market itself. It seems that the conditions of contestability do exist as sunk costs are low, even though there are some barriers to entry and exit, and all operators have access to the same technology. Where the market is less contestable is in the quality factors such as access to bus stations, the availability of service information and experience, and the requirement for 42 days' notice for changes in registration. These factors have made it difficult for 'hit and run' operations where the new entrant sees a market opportunity and enters the market for a short while to make a profit and then withdraws when the incumbent operator reacts. The market position of small operators seems to be with the tendered services and not on the commercial network. Competition on the main corridors of the commercial network in the Metropolitan Areas seems to be restricted to the larger operators where competition takes place among equals and where incumbent advantages are limited. This means that smaller operators may have a greater potential to compete in London where services are contracted out. As the competitive market becomes more stable it seems that larger companies are formed either through mergers or through holding companies owning several operators. The natural sequence in the competitive market may be the re-establishment of oligopolistic or monopolistic operations, and it will only be on the tendered routes that the small operators will be able to compete as they are granted monopoly rights, if successful in the bidding process. In the Metropolitan Areas there may be a few large operators running the vast majority of services with small operators running special niche services and some tendered routes. It may be in London that the greater variety of operators will be found as all competition takes place off the road and small operators can compete on equal terms with the large operators.

The Metropolitan Areas have been the acid test of the 1985 Transport Act and the main effects seem to have been a reduction in revenue support on buses at no great loss to service frequency (Table 4.7). Tyson (1989) estimated that about 70% of this saving to the tax and rate payer has been passed on to the traveller through higher fares. However, due to the uncertainty caused by a fairly traumatic period of transition there has also been a significant downturn in patronage which has in turn accelerated the well known downward vicious spiral. Permanent damage may have been caused to the quality of bus services. Competitive regulation as practised in London seems to offer an alternative which allows similar savings but maintains the stability in services which is so important to the traveller. All competition for services takes place off the road so that cost savings can be made through the tendering process and the quality of service can be maintained through the terms of the contract.

Table 4.7 *Summary of changes over the initial period of deregulation (1985–87).*

	Full deregulation Metropolitan PTCs	Competitive regulation London Buses Ltd
Passenger journeys	− 16.2%	+ 10.2%
Vehicle kilometres	+ 7.5%	+ 1.8%
Fares	+ 27.5% in real terms	+ 4% in real terms
Ticketing	Travelcards can be used on most services	Travelcards and Capital Cards on any service
Stability	Low but improving	High
Staff employed	− 26%	− 23%
Passenger receipts in real terms	− 1.1%	− 8.1%
Revenue support	− 22%	− 18%
Proportion of network tendered	14%	25%

Note: In the Metropolitan Areas only the non-commercial services are put out to tender, while in London all services on certain routes and networks have been put out to contract.
Source: DoT (1989)

If competitive regulation had been introduced in the Metropolitan Areas then the cost savings achieved in London through the increases in productivity could have been further augmented by the savings made in labour costs due to the differences in the local labour market conditions outside London. Net savings seem to have been similar under the two types of competitive regime but the costs of full deregulation are much higher. It seems that if competitive regulation had been introduced in the Metropolitan Areas even greater cost savings could have been achieved with less instability and loss of patronage. There seems to be a strong case to delay the decision to fully deregulate bus services in London until the longer term effects of the two types of competitive regimes are evaluated as competitive regulation may offer significant advantages over full deregulation.

Acknowledgements

The research on Metropolitan Areas reported in this chapter comes from a major monitoring study of the effects of the 1985 Transport Act on the Metropolitan Areas funded by the Association of Metropolitan Authorities and the Passenger Transport Executive Group. The work involved a team of researchers at Oxford University Transport Studies Unit – Gordon Stokes, Shirley Meadowcroft, Phil Goodwin and Francesca Kenny as well as the joint author. Bill Tyson was the coordinator of that project. Discussions on the London situation were held with Martin Higginson and Peter Livermore. Their various contributions to this chapter are all acknowledged although the views expressed remain those of the chapter authors.

References

Balcombe, R. J., Hopkin, J. M. & Perrett, K. E. (1988) Bus deregulation in Great Britain: a review of the first year, *Transport and Road Research Laboratory* RR161.

Banister, D. J. (1984) Central–local relations in Britain: the case of the Fares Fair policy in London, *Transport Policy and Decision Making*, 2(3), 275–89.

Banister, D. J., Mackett, R. L. and Bird, J. (1989) The minibus – theory, recorded experience and their implications. Report to London Regional Transport. Published in *Transport Reviews* 1990.

Bayliss, D. (1987) Deregulation or competitive regulation? Keynote address to the 1987 Australian Bus and Coach Conference, Alice Springs, Australia.

Beesley, M. & Glaister, S. (1989) Bidding for tendered bus routes in London. Paper presented at the International Conference on Competition and Ownership of Bus and Coach Services, Thredbo, Australia.

DoT (Department of Transport) (1988) *Transport Statistics for London*, London: HMSO, Statistics Bulletin (88) 51.

DoT (Department of Transport) (1989) *Transport Statistics Great Britain 1978–1988*, London: HMSO.

Dodgson, J. & Katsoulacos, Y. (1989) Competition, contestability and predation: the economics of competition in deregulated bus markets. Liverpool Studies on Bus Deregulation WP 6, University of Liverpool.

Donald, R. & Pickup, L. (1989) The effects of local bus deregulation in Great Britain on low income families – The case of Merseyside. Paper presented at the International Conference on Competition and Ownership of Bus and Coach Services, Thredbo, Australia.

Higginson, M. (1988) Competition and London's bus services. In Harrison, A. & Gretton, J. (eds) *Transport Policy in the UK – 1987*, Policy Journals, Newbury, pp. 52–57.

Higginson, M. (1989) Deregulate: who dares? – the London experience. Paper presented at the International Conference on Competition and Ownership of Bus and Coach Services, Thredbo, Australia.

Huntley, P. G. (1989) *Tendering and local bus operation: the practical handbook*, Kingston: Croner.

LRT (London Regional Transport) (1988) Annual Business Plan 1988/89, LRT, Broadway, London.

Pickup, L. *et al.* (forthcoming) Monitoring the effects of the 1985 Transport Act in the Metropolitan Areas. Oxford University Transport Studies Unit report to the Association of Metropolitan Authorities and Passenger Transport Executive Group, Oxford: TSU.

Tyson, W. J. (1988) A review of the first year of bus deregulation. Report to the Association of Metropolitan Authorities and Passenger Transport Executive Group.

Tyson, W. J. (1989) A review of the second year of bus deregulation. Report to the Association of Metropolitan Authorities and Passenger Transport Executive Group.

CHAPTER 5

Deregulation in the Outer Metropolitan Area

Peter Stanley

5.1 Introduction

The 1985 Transport Act represented a fundamental change in the philosophy of planning and controlling bus services in the United Kingdom outside London. It reversed the trend, seen in the legislation of the previous two decades, to increase the involvement of local government in the co-ordination, financing and planning of local bus services. The legislation relied instead upon a belief that the forces of the market were capable of stimulating adequate responses to maintain local bus services; provoke innovatory responses in supply; and above all generate an increased efficiency in operations. This was to occur in a market where the secular trend of demand, over the previous 30 years, had been one of continuous decline.

To achieve this dominance of market forces in the provision of services the Act adopted a two-pronged strategy of change:

(a) Deregulating the market for local bus services – easing the conditions of provision to slacken the requirements of market entry and hence potentially allowing increased competition to take place.
(b) 'Privatisation' of publicly owned local transport services – to remove the direct influence of public agencies from the operation of services and hence to engender a more commercial attitude in its management.

The implementation of these two thrusts of policy overlapped. Complete deregulation of the market was achieved as from January 1987, ending the period of transition that had been operative from January 1986. The process of privatising the National Bus Companies (the major operators in the South-East of England outside the London area) began as early as August

1986 but continued for nearly two years before all the companies had been sold. It is important to realize that these two processes strongly interacted and that the resulting changes seen in the bus services operated owe at least as much to the changes in the ownership structure of the industry as to the deregulation of the market. Equally it should be appreciated that in the Greater London area the policies of the 1985 Transport Act did not apply. The publicly owned major bus company, London Buses, was not and is still not, privatised. Also the local market was not deregulated and bus operations seen in the capital are rigidly controlled by London Regional Transport through a system of franchising routes, after soliciting bids for their operations through competitive tendering. The indications are that this situation will at least apply until 1992.

5.2 The interaction of deregulation and privatisation

This interaction between the two main policies, flowing from the 1985 Act, has been especially important in conditioning the changes seen in the Outer Metropolitan Area of the South-East of England. The timing of the privatisation of companies varied throughout the region. Some companies, such as the City of Oxford Motor Services, were of the first contingent to be sold, mainly to management buy-outs and according to some sources at relatively knocked down prices, while others came much later in the process when interest from external bidders had increased and prices had correspondingly risen.

The companies that were sold early into the cycle were left with capital debts, often low in relation to the worth of the assets they held and the anticipated value of their future cash flows. This created enormous potential for future growth in these companies. It is significant that the greatest expansions, through acquisition and establishment of new companies, has been associated with those NBC companies that enjoyed early privatisation, such as Devon General and Badgerline. Also most of the early sales were predominantly through management buy-outs, where the pre-existing managerial team continued in control and the main management thrust could be aimed at improving the efficiency of operation but within an overall concern to remain in the bus industry and make profits, if possible, from bus operation. Early sales gave companies a competitive edge through the new managerial freedom they could exercise. Long-term plans and strategies could be instituted and new bus acquisition policies defined, that could be backed by their healthy resource base. This has led to firms such as the City of Oxford Motor Services and East Kent returning some of the best financial returns, relative to their assets, seen in the industry today. Equally they felt a general relief that the distraction of a time consuming process of competing in the privatisation process, was behind them and that they could now concentrate on running bus services. The companies that were considered later in the privatisation found themselves doubly handicapped in the new deregulation environment. The uncertainties surrounding their future and the managerial time needed to try to put forward their own management buy-out bids in the face of growing external interest in the sales, eroded their ability to respond to the new environment. No long-term plans could be formulated and strategies of just holding their current position, as well as they could until the uncertainties were removed, tended to predominate. This undermined positive responses to the new deregulated market.

Also the growth of the external interests in sales, certainly in the South-East, became far more centred upon the property holdings of companies and the profits they could realise through redevelopment, than upon the potential profitability of the bus operations themselves. The case of Alan Souter's purchase of Hampshire Bus is well known in the industry, where the purchase of the company was soon followed by the resale of elements of its property in Southampton at, reputedly, double the value of initially purchasing the whole company. This in turn appears to have financed his subsequent purchase of East Midland Motor Services.

The concentration on the value of property assets even led to some sales being completed where the bus operation was sold separately from the land and buildings the company held, for example in the case of the sale of London Country South West. This in turn imposed considerable constraints on the future possibilities of bus operation. The denuded bus companies have had to make either lease back and rental agreements with the new property owners, or acquire new facilities. Often this situation was resolved by the purchase of small local independents to acquire replacement depots hence releasing the rental sites for redevelopment. This strategy also held the benefits of simultaneously removing a local competitor. This has been the case in Hertfordshire, an example that will be considered in more depth later.

The point to stress, therefore, in considering the picture of the nature of changes seen in the Outer Metropolitan Area of the South-East, is that because of the parallelism of the processes of deregulation and privatisation, the impact of just one of these processes cannot be disentangled. Also, given that these forces of change have been current during a period when the underlying economic fortunes of the area were rapidly moving from one of relative economic depression to one of considerable growth, the identification of the real causes of change is extremely difficult. An appreciation that the labour shortages, rapid escalation in property values, and the re-emergence of central London as a growing employment centre, have had profound impacts on the South-East, is needed, for these have in turn conditioned and constrained the nature of changes in the local bus industry.

5.3 The nature of the market for bus services in the Outer Metropolitan Area

The Outer Metropolitan Area of South-East England is on average the wealthiest region in the United Kingdom. The high level of personal incomes is reflected in the high levels of household car ownership, with areas such as Surrey and Hertfordshire heading the national figures. The relationships between income, car ownership and bus use are now well established, with the propensity to use the bus having a strong inverse correlation with personal access to a car. In general it would be expected that the levels of bus use per capita in the South-East would be below the national average. Few statistics are available to attest to this pattern but the 1981 census returns show that even in the relatively depressed area of Thurrock in south-west Essex only 8% of the journeys made to work, were by bus. One contributory factor to this situation is the highly developed rail commuter system and the growing re-emergence of Central London as a growing employment centre. The use of rail for the journey to work has grown enormously over the period since 1982.

The importance of the bus for work purposes in some localities should not, however, be understated. In places such as Brighton over 24% of journey to work trips in 1981 were made by bus (national average 16%), while in locations such as Oxford the large student population still generates a considerable volume of traffic, sufficient, it seems to keep two competing bus companies in profit. Much of the basic market for local movement is associated with school traffic and shopping, with some significant localized demand for the journey to work.

In London itself, however, the sheer size of the local population and the difficulties of using and parking a car, mean that large volume movements on the bus are encountered. Although the share of total travel performed by passengers on buses in London has declined in the 1980s, this has been within a generally rising travel market and unlike elsewhere in the United Kingdom, which has witnessed passenger declines since deregulation, volumes have slightly risen. This has meant that the newly privatised ex NBC subsidiary companies, have looked towards London Regional Transport contracts as a way of obtaining a stable income in a high volume market and hence offsetting the instabilities of their local markets. This preference for obtaining these London contracts has led some companies into difficulties as they have overstretched themselves and have failed to perform their scheduled mileage on local county council contracts and on their locally registered services. There is also some evidence that the potentiality of large profits in a deregulated London, that may be realized in the near future, have caused some companies to hold back resources ready for a launch of new services in the capital when the chance is offered. So although London itself has not been part of the bus deregulation and privatisation process, it still wields a considerable influence on the services seen in the South-East and the volumes of trade possible there, stand in marked contrast to those witnessed elsewhere in the region.

5.4 Commercial registrations

A major change evoked by the 1985 Act was to give the freedom to operators, who had already established their competence with the Traffic Commissioners, to register any commercial services they wished. Although such registrations could be questioned, in certain instances by local authorities on the grounds of inducing unacceptable levels of local congestion, in reality such constraints have been non-operative. In the centre of Oxford, for instance, the number of buses moving through the pedestrianized shopping streets of the town centre more than doubled when Thames Transit began its minibus services in competition with the services of the City of Oxford Motor Services. The local authority, however, failed ultimately to obtain curbs on non-local bus traffic using the streets.

At the advent of the deregulated era the level of commercial registrations in the South-East was surprisingly high. Eastern National, the main operator in the southern parts of Essex registered 92% of its pre-deregulation mileage, while similar high levels were seen in Brighton and on London Country operations in Stevenage. Elsewhere figures of about 75–80% were commonplace.

Through time these levels appeared to have fallen with (in 1988) 37% of all bus mileage in Hertfordshire being operated under county council tendered contracts and over 20% similarly operated in Essex. One of the most dramatic deregistrations was seen in Berkshire where the County Council found themselves faced with the complete deregistration of Bee Line Bus Company's routes in Maidenhead, Newbury, Bracknell, Windsor and Wokingham. This move seemed to have been generated by the poor financial state of the bus company. The routes selected related far more to the perception by the company that the County Council would be forced to reinstate them, than their general poor financial performance. After tendering the company won back all but one of the routes at a total additional cost to the Council of £367,000 which breached their budget for 1986/7. Similar curtailments of commercial services by Maidstone and District in the Medway area in 1987 caused Kent County Council to face an increase in its local costs, after retendering, from £385,000 to £716,000 (an 86% increase in one year). Maidstone and District secured the larger part of the new contracts offered.

Non-registered services have mainly fallen into the groups that were commonly witnessed throughout the country: evening and Sunday services being withdrawn completely, while low demand routes, such as rural services, were registered with much reduced frequencies. Most of the counties in the area took as their initial aim to re-establish the services lost by the new competitive tendering procedures and hence reconstitute the previous network. This reflected the short period of time available for the work to be completed on the first round of tendering and the need to consider all routes simultaneously. In subsequent rounds of tendering, the process was generally staggered by area so allowing greater time to be spent on the exercise and so facilitating the generation of general policies and a deeper analysis of the routes that should be offered to operators.

Deeper analysis of the spread of commercial registrations, however, showed an interesting relationship between non-registrations and the configurations of local land uses. In the new towns of Harlow, Stevenage and Basildon these associations were extremely marked. In Stevenage and Basildon routes serving the main hospitals were lost, reflecting their eccentric positions relative to the main passenger flows in the town and the fragmented nature of their passenger demand. Early morning services to the peripheral industrial areas in Harlow and Basildon were also disproportionately affected. Both cases demanded reinstatement by the County Council, in the case of the industrial areas at considerable expense, for the services needed attracted relatively high cost bids from operators reflecting the high costs of providing more capacity in service provision in the morning peak. It would appear that the strong land-use zoning patterns seen are not conducive to the operation of commercial bus services. For a full development of this point see Stanley and Pearmain (1987).

5.5 Competitive registrations

This freedom to establish services where operators perceived the potentialities of making profits should have encouraged the registration of numerous competing services but in general there have been few examples of sustained competition between operators in the South-East. The notable exception has been in Oxford.

Competition has been seen, at various times in a variety of locations in the region. Acrimonious and quite fierce battles have ensued, most of which have been quickly resolved one way or the other. The South Coast resorts of Poole and Bournemouth have been notable in this respect. In Poole, for instance, there were at one time six different operators competing for the limited traffic available. The area had been an established component of the Wilts and Dorset territory prior to deregulation and for some period after. In the autumn of 1987, however, a perfect mix of former NBC subsidiaries, under the control of both management and outsiders, a municipally owned company, and old and newly established independent operators, moved into the area. Single and double deckers plied for trade in competition with new minibuses as Shamrock and Rambler, Southern Vectis, and Badgerline moved in to take on Wilts and Dorset who responded with increased services. By April 1988, however, the companies began to withdraw leaving the field to the traditional local operator.

Similar competitive intrusions have been seen elsewhere but, in general, the traditional established operator has won through by shaking off their complacency and retaliating either through improved local services, or in some cases, by buying out the opposition. It would appear that 'playing at home' gives companies a distinct edge in any competitive confrontation. Perhaps the depth of local knowledge about the market linked with some passenger expression of brand loyalty to the established operator, gives just sufficient support to undercut the impact of the intrusions. Equally, management may be willing to fight harder, and hence devote more resources, for the continuance of what they see as their rightful local market than they are to preserve and develop what are often speculative invasions of others' territory. Certainly the territorial perception, so strong in the days of the NBC operations, still appears to dominate in the post deregulation environment.

Sustained competition, should logically, be only possible if long-term profitability can be achieved by all parties involved in that competition. There was considerable argument about the 'contestability' of local markets for bus transport in the academic press at the time of the 'Buses' White Paper in 1984. It would appear from the evidence of post deregulation activities in the bus industry in the South-East that it is possible to generate profits from bus operation, if the companies are efficiently run. What is questionable, however, is whether there are sufficient profits available to simultaneously sustain two competitive companies. In the short term it is plausible for a company to continue to operate a service, after it has committed the initial capital outlays, if it generates sufficient revenue to cover the direct costs of operation and to contribute something towards overheads. The company would actually be worse off if it stopped operation if this level of revenue was forthcoming. Given the short spells of competitive activity seen it would appear that not even this level of revenue generation has been possible from some of the competitive ventures.

In the longer term, however, revenue must not only cover direct costs but also give a return to replace the assets being utilized. When revenue falls between these two levels the crucial question of whether to withdraw the service is often associated with the need to replace vehicles, maintenance and garaging facilities, etc. That is, capital replacement decisions are involved. This would appear to be the case in Oxford where Thames Transit established (January 1987) a comprehensive network of services, based upon minibus operation, to compete with the incumbent City of Oxford Motor Services. The initial surge of alleged competitive dirty practices has settled and now a seemingly stable relationship between the operators has evolved, two years on from the invasion by the new company. Competition has been based solely on quality of the service offered, for the fares of each operator have matched each other from the beginning of competition. The point worth noting is that the minibuses being used by Thames Transit are being depreciated over six years, according to the company's accounts. If the revenues being generated by Thames Transit fall into the range, noted above, then continued competition would be possible for a few years more before vehicles are theoretically needed. Evidence from elsewhere, however, would imply that an assumed six-year life for transit minibuses, being used on continuous stage carriage operations, is optimistic, and that even if this could be accomplished, maintenance costs, and hence the direct costs of operation, are likely to rise dramatically as the vehicles approach this age. If Thames Transit are in this position, then withdrawals and recasting of services are likely to be seen in about two years' time. If revenue generation has been sufficient to cover all long-term costs then the competition is capable of being sustained seemingly for an indefinite period.

The Oxford situation also raises some other interesting issues concerning the impact of competition. When two companies match fare levels for a long period it is extremely difficult for either of them to raise fares to reflect rising costs. This is the case on the two companies' coach services to London where fares have remained almost constant since 1987. If either raises their fares there is the fear that they will lose a substantial proportion of their market share, while if the fares are simultaneously moved together there is the possibility of being taken to the Office of Fair Trading for practising collusion and uncompetitive practices. Yet if the fares remain at a constant level in a period of rising costs then profitability suffers. If either strategy is adopted the companies will financially suffer, but obviously in the interim the passengers enjoy an extremely low cost service.

The final aspect to note about the impact of competition is upon the timing of services. A situation analogous to Hotelling's classical study of two ice cream sellers on the beach would seem to arise. Here, however, the supply of services is conditioned in respect of the timing of services rather than in the spatial domain. Competing companies will always find a competitive advantage by running their services just before those of the opposition. Retaliatory strategies would ultimately mean that the services would have the same scheduled time. From the public's point of view, equally spaced services are the best for they reduce average waiting time, yet to achieve this situation the operators must come to some agreement. Such agreements have been considered by the Office of Fair Trading and found to be contrary to competition. In such cases competition can, therefore, actually result in worse services for the public than could be achieved by cooperation.

5.6 Tendering and local authorities

Local authority subsidization of socially necessary but unremunerative bus services has been allowed in the United Kingdom from 1968 in respect of rural services, and from 1974 in a general way. Such public involvement in financially supporting bus services has always been discretionary and hence wide variations in local government's response has been encountered, often associated with the political colour of the authority and their perception of the local need for such services. Local authorities, however, do have a statutory duty to provide school transport to certain categories of children, and have had a growing role in providing concessionary fare schemes for the elderly and disabled and performing social-service-based transport schemes. Financially supporting loss-making local bus services has been only one of their transport roles and generally the sums devoted to this by county councils are, in most instances, now substantially lower than their spending on school transport.

The 1985 Act removed the general co-ordinating role of county councils for all public transport services in their area and instead limited their planning concerns to just the tendered services. All commercial services were, therefore, beyond their sphere of influence and they were charged in the implementation of their new role in avoiding any practice that could inhibit competition in that sector. Their role in securing school transport and of maintaining concessionary fare schemes was not fundamentally altered but some stress was laid in the legislation upon increasing the integration of educational and social service transport under their control more fully with the tendered sector. The general levels of per capita spending seen in the county council areas of the South-East for 1987/8 are shown in Table 5.1.

Table 5.1 *1987/8 per capita budgets for all passenger transport expenditure (all in £/head).*

Area	Public transport support		Concessionary payments	Schools	Total
	County	District			
Buckinghamshire	2.36	0.00	2.20	5.97	10.53
Hertfordshire	3.03	0.93	3.53	2.48	9.97
Isle of Wight	2.07	0.00	2.55	5.22	9.85
Hampshire	2.80	0.65	3.55	2.43	9.43
Essex	2.56	0.04	2.01	4.39	9.01
Kent	2.20	0.02	0.83	5.06	8.12
Berkshire	1.40	0.07	3.72	2.40	7.59
Oxfordshire	1.44	0.24	1.78	3.66	7.13
Surrey	2.70	0.00	1.28	2.65	6.63
Dorset	0.78	0.14	1.07	4.27	6.26
East Sussex	1.70	0.33	1.46	2.05	5.54
West Sussex	1.37	0.00	1.49	2.50	5.36
English counties Median values	1.70	0.07	1.93	4.21	8.12

Source: derived from Chartered Institute of Public Finance & Accounting statistics

One of the government's main objectives in introducing competitive tendering was to reduce the cost of public transport support by local authorities, but as can be seen from the figures in Table 5.1, this approach was only to affect a small proportion of total expenditure in this field. In the first round of tendering, savings were forthcoming to some county councils but the response to offered services was extremely variable. In Hampshire for instance, of nearly 500 tenders offered, 141 attracted only bids from a single operator and just 47 solicited bids from three or more operators. Some offered routes in Essex actually attracted no bids at all and services were only secured after operators were subsequently prompted to offer bids. The patchiness of competition for tenders reflected the general dearth of operators in some areas and the difficulties in obtaining more drivers if new business was won. This problem has grown through time.

The tendering of services generally worked, initially, against the larger operators and many independents took it as an opportunity to safely establish themselves in stage carriage operations. It represented a method of entering the larger company's area of operation without having to suffer the full impact of their counter competition. Local authority contracts represented a stable income, one against which new capital could be borrowed to facilitate expansion. It was, therefore, a safe way to expand. Many of the larger companies were aware of these possibilities and there is some belief that the level of initial commercial registrations was deliberately overstated to keep out such intrusions from other operators through the tendering process. Once the fact that little competition was forthcoming from this avenue was realized then deregistration of marginal routes could be accomplished knowing that a high probability existed that they could be won back with local authority financial support. It is this strategy that probably underlaid the route changes of Beeline in Berkshire noted above. The lack of substantial local competition and the general deregistration of formerly registered commercial services has gradually pushed up the number and costs of contracts and the initial savings have been quickly eroded.

The process of tendering

There were two possible avenues that the county councils could have adopted in the structuring of the financial arrangements for the payment of tender prices. Most of the contracts were arranged on a net subsidy agreement. Here the contracts aimed to compensate the operator for the shortfall between revenue and costs on the route. The bids solicited related to operator perceptions of the anticipated shortfalls. The risks of being wrong fell totally on the operator but equally it gave the successful operator an incentive to maximize revenue by marketing the service. This form of contract, however, favoured the pre-existing operator on the route for they were in the best position to reliably gauge the revenue take available. Hence it favoured a position of little change or of small operators taking something of a leap in the dark and subsequently suffering, because they had been too optimistic in their initial estimates of the revenue earning capabilities of routes.

The other form of contract was minimum cost based. Here the operators bid for the sum they required to operate the route. All revenues generated would be considered the property of the county council. This put the risk of failure totally on the county council. Essex County Council adopted this approach for they believed that all operators were capable of estimating the costs of operation and hence there would be a greater degree of open competition for the tenders. Secondly it gave the Council an opportunity of marketing all their supported services as a coherent network with ticket promotions, interlinked timetables, etc. The offer of reduced cost tickets, to particularly promote weekend travel by bus in Essex, has been viewed as extremely successful, and the County Council has maintained this approach.

The operation of tendered services and staff costs

The tendering system resulted in a firm legal contract being drawn up between the bus company and the county council. The operator was to deliver a certain service level, at the required time, often using a specified capacity of vehicle, in return for a payment of the bid sum. Normally payment was made on a quarterly basis. To safeguard their position in acquiring the best value for public money, and to ensure that the terms of the contract were being fulfilled, county councils monitored the supported services and encouraged the public to write in if buses failed to arrive as timetabled.

Certain county councils have had considerable problems in the failure of bus companies to deliver their contracted services. The case of Hertfordshire, foremost among the councils taking operators to task for such failures, will be considered more closely below. Much of the problem seems to stem from the nature of the local labour market in the South-East. In the first 18 months following deregulation, competition for tenders was sufficient to allow county councils to secure services at reasonable cost. Most tendered services were operated in a satisfactory way. More recently, however, there is growing evidence that interest in certain types of operation is falling off. Usually the services to which this applies are ones that require a new driver commitment, either for all of the day or for evening work. When operators have been questioned about their failure to submit bids most have given the same answer, the lack of drivers and the inability to recruit more at current wage levels.

Bus operation is labour-intensive. In fact about 70% of the costs of bus operation can be attributed to staff inputs and hence keeping down staff costs is fundamental to profitable operation. The rapid growth of minibus services elswhere in the country has been facilitated by the bus companies' abilities to offer low wages and still attract drivers from the relatively large pools of the unemployed. In the South-East this has not been so easily accomplished. Substituting minibuses for conventional bus operation usually means increasing the number of drivers employed. In the South-East extensive schemes for such minibus substitution have been made by some operators but subsequently have had to be abandoned or reduced when insufficient drivers have been recruited.

The problem now, is not only acquiring new drivers for extending services or undertaking new ventures, but in retaining those already employed by the firm. Trained drivers with PSV qualifications are in short supply. Taking on new staff, training to the standard required, and then getting them through the required test, is expensive. The current waiting time for tests is about eight weeks in the South-East, with a subsequent two weeks until the badge is through. This means a company has to pay ten weeks' wages, at say £200/250 basic per week, before that person can be productive for the company. Also each person lost generates a gap of ten weeks before they can be fully replaced. Inevitably the coverage of work suffers, services are not covered, and if the shortage continues deregistrations of commercial services may follow. This in turn causes a new tender to be generated by the council to cover the loss and obviously the existing operator is not interested in even offering a bid. Ultimately the loss of services through lack of interest could occur.

This scenario is perhaps a little overdrawn but the fundamental trend in the bus industry of staff losses is certainly real. Companies such as Kentish Bus are now contemplating giving loyalty bonuses to staff that stay with them for more than a year. Municipally owned Brighton Buses was forced to recruit in the North-East of England. It managed to obtain 15 drivers being laid off by United Automobile, but also had to give hotel accommodation to secure their services. These instances just mirror growing problems being encountered throughout the South-East where lost mileage due to staff shortages appears to be generally rising.

5.7 Services in Hertfordshire

A consideration of the situation in Hertfordshire since deregulation offers a detailed picture of most of the themes alluded to above. It offers an opportunity to see how these different trends intermingle and contribute to problems in other areas of bus operation.

At deregulation most of the services in Hertfordshire were operated by London Country. The company ringed the whole of London, operating in Surrey, Essex and Kent, and was ultimately to be split into four operating units on privatisation – Kentish Bus, London and Country (formerly South West), London Country North East and North West. All were late in being privatised from the National Bus Company.

Prior to deregulation London Country North East, especially, had a reputation for having problems in performing all of its scheduled mileage. In the 1970s the percentage of route mileage performed fell as low as 95%, much of it attributable to staff shortages in the company. In fact since that date the company seems to have been plagued with staff problems which all contributed to the low perception of the quality of their services held in such places as Harlow and Stevenage. In 1987 the company was short of 60 drivers.

On deregulation the company lost a considerable number of services in the tendering process. Jubilee Coaches gained four contracts in Stevenage while London Country withdrew from offering any services in the Hatfield and Welwyn areas. This should have helped the ailing company to fit their service pattern more satisfactorily to the staff available but only moderate performance was seen on services until June 1987 at which time they took on three London Regional Transport contracts amounting to an annual increase of 14,000 route miles. In doing so it seems to have overcommitted itself and a host of problems ensued as its shortage of driving staff and engineering facilities cut into its ability to maintain the coverage of its committed scheduled mileage. Numerous meetings with Hertfordshire County Council followed and because the company was unwilling to scale down its activities the Council had no choice but to take them in front of the Traffic Commissioners for failure to perform their registered services.

Paralleling this series of problems was the involvement of the company in the run up to its privatisation. It would appear that as part of the process of rationalizing its internal structure, to make the company attractive to bidders, the management tried to impose a new wage and conditions agreement on the work force. The end result of this was a ten-day strike in early 1988 which in turn caused London Regional Transport and Essex County Council to withdraw their contracts and place them with other operators. Jubilee Coaches also took this opportunity to launch a full minibus network in Stevenage. The rapid return to work of the staff in the face of the loss of so much of the company's services did little to stem the tide. In April the new owners of the company brought out a reorganization scheme, where all of the premises were transferred to the investment and property company Parkdale Holdings, leaving the bus operations in the hands of Alan Stephenson. The forecast was a complete shake-up of operations, loss of jobs and closure of depots, so releasing them for redevelopment.

The hearing before the Traffic Commissioners took place in May 1988 and considerable evidence, on the problems of London Country North East, was presented. In total the County Council presented details of 330 specific failings on ten routes based on their own monitoring of services and public complaints. LCNE in reply admitted they had gone through a period of poor performance and blamed the impact of deregulation, staff shortages, the uncertainties in the run-up to privatisation, the loss of engineering backup when London Country had been split into four parts and the general ageing of its bus fleet. Certainly poor morale was widespread amongst the staff of the company, so much so, that ten drivers walked out of the Hatfield depot to establish their own competing bus company, and later a similar process occurred in Harlow. It was finally admitted at the hearing that taking the LRT work had been a fundamental error that had overstretched the company at a time of extreme internal problems. Given that total committed route mileage had then fallen to 165,000, relative to the 217,000 p.a. operated before the loss of the LRT contracts, it was felt that the decline had stabilized and that given the new management structure, much better performance could be achieved in future. The only penalty imposed on the company was the restriction that they could not register any new services in the next six months.

In fact the saga of problems continued to beset the company with further deregistrations and loss of tenders to small companies in Hertfordshire. Jubilee Coaches, who took over some of the tenders, however, also ran into problems as the County Council became more aggressive in its policy of making certain that its contracts were performed properly. Ultimately, at the end of 1988 LCNE removed the problems of competing with Jubilee for traffic in Stevenage by arranging to buy out the firm. This gave the double advantage of inheriting a readymade minibus network in the town and also a new bus depot which in turn freed the existing town centre garage site for redevelopment by Parkdale. This policy of buying out competing independent operators continued by the purchase of Sampsons of Hoddesdon which allowed LCNE to contemplate moving out of its Hertford garage site. The final move in the restructuring of the company was the creation of two separate entities which were relaunched with new names and liveries.

5.8 Conclusions

Although LCNE must have been the most troubled bus company in the South-East since deregulation, the general problems it faced have also occurred elsewhere. The lateness of the privatisation process also affected all of the former London Country companies. London Country North West was also taken to the Traffic Commissioners by Hertfordshire County Council in May 1988, for failing to maintain their scheduled mileage. London Country South West suffered even more directly from the separation, on being privatised, of the bus operations and property holdings of the former NBC company. Although the agreement was to allow the company to continue renting its premises, the rentals paid were scheduled to rise to full market level over a transitional five-year period. In the case of the Guildford depot this would have meant an increase from an anticipated £8,000 p.a. in year one to over £62,650 in the fourth and subsequent years – a heavy burden for a new company to bear. The privatisation process at that stage was very much about obtaining the greatest return to the government from the sale of companies, irrespective of the difficulties it would present for the future continuance and development of local bus services. Kentish Bus, the fourth element of the former London Country empire similarly suffered initially from staff problems and uncertainties but now under new management the company now seems to be heading for better times. It is significant that Kentish Bus retained the ownership of its premises in the privatisation process.

The second issue to note, that interacts with the discussion on competitive practices above, is that expansion of a company by acquisition rather than by entering the territory of other companies, appears to be the favoured method within the industry. There has always been a tradition in the bus industry of expansion by acquisition, and the deregulation of the market, although seemingly favouring the establishment of new companies and expansion into new territories, has done little to change this tradition. Even when new large-scale ventures were set to mature, such as Transit Holdings going into the territory of Hampshire Bus at Basingstoke to establish a comprehensive town network of services, the reaction from Hampshire Bus was to buy out the venture and run the scheme as part of their existing package of services, rather than compete.

Acquisition of companies has certainly become the dominant strategy of growth and the emergence of holding companies like Stagecoach and Badgerline point the way to just possibly five or six large companies controlling the whole of the bus industry in this country in the near future. Only Transit Holdings, so far, has been willing and able to sustain the high risk raids into the territories of other companies. Its ventures into Oxford and latterly the London Docklands are notable because they are still the only large scale attempts at competition to be seen in the South-East.

The 1985 Transport Act sought to promote widespread competition in the bus industry, but the risks associated with long-term battles have soon dissuaded the majority of companies that have entered the competitive arena. Certainly there is an underlying fear that bitter conflicts can only lead to the bleeding of both companies and, given the spate of acquisitions in the industry, leave both combatants open to take over at knocked-down prices to third parties. The risks of direct competition, therefore, appear to be too great for companies to take, especially if acquisition remains an easy, low-risk option. The general perceptions of the low level of potential profits available in the industry must also contribute to the dominance of this strategy.

The growing problems of finding adequate staff and premises to support large-scale new ventures are also reinforcing this means of growth. Acquisitions of pre-existing companies imply gaining new staff and premises, and equally can release existing premises for profitable redevelopment. It would also appear that these joint forces of staff shortages and the rising opportunity costs of retaining premises, now current in the industry, must inevitably raise the long-term costs of bus operation with direct consequences on the consumer and local authorities. Higher tender costs and more routes being deregistered, that need to be covered through tendering, is the likely scenario that local authorities will face. Ultimately, given the present constraints on local authority finance, this may lead to fewer but higher volume routes being supported. From the consumer's viewpoint, fares are likely to rise considerably faster than general inflation levels. Hertfordshire County Council, for instance, reported that bus fares had increased by 20% in the period 1988/9.

Rising labour costs will also tend to erode the general profitability of the industry. Already the bus industry, in general, does not give the return on capital employed that can be expected from other industrial activities and this is despite the fact that many of the new companies are eating into their assets through sales of surplus premises. Diversification away from bus activities has not been seen on any wide scale in the industry so far. Badgerline's excursion into retailing was short-lived, but more significant, in the long term, may be People Provincial's role in a consortium promoting the idea of a light rapid transit system in the Portsmouth area. If profitability cannot be maintained (and in this respect it should be remembered that the downward secular trend in the demand for bus services has not been arrested by the deregulation process) then the flow of capital out of the industry into more healthy sectors of the economy must begin. The entrepreneurial thrust already seen in the industry could easily be turned to other areas.

The impact due solely to deregulation, in this picture, seems to be submerged by the greater forces of privatisation and the changing nature of the local labour market. It has not generated the anticipated levels of competition nor has it contributed to a long term reduction of the level of public support for local public transport services. It can be argued, as in Stanley (1987), that ultimately the privatisation process will be seen as the more fundamental process at work, having the greatest consequence upon the future of bus operation in the South-East. Deregulation, although being a necessary adjunct of the privatisation process, will be seen as having worked in a way that has allowed the new managements to speedily adjust their networks to changing conditions in the market, but it has failed to stimulate the promotion of new competitive ventures. The reason for this can be seen in the market for local bus services. Given its continued general decline, it would appear to be ultimately not worth contesting.

References

Stanley, P.A. (1987) *All change – A study of bus transport planning, deregulation and privatisation in seven towns.* South East Economic Development Strategy – Strategy Study no. 4, Stevenage.

Stanley, P.A. & Pearmain, D. (1987) *Transport in Basildon District – A study of public transport provision and accessibility.* Basildon District Council.

CHAPTER 6

Bus deregulation in rural localities: an example from Wales

Philip Bell and Paul Cloke

6.1 Privatisation and rural areas

One of the most striking features of the political and professional debates about deregulation prior to the 1985 Transport Act in Britain was that rural areas were frequently used to depict locations which would suffer from the proposed changes. Part of the concern appeared to be opportunist, in that those who opposed deregulation on ideological or pragmatic grounds were casting their nets very widely for apparently logical arguments to employ against the government. In cases such as this, the newfound concern for rural areas and the people who resided there was always likely to be a short-lived campaign device, particularly given the wider lack of political concern for rural community issues to be found in British national politics (Cloke & Little, 1990). Alongside the pragmatists, however, there were those whose appreciation of the recent history of rural transport provision gave them genuine cause for concern. Analysts of this history (see, for example, Banister, 1980; and Moseley, 1979) have highlighted trends of route reduction, patronage reduction and fares increases in rural bus services. Even though significant government subsidies have been attracted to these services, the competition between public transport and private car ownership has been one-sided in favour of the latter. The rural transport 'problem' has thus changed from one of general access to one of securing access for residual but significant non-mobile groups living in the countryside. Given this history, there seem to have been legitimate grounds for concern that a new emphasis on competition and a new focus on the economic viability of particular services would merely hasten the already established demise of rural public transport in post-war Britain.

Our current understanding of the relationship between wider issues of privatisation and the likely impact in rural areas is largely speculative. We have suggested elsewhere (Bell & Cloke, 1989) that there are four important areas where research work is urgently needed in this context:

(a) *Rural areas as arenas of production*

Here it seems significant to acknowledge that rural areas are characterized by geographical dispersal of settlements and are therefore regarded as expensive and difficult locations in which to provide services. Such areas may therefore be fruitless arenas for competition compared with more densely populated urban centres. Clearly, it should be stressed here that there is no such thing as a characteristic rural area. The heterogeneous places we label 'rural' will represent a range of competitive environments.

(b) *Rural areas as arenas of production*

The key questions in this context are the type of capital and entrepreneurial interests which are attracted to particular rural locations at particular times, and the type of production or services which results from this interest. Deregulation of the economy may induce a 'footloose' element to particular firms or entrepreneurs who in turn may be attracted to rural areas as a base for their production. On the other hand, deregulation of existing rural production may, as in the case of agriculture, shake out many producers in a newly competitive and unsubsidized regime, or may, as in the case of transport, expose a dearth of local entrepreneurial drive or capital interest which would be required to rise to the challenge of competition.

(c) *Rural areas as arenas of continued regulation*

The outcome of privatisation can be the removal of one role for the state, for example as producer or controller, and the adoption of a replacement role of ensuring that the newly deregulated markets are operated within certain prescribed rules. Privatisation of infra-structural services in Britain has been accompanied by the establish-ment of 'watchdog' agencies. One of their tasks will be to safeguard commitments (required by government and endorsed by the new private companies) to continued service provision in rural localities. The upkeep of the watchdog role is crucial to counteract the risk that in the longer term uneconomic rural services will be vulnerable to the profit motive.

(d) *Rural areas as arenas of planning*

A further layer of protection for vulnerable rural consumers is the formal planning apparatus within public sector agencies. Strong planning to advance the interests of the market-disadvantaged would be a useful bulwark against the excesses of a competitive system in a non-competitive arena. Such planning is, however, anathema to the privatising state, and care must be exercised to review deregulation in all related sectors (including deregulation of the planning system) rather than taking a blinkered unisectoral view of deregulation of transport.

These four concerns provide a framework for a long-term research programme with which to understand the impacts of privatisation and deregulation in rural areas. The study which follows can only be a small part of that jigsaw, focusing as it does on one sector and on a relatively short timespan immediately before and after the implementation of the 1985 Act. Even so, rural areas *had* become arenas for public transport competition and the question of a 'rural' or 'dispersed' factor in the differentiation of competitive environments must be addressed; the role of capital and entrepreneurial interest in commercial services *was* fundamental to the construction of rural areas as arenas of production; the deregulated system *was* operated within prescribed watchdog rules, notably with the continued subsidy for socially necessary but uneconomic routes; and the planning role of local authorities *continued* to be important, although in a different manner from their previous role. Therefore the fears for the future of rural bus services can to an extent be put to the test through the study of deregulation in practice in particular areas.

6.2 Bus deregulation in rural Wales: a case study

The area covered by this study includes the four administrative districts of Colwyn, Glyndwr and Rhuddlan (Clwyd) and Montgomery (Powys) and was selected to represent varying types of rural locale from the relative remoteness of mid-Wales to the relatively urbanised north Wales corridor, with its significant tourist industry. The study was timed so as to investigate the network of services prior to and after deregulation, and to uncover the impacts of the 1985 Act on local authorities, bus operators and passengers. There are obvious problems here in attempting to 'freeze' a dynamic system into snapshots of bus service networks at particular times, but by establishing key dates – November 1985 (a year before deregulation), October 1986 (when deregulation was implemented), January 1987 (when the first changes were made to registered services) and January 1988 (the end of the monitoring period) – a clear impression can be gained of the 'before-and-after' experiences surrounding deregulation.

The pre-deregulation network

The most remote of the districts (Montgomery in Powys) is characterized by a history of steady service withdrawal and increasing subsidy payments. With the exception of key routes which were boosted by the demise of parallel railways (for example, between Newtown and Machynlleth where wayside stations were closed) there had been few service innovations in this area. Immediately prior to deregulation, the National Bus Company (NBC) operator, Crosville, ran all the inter-urban routes, most of the town services and some of the rural services in the area (Figure 6.1). Private operators ran some regular services in East Montgomery as well as market day services on a wider scale, and four post bus and three social car schemes augmented the network. Table 6.1 summarizes the initial route network. Private operators

Figure 6.1 Powys study area: the base network.

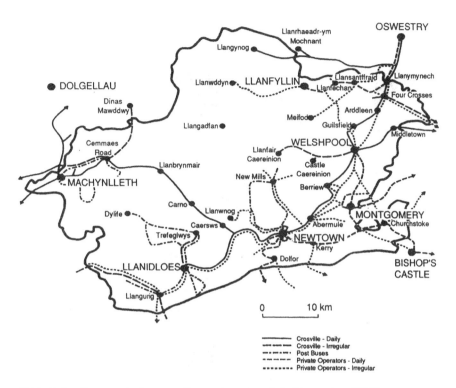

Table 6.1 *Powys study area: the route network in November 1985.*

	Route miles	*Vehicle miles/week*
Crosville	268.2 (34%)	8,757 (62%)
Private operators	523.5 (66%)	5,366 (38%)
Total	791.7	14,123

ran two-thirds of the route miles, but less than one-third of the vehicle miles per week.

Crosville were in a dominant position in the Clwyd districts of Colwyn, Glyndwr and Rhuddlan (Figure 6.2). The north coast corridor contrasts sharply with the rural interior, with services being far more frequent, and their potential for profit being correspondingly greater. Table 6.2 shows that Crosville's role in providing local bus services, both on the north coast and (at lower frequencies) in the rural interior, was even more secure than in Powys. Private operators were most active in the Wrexham area, and there existed a sizable number of firms who might have been tempted to enter the local bus service market, especially summer excursion and tour operators in the north coast area.

Figure 6.2 Clwyd study area: the base network.

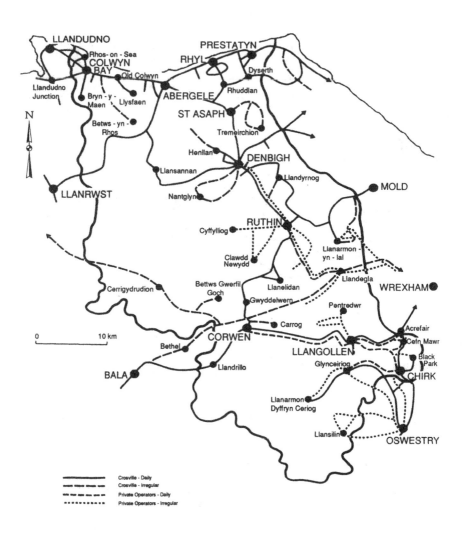

		Crosville - Daily
		Crosville - Irregular
		Private Operators - Daily
		Private Operators - Irregular

Table 6.2 *Clwyd study area: the route network in November 1985.*

	Route miles	Vehicle miles/week
Crosville	721.5 (66%)	45,487 (89%)
Private operators	364.5 (34%)	5,837 (11%)
Total	1,086.0	51,123

It is important to note that the base networks briefly described here were largely the product of a long period of decline. Aside from the north of the Clwyd study area, the levels of service were very basic, and were already associated with potentially severe problems of access for the local population. Given this baseline, further reductions in services could result in the total loss of particular routes, or at least of those routes in off-peak hours.

The post-deregulation network

The network subsequent to deregulation consists of a number of phases. First there was an initial period during which operators registered the routes which they intended to run on a commercial basis. Then the county councils reviewed this 'commercial' network and decided which gaps should be plugged with socially necessary services. These services were then put out to commercial tender. Finally operators made numerous changes to their services when the pattern of provision and competition became evident.

The results of these phases of decision-making are illustrated in Figures 6.3, 6.4 and 6.5 for the Powys area and 6.6, 6.7 and 6.8 for the Clwyd area. Very little of the previous network in the Powys study area was registered as commercial. The busiest corridor prior to deregulation had been that between Newtown, Welshpool and Shrewsbury. Even here, Crosville only registered restricted peak-time services, hoping to tender for subsidized working of early, late and weekend services on these routes. Most existing private bus operators registered their market day services, and one – the charmingly named Mid Wales Motorways – registered an expanded service in the town of Newtown. In total, while 50% of the immediate pre-deregulation route mileage was registered commercially, only 24% of the vehicle mileage was so registered.

Powys County Council therefore invited tenders for almost all services that were not registered commercially, so as to restore the network to that operated before deregulation. The overall result was a loss of route mileage (– 2.6%) and vehicle mileage (– 11.3%), but a continuing dominant role for the newly privatised Crosville Wales, which won 63% of the tendered vehicle miles and retained all the main routes (Figure 6.4). Almost all of the services previously operated by independents were retained by their existing operators, despite some competition within the tendering procedure.

Subsequent alterations to services by operators in reaction to the publication of commercial and subsidized routes were few and far between. There have been no innovatory services introduced in this Powys sector of the study area, and no competition between operators, except on a small scale between Crosville Wales and Mid Wales Motorways in Newtown itself. Perhaps the most interesting change arose when an independent operator – T. R. Morris of Llanfyllin – requested subsidy for all of their routes which had been registered as commercial at deregulation. This was agreed to by Powys County Council, as these services had been supported prior to deregulation, and the actual costs involved were only some £2,000.

Figure 6.3 Powys study area: the commercial network.

	Crosville -Full Registration
	Crosville - Partial Registration
	Private Operators - Daily
	Private Operators - Irregular

However, were this precedent to be widely repeated, such requests for subsidy would pose serious financial problems for local authorities.

In the Clwyd study area there were rather more changes associated with deregulation. The registration of commercial services was concentrated almost entirely in the northern coastal zone (down as far as Denbigh) and in the area to the south of Wrexham. Even in these areas where routes were considered commercial, very few evening and Sunday services were registered. In the southern, more rural, part of this study area, there was little commercial registration of routes except by existing independent operators seeking to defend the intermittent services which were already in

Figure 6.4 Powys study area: the subsidized network.

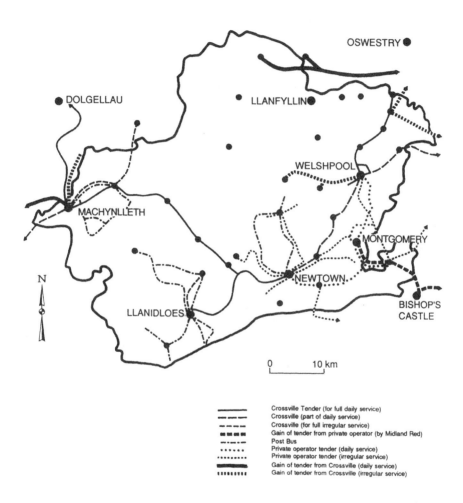

————	Crossville Tender (for full daily service)
— — —	Crossville (part of daily service)
— — — —	Crossville (for full irregular service)
▪▪ ▪▪ ▪▪	Gain of tender from private operator (by Midland Red)
—·—·—·	Post Bus
•••••	Private operator tender (daily service)
··········	Private operator tender (irregular service)
▬▬▬▬	Gain of tender from Crossville (daily service)
ⅼⅼⅼⅼⅼⅼⅼⅼ	Gain of tender from Crossville (irregular service)

place. Overall then, the registration of high frequency services in urbanized areas, and the neglect of longer inter-town routes in the rural hinterland meant that only 39% of route mileage, but 53% of vehicle mileage was registered as commercial and thereby required no subsidy.

Clwyd County Council sought to restore the original network by putting virtually all unregistered routes out to tender. There was, however, an overall decline of 7.7% in the route mileage of the network compared with that before deregulation, although vehicle mileage actually increased by 0.8%. This increase was due to the incidence of competition between Crosville Wales and independent operators both in the Colwyn Bay area

Figure 6.5 Powys study area: the initial service changes.

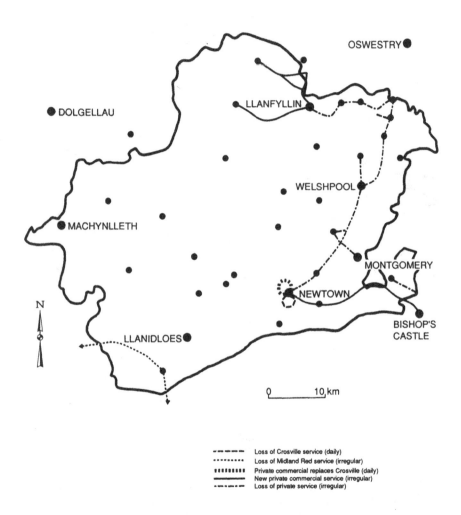

– – – – –	Loss of Crosville service (daily)
· · · · · · · · ·	Loss of Midland Red service (irregular)
IIIIIIIII	Private commercial replaces Crosville (daily)
▬▬▬▬▬	New private commercial service (irregular)
– · – · – · –	Loss of private service (irregular)

(with Alpine Travel) and in the Wrexham area (latterly with Wrights). This competition led to important changes after January 1987, with Crosville Wales reacting to competition in the north Wales corridor by introducing high frequency minibus services. By January 1988 the total route mileage for the study area had thereby increased by 10% compared with 1985 levels, and vehicle mileage rose by 30% over the same period. The introduction of minibuses was the only substantial innovation arising from deregulation. So,

Figure 6.6 Clwyd study area: the commercial network.

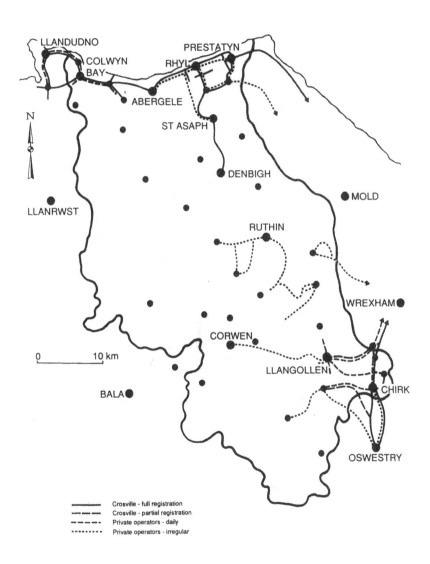

LLANDUDNO

COLWYN BAY

PRESTATYN

RHYL

ABERGELE

ST ASAPH

N

DENBIGH

MOLD

LLANRWST

RUTHIN

WREXHAM

CORWEN

0   10 km

LLANGOLLEN

CHIRK

BALA

OSWESTRY

Crosville - full registration
Crosville - partial registration
Private operators - daily
Private operators - irregular

whereas very few places in the overall study area lost their bus service (one or two formerly independent routes were not fully replaced) there are few new services in operation, and the beneficial aspects of change have all occurred in the most profitable zone of the north Wales corridor.

Figure 6.7 Clwyd study area: the subsidized network.

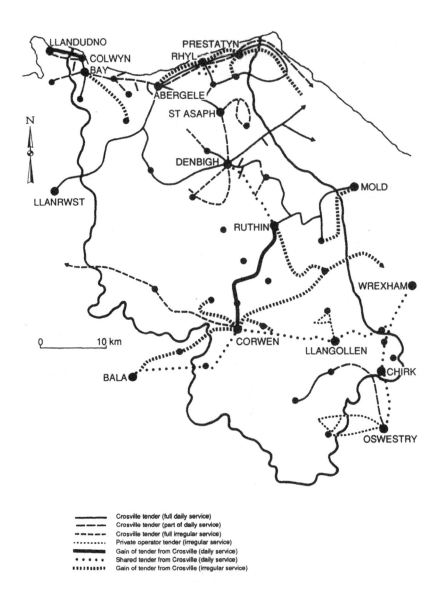

———————	Crosville tender (full daily service)
— — — —	Crosville tender (part of daily service)
━ ━ ━ ━	Crosville tender (full irregular service)
············	Private operator tender (irregular service)
▬▬▬▬	Gain of tender from Crosville (daily service)
• • • • •	Shared tender from Crosville (daily service)
▪▪▪▪▪▪▪▪▪	Gain of tender from Crosville (irregular service)

Figure 6.8 Clwyd study area: the initial service changes.

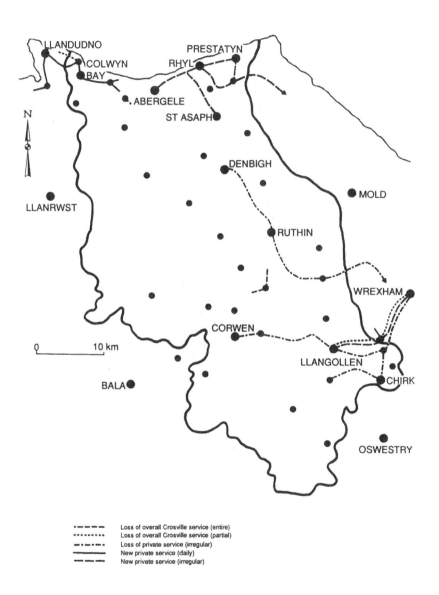

Loss of overall Crosville service (entire)
Loss of overall Crosville service (partial)
Loss of private service (irregular)
New private service (daily)
New private service (irregular)

6.3 Attitudes of bus operators to deregulation

The actions of operators, both in registering (and withdrawing) commercial routes and in competing for the tenders offered by county councils have obviously been crucial in moulding the network changes outlined above. Extensive consultations with operators as part of our study yielded important information of the attitudes which underlay operator behaviour during deregulation.

Crosville Wales

Prior to deregulation Crosville were the NBC operator in the study areas. They were based in Chester and operated more intensive services in Cheshire, Shropshire and parts of Merseyside as well as those in Gwynedd, Clwyd, Powys and Dyfed in Wales. At deregulation, the initial commercial registrations and the initial tenders were made from the Chester base, and this may explain the reluctance to make any strong tactical bids for some of the less intensive routes in rural Wales. On 9 August 1986, Crosville was divided into English and Welsh companies, and the latter became Crosville Wales, based in Llandudno Junction. By the summer of 1987 a management buy-out was selected as the preferred form of privatisation, and this was completed by December 1987. More recently, Crosville Wales has been sold to National Express (ex NBC themselves), one of the emerging big few companies who are gradually purchasing the privatised fragments of the former NBC operation. One important factor to note is thus that most of the commercial decisions taken by Crosville Wales during the period of this study emerged from an uncertain producer environment.

The original registrations and tenders issued from Chester were scrutinized by the more locally-based management in Llandudno Junction, and even before October 1986 changes were planned to the company's response to deregulation. Registrations made by Chester had been too cautious, and it was considered that there had been an under-registration of commercial routes. These gaps had permitted a major competitor – Alpine Travel – to become established in the Colwyn Bay area, and Crosville Wales decided to compete aggressively with the extensive use of minibus services. This tactic paid dividends and by January 1988 Alpine's one remaining commercial service was not viewed as any kind of threat. Similarly, potential competition in Rhyl and Prestatyn from Gold Star Line (who had already competed briefly in the run-up to deregulation) was seen off with the operation of intensive minibus services in the summer of 1987. The competition in Newtown has also been responded to by minibus operations.

Crosville's aggressively competitive attitude which was employed so effectively against Alpine, Gold Star, Wrights and Mid Wales Motorways, was not extended to the procedures of tendering for socially necessary routes. Here, a far more relaxed attitude was taken, and tenders were only submitted for those contracts where a reasonable rate of return seemed likely. There was no attempt to maintain all of the network of services previously run by Crosville with local authority subsidies. Indeed, they have proved prepared to relinquish one or two contracts for minor routes which they won initially, and have equally been happy to work jointly with independent operators on particular contracts.

Independent operators

The relatively aggressive attitudes of the few independent operators who decided to compete directly with Crosville for high volume (and therefore profitable) routes were not matched by the majority of local operators. It was far more the norm either to pull out of stage carriage work at deregulation (concentrating instead on schools work and excursions) or to limit their involvement to tendering for contracts for socially necessary services, and perhaps to registering existing intermittent services. In the Powys study area several private firms registered their existing services even when they had been in receipt of subsidy beforehand. This could be interpreted as a case of deregulation removing the practice of payments of unnecessary subsidy. However, in these cases it seems clear that operators acted in this way to ensure that their main services were retained, provided that the cost of doing so was not too high. School contracts tend to be the major areas of profit for such firms, and fares were often raised on registered routes in order to compensate for lost subsidies.

Most operators in the Powys area appeared to want to ride out the changes with as little disturbance as possible, and even those firms tendering against each other were often inspired rather more by fear of losing their own work than through real predatory instincts. Very few routes changed hands in practice as a result. A loose form of cartel was thought to have existed in the area in previous years, but this seems already to have weakened well before deregulation.

The pattern of operator attitudes in the Clwyd study areas was similar. There were many defensive registrations of existing services run by the independents and there were very few new commercial registrations. More new operators were involved in the local bus service market after deregulation, but these were almost entirely existing local firms who were expanding out from schools and excursion work, or local bus operators already operating outside the area who succeeded in winning tenders within it. The only significant commercial competition with Crosville, involving Alpine Travel in the north and Wrights in the Wrexham area, has effectively been swamped into relative submission by the Crosville tactic of employing the full force of its scale of operations in particular competitive arenas.

The impact on employees

The conditions of employees are a major factor in the assessment of deregulation. Most companies in the study areas have seen little change in the scale of their operations and so the numbers of staff, and their terms of employment have accordingly also changed little. Employment by the small independent operators did fluctuate during deregulation, but job gains and losses were cancelled out according to which firms benefited from tendering procedures and which registered new commercial routes. Even Alpine Travel, which has already been identified as the major competitive independent operator in the network, had only recruited 24 drivers by 1986. Many of these were employed on a part-time basis, and all were recruited at rates of pay which were below the equivalent received by Crosville drivers.

The changing management of Crosville's operations resulted in more dramatic changes for some of their employees. The company has sought efficiency in three areas:

(a) *Tighter scheduling*

This usually involved faster journeys and faster turnarounds. Some drivers suggested that these schedules were both over-ambitious in terms of speed between stops, and resulted in additional mechanical problems for the vehicles concerned. Crosville management dispute both of these suggestions.

(b) *Redundancies*

Information on this aspect was extremely sensitive, but 25–30 staff are believed to have gone initially from Crosville's Rhyl and Llandudno Junction depots. The steady increase in minibus work later led to extra jobs, but these were not at standard bus driver wages. The reductions in management staff evident in some ex-NBC companies following deregulation was not deemed necessary at Crosville Wales. This was in any case a management buy-out initially, and it was further claimed that the new company had 'no entrenched bureaucracy'.

(c) *Terms of service*

When Crosville Wales was created, wage rates were decoupled from those used by the NBC Crosville which in turn had been based on conditions pertaining in the Merseyside area. Employees of Crosville Wales were paid on a flat rate, with previous special overtime rates being abandoned. This again, was a sensitive area of information, but according to one driver the decoupling from Crosville NBC wage rates resulted in a 9% cut in wages, and this could become a cut of 35% if the loss of overtime rates of pay are taken into account. In addition, drivers hired to drive minibuses were paid on a rate which was reported locally to be some 50–60p per hour less than the new standard rate.

Taking these three factors into account, it is clear that one significant impact of deregulation has been experienced by the former and existing workforces of the newly privatised ex-NBC company.

6.4 The roles and responses of county councils

The 1985 Act has reduced the powers previously held by county councils to plan and co-ordinate transport services. According to the Act, their main role is to secure by means of commercial tenders the provision of such routes that they deem to be socially necessary and that are not already registered commercially. This can involve: providing a service on a route which ran before deregulation but which has not been registered; or extending a registered route beyond that which is considered commercial by the operator concerned; or adding additional journeys to existing routes, usually at the margins of the timetable, or at weekends.

Where commercial interest in the bus service network is relatively low (as is the case with nearly all our study area) the role of transport planners in county councils is effectively little changed. The main difference in these circumstances is the requirement to carry out procedures of tendering for subsidized services, rather than merely deciding whether to support operators who are already running particular services. Indeed a representative of one of the county councils concerned suggested that they now had much greater power over the routes that they were subsidizing, and in some ways they can be seen to have returned towards the situation that existed before revenue support became widespread.

Both of the county councils in the study areas played a crucial role in the aftermath of deregulation. The response of each is briefly dealt with here.

Powys County Council

Powys County Council is controlled politically by an Independent group of councillors. Their policy decision relating to deregulation was to attempt to maintain their base network of bus services (see Figure 6.1) insofar as budgetary constraints permitted this. The resources devoted to public transport matters in the council are, however, limited. Their personnel in this section initially comprised one officer who also had responsibilities for traffic matters. One extra staff member was employed from April 1986 to assist in the computerization of records, but even so extensive surveying and monitoring of service changes was beyond the scope permitted by the resources available to the department.

The County Council faced a major challenge in implementing their policy of maintaining the pre-deregulation network. Their most pressing difficulty was their location at the extremities of the major longer bus routes, as decisions made elsewhere (for example by Shropshire County Council on their end of the Shrewsbury-Welshpool-Newtown route) could have severe repercussions in Powys. Those sections of the routes in Powys were frequently unprofitable, and dovetailing tenders with commercial services over the county boundary was a major source of concern.

In the end, the County Council succeeded in replacing most of its base network for the same cost as previously (£330,000 per annum for the whole county). Some routes cost less than before; others cost more. Tendering in this area did not result in a universal reduction of subsidies. This balancing of required subsidies and available finances was not predictable, and had financial provision not proved sufficient, the county would have had to resort to some form of crisis management as there were no ranked lists of priority routes prepared for such an eventuality. In the event of any sudden shortfall in funds to meet subsidy costs, the County Council has *no* formal contingency allocation, although there would be an expectation (but no guarantee) that they would in these circumstances receive favourable consideration from the county treasurer.

So far, Powys County Council have maintained public transport at its pre-deregulation level (which was in any case not high in most places) but retendering will be a key test. Councillors have demonstrated concern over the transport issue, but initially were content to let officers deal with the details. This approach appears to be hardening, however, and the fact that a particular service has existed for years no longer renders it inviolate. Rural areas such as Powys depend heavily on subsidy from central and local government to maintain public transport, and this position has not been altered by deregulation. The new system does provide the County Council with more detailed information on individual routes than before, but the continued support for such routes will inevitably be a political rather than a technical decision. Future levels of available finance are, therefore, crucial. Virtually all of the bus network in Powys was eligible for the transitional rural bus grant, and so one significant problem for the near future is the possibility of a rise in tender costs as this grant is phased out. Crosville and the larger operators may already have taken this into account in their future costings (although tender prices could rise as a result) whereas smaller operators may be less aware of the conditions of this grant and therefore may have to withdraw their operations if this reduction of support is serious. Although in national terms these grants represent a small proportion of total revenue, the position of rural bus grant has a special significance on economically marginal routes in areas such as Powys.

Clwyd County Council

Clwyd County Council adopted a similar objective to that in Powys – namely to replace the existing bus network at least cost in terms of subsidy. The Council is controlled by Conservatives and Independents, and the Transport Department has greater resources of finance and staff than in Powys due to the greater scale of public transport operation.

Tenders were invited for practically all the routes which were not registered as commercial, and the task for the County Council was to subsidize most of the rural services as well as evening and Sunday services in the largely urbanized north. 262 bids were attracted for the 1000 contracts on offer across the whole county, of which 75% were contested. As a result, the network was brought to its pre-deregulation status with a reported saving of some £200,000 out of a previous budget of £1,536,000. The exact source of these savings is not easy to establish, and the effects of rural bus grant and extra spending on publicity reduce the total figure saved. However, the most obvious economies have been made in the Wrexham area, where competition is greatest. Some savings were made in the study area referred to in this chapter (mainly in the northern coastal strip between Prestatyn and Llandudno), but it would appear that it was *not* possible to make major economies in rural bus operation without putting current levels of service in jeopardy.

Although Clwyd County Council can claim some success in maintaining services at the lower cost, there remain fears about what would happen if unexpected demands for subsidy were to occur. Such fears stem not only from the phasing out of rural bus grant, but also from the expectation that current levels of competition may not be sustained. Contemporary competition may be viewed as a tactic being used by larger operators in order to gain supremacy over particular routes. Once supremacy has been gained, there are legitimate fears that a monopolistic position may be exploited by a sharp reduction in service schedules followed by requests for local authority subsidy to cover the axed routes which are no longer seen as commercial. In other words, uneconomic routes may currently be operated as 'commercial', in order that competitors can be seen off. There will come a time, however, when the uneconomic status of these routes will be the subject of bargaining between dominant operators and the county council.

The future, then, is uncertain. Both county councils have managed to buy back almost all of their existing networks, but at little saving in subsidy. The effects, then, of any future reduction in rural transport subsidy could be very serious. There is little evidence from this study that deregulation has led to any significant improvement in the provision of rural transport services. Moreover, the future levels of provision could be precarious as they will continue to rely heavily on political decisions and allocations of subsidy at both local and central levels. It seems that county councils are acquiring more experience in the management of those aspects of public transport which remain within their control, but that such management skills *per se* cannot prevent the impact of detrimental policy decisions in the wider sphere.

6.5 Attitudes of passengers to deregulation

Given the previous account of largely conservative attitudes by rural bus operators and of local authorities attempting to secure the retention of pre-deregulation networks of services, it should come as no surprise that many passengers experienced little change to bus services in these case study areas. A more detailed examination of fares, publicity and service reliability suggests that this simple conclusion glosses over some actual and potential impacts of deregulation on rural passengers.

In general, the bus fares charged to passengers in the rural areas of Powys and Clwyd have been little changed during the deregulation process, with few climbing above the rate of inflation over this period. So far as private operators are concerned, there is wide variation in decisions as to whether or not fares should be increased, and there is certainly no consistent pattern of increases as a direct response to deregulation. Crosville had raised their fares immediately prior to deregulation, and many were not altered over the initial two years of the new system. Both Powys and Clwyd county councils stipulated a maximum fare level for subsidized services based on the previous fares charged on that route. In the event, most operators of subsidized services set fares at this maximum level, although a few did reduce fares slightly on subsidized routes. County councils had no control, however, over fares on commercial routes. Here some operators raised their fares so as to render economic some of the more marginal services they had registered as 'commercial'. Elsewhere, particularly in the competitive north Wales corridor, passengers have been able to achieve savings on fares by taking advantage of return, bulk or rover tickets, all of which have been discounted in a bid to attract customer loyalty.

Some initial problems were encountered with access to information and publicity about the new service schedules coming into operation on deregulation day. The changeover of timetables and operators led to considerable initial confusion for passengers, and in some blackspots (such as Llangollen) the chaos arising from poor publicity and service changes led to a marked but seemingly temporary decline in patronage. The key to this chaos was the newly divided responsibility for information about routes subsidized by county councils and those run commercially by different operators. With commercial operators being unwilling to co-operate with potential competition in developing a comprehensive timetable, there was real difficulty in getting complete service information to passengers. Crosville Wales, for example, produce their own publicity with information about their own service, and this exclusivity is seen as part of the normal tactics of service competition. County councils have now assumed the task of producing computer-derived and regularly updated comprehensive timetables for their areas.

Those difficulties in gaining access to official timetables mean that it has been difficult to measure the reliability of post-deregulation services. There were few Buswatch reporters in these study areas, but the general picture seems to be one of little change in service reliability. It must be borne in mind, however, that rural passengers are historically well adapted to slippage in the punctuality of bus services, and so this lack of change may mask significant existing problems of reliability.

Overall, the attitudes of passengers are perhaps best gauged by their patronage of post-deregulation services. In the commercially sensitive environment of commercial services and tenders, operators have been unwilling to release accurate statistics on patronage. However, a series of passenger demand surveys in the case study areas (see Andrews et al., 1986; Bell et al., 1987) suggest that:

(a) the claims by Crosville Wales, that new minibus services in the north Wales corridor have increased patronage by some 30%, appear to be substantiated;

(b) in the more rural localities, deregulation has neither led to a widespread collapse of patronage nor sparked off any increase in the usage of bus services.

It should again be stressed that this short-term pattern is dependent on the maintenance of current service networks in any future period of financial cutbacks in the public sector.

6.6 Conclusions

Much of the vigorous and even sensationalist debate over the impact of the 1985 Transport Act for Britain's less accessible rural areas will find little comfort or support in the findings of this case study. The hard-nosed reality of implementing the Act in rural Wales suggests that many of the fears and expectations mentioned at the beginning of this chapter have, as yet, proved groundless. High expectations of innovatory rural transport services have been disappointed. The minibus services introduced in the north Wales corridor have focused on the most urbanized part of the study area, and there have been no significant innovations elsewhere. The rural consumer has certainly not received any major benefits from deregulation. On the other hand the doom-and-gloom predictions of major service losses in rural areas have not materialized either. The short-term picture suggests little overall change between the regulated and deregulated system of bus transport.

It would, however, be a mistake to evaluate deregulation merely on the evidence of the first two years after its introduction. Clearly, the decisions being made by operators and local authorities are ongoing, and the underlying foundation for central government funding of local operations is consistently reviewed and subject to policy shifts in the immediate and mid-term future. This case study in rural Wales does highlight a series of significant factors which aid our understanding of the potential longer-term effects of bus deregulation in deep rural locales.

(a) Crosville Wales (the ex-NBC operator) was willing to give up routes in rural localities which it had previously been running over a long period of time. The judgement here was that tenders for these routes could not be secured at a sufficiently profitable level, and so the competitive instincts of the company were directed towards the more dense passenger traffic flows of the more urbanized areas. It seems likely that in future years the search for profit in bus operations will increasingly be directed at the more profitable arenas of competition – that is away from many areas traditionally viewed as rural.

(b) There was a marked absence of new operators emerging under deregulated conditions to run tendered or commercial services in the more rural zones.

(c) The private operators in the remoter rural zones of the study area certainly were very familiar with each other, being used, for example, to subcontracting private hire jobs to each other in many cases. It has even been suggested that some form of unofficial cartel may have operated there. These factors may not be unconnected with the evidence that competition for local authority tenders was, and in all probability will remain, below the national average level. In this climate, operators of some socially necessary routes may feel able to request additional subsidies from local authorities without fear of undue competition from other operators for their tender.

(d) The two local authorities have not made significant financial savings by putting their subsidized rural routes out to tender.

(e) The phased withdrawal of Rural Bus Grant *is* likely to have severe implications. In Powys, it seems likely that operators will attempt to pass on at least some of the revenue deficits caused by the stopping of Rural Bus Grant to the local authority in the form of bids for increased subsidy. Without additional funding, the county council is ill-placed to fund such demands, and hard decisions may have to be made about network reductions. Clwyd County Council are in a better position to meet the inevitable demands for increased subsidy payments where the loss of Rural Bus Grant is not absorbed by operators. However, their contingency funds are small, and the transport budget thereby appears more vulnerable than that of other counties facing similar bids for increased subsidies.

(f) Given this vulnerable position of *not* having made financial savings due to deregulation, any real decline in the wider financial provision to local authorities would create considerable difficulties for the two councils to maintain their current subsidized networks.

(g) Any reorganisation of local government which alters the relationships between and responsibilities of county and district councils could also lead to specific problems in continuing to support existing networks of transport services. If, for example, responsibilities for transport planning were to be given to district councils, mayhem could ensue. Currently, the more rural districts, because of the geographical distribution of socially necessary services receive cross-subsidy from other districts within the county-level framework of planning. If district councils were granted powers of planning transport services, such cross-subsidy is unlikely to be maintained. The current climate of inter-governmental relations suggests that the districts' star is rising and that of the counties is falling.

The evidence presented in this chapter is one where rural areas may often be seen as poor arenas of competition. As a result the supposed benefits of competition – price reductions, better quality service and the like – are not being experienced simply because service provision has notionally been opened up to competition. This low competitive status of deep rural areas is related both to the low density of population and to the apparent lack of a new breed of entrepreneurs who are willing either to expand existing businesses in a competitive market or to innovate in these particular localities. In view of these competitive conditions, many rural areas appear eligible for specific protection from the central and local states in order to protect whatever are normatively designated as necessary levels of service. The use of subsidies to fund socially necessary routes in these areas represents a form of continued regulation and planning in the transport sector even though the 1985 Transport Act was born in an ideological context favouring privatisation, deregulation and anti-planning. The designation of what is 'necessary' is therefore a delicate political judgement, which can easily change. Although these studies suggest that the status quo has been maintained in the short term, there would seem to be real dangers ahead for the financing of rural transport services. The basic contradictions between interventionist and regulatory state action on the one hand, and permitting a free reign of market forces on the other, may have as yet been minimized by short-term palliatives such as interim grants, continuing subsidies, and continuing public sector involvement. However, in the longer term these contradictions are likely to become more severe, and a continued monitoring of rural transport provision appears essential.

References

Andrews, I., Bell, P. & Cloke, P. (1986) *Clwyd–Powys study area: a preliminary demand survey* Bus Deregulation Project, Working Paper No. 1, Department of Geography, St David's University College, Lampeter.

Banister, D. (1980) *Transport, Mobility and deprivation in outer urban areas* Farnborough: Saxon House.

Bell, P., Burns, T. & Cloke, P. (1987) *Clwyd–Powys study area: a study of competition in Colwyn Bay* Bus Deregulation Project, Working Paper No. 2, Department of Geography, St David's University College, Lampeter.

Bell, P. & Cloke, P. (1989) The changing relationships between the private and public sectors: privatisation and rural Britain *Journal of Rural Studies* 5, 1–15.

Cloke, P. & Little, J. (1990) *The rural state?* Oxford: Oxford University Press.

Moseley, M. (1979) *Accessibility: the rural challenge* London: Methuen.

PART III
International Experience

CHAPTER 7

Deregulation in a European context – the case of Sweden

Brian Fullerton

7.1 Introduction

Deregulation of transport services has proved as attractive to welfare states as to free market economies. It has encouraged the adaptation of services to changes in demand and increased their efficiency. Deregulation conflicts with the objectives of the welfare state however, where it threatens the viability of minimum public transport services or restricts the access of those citizens without the use of a car to employment, shops and welfare services. It may also be necessary to continue to regulate transport in order to protect the long-term environmental welfare of the population. Such considerations are often more easily appreciated in welfare states than in free market economies. The experience of Sweden since the 1950s provides a clear and particularly well-documented case study of the possibilities and limitations of deregulation in a welfare state with high living standards.

The major political parties (including the Social Democratic party, which has formed Swedish governments from 1932 to 1976 and from 1982 to the present day) agree that Sweden's prosperity depends upon her ability to sell relatively high value goods and services to Europe and the world and that Swedish manufacturing industry must therefore be subject to the disciplines of free trade and a free market. Social Democrats also believe that the wealth created should be shared amongst the whole population in all parts of the country and that there should be high levels of employment everywhere. Equality of access to services is fundamentally important in providing both the opportunities and the incomes to allow real freedom of consumer choice. High levels of personal taxation support generous levels of public service. Narrow earnings differentials and extensive training programmes facilitate labour mobility and help to maintain very high levels of employment.

Seats in the Swedish parliament are distributed in proportion to the total number of votes cast nationally for each party. Ministries are small and primarily concerned with general policy issues. There have been only three major Transport Acts since World War II. Policies are administered by a variety of executive agencies, some of which are required to act commercially. Political parties and interest groups (including trades unions and employers' organizations) are represented on the boards of these agencies. This structure favours consensus. So does voting behaviour since neither the Social Democrats nor the group of three non-socialist parties can rely on more than 45% of the votes at national elections. There are strong incentives for each group to attract as many votes from the narrow middle ground as possible.

The patterns of demand for passenger and freight transport in Sweden make it difficult to provide a transport system which is both economical and equitable. Sweden has 8.4 million people – equivalent to the population of Scotland and Wales – but spread over an area twice the size of Britain. Three million people (36% of the population) live within 40 km (25 miles) of the centres of the three big cities of Stockholm, Gothenburg and Malmö. Stockholm is 400 km (250 miles) from Gothenburg and 500 km (310 miles) from Malmö. Gothenburg and Malmö are 250 km (155 miles) apart. It is as if London, Edinburgh and Preston were the only big cities in Britain. The average distance between towns of 50,000 population or more in southern Sweden is 90 km (56 miles). Population densities outside large towns range from 50 to 60 per sq km in Skåne (just over half of the population density in rural East Anglia) to about 25 per sq km in the rest of southern Sweden (comparable to densities in mid-Wales). The forested plateaux of northern Sweden, which reach to within 160 km (100 miles) of Gothenburg and Stockholm, have a population of only 1.6 million with densities of 2 to 6 per sq km – roughly half of the population density in the Scottish Highlands.

The cost of transport provision is raised by the long snowy winters and the damage done to roads and permanent ways during the annual thaw. The granite upon which Stockholm, Gothenburg and many other towns are built adds to the building costs of streets, underpasses and underground transport.

Car ownership levels are high, with 2.5 persons per car in 1987 (Britain 3.2). In 1987 Swedes generated 11,900 passenger km per head (9800 in Britain) and 8700 tonne km per head (3528 in Britain) showing the effect of low population densities, longer inter-regional journeys and the isolation of the iron ore and timber resources of the North. With 2.1 million traffic units per km in Sweden the intensity of railway track use is lower than in Britain (3.0).

In this economic and political context, deregulation may allow a clearer recognition of those parts of the transport system which serve the market economy (especially the competitive export/import sector) and should therefore respond to market forces and those transport services which must be retained if the whole population is to share roughly equal access to jobs, education and health and welfare services. It raises problems as to what to do when commercially viable and socially necessary transport services are jointly produced and how to allocate investment between them. On routes with sufficiently high levels of demand, modal competition may provide an efficient use of resources and deregulation may become the spur to a rationalization in which individual markets are more clearly distinguished, enterprises are subdivided, managers are made more responsible for sectoral profits and losses and cross-subsidies are reduced as far as possible. Rationalization is particularly relevant to large nationalised corporations like the state railways (SJ) which may over time have assumed a great variety of obligations and services. Private investment might be attracted into parts of the public transport sector. Wherever levels of demand would not support modal competition the devolution of regulation and investment decisions to local authorities may make transport services more cost-effective and more sensitive to local needs. Sweden has practised both deregulation and devolution since the 1960s, as the following account shows.

7.2 Deregulation in the 1960s

The regulation of Swedish road transport must be seen in the context of a railway network which, having been built at rather low capital cost, was circuitous and heavily graded. The railway network had been designed to encourage local economic development and to serve through transport. Main lines avoided existing towns which were thought to be able to link themselves with the state network at their own expense. Thus important regional centres, such as Jönköping (present population 109,000), are still on branch lines. In contrast to Norway and Denmark, where unregulated coastal shipping has always offered significant competition to inland transport, the Swedish state controlled internal transport through its railway system.

When the first road hauliers appeared in the 1920s they had to satisfy the authorities as to the need for their proposed services and their fitness to carry them out. Firms were allowed to carry their own goods in their own vehicles but once a service was established, the controls, in Kritz's (1976) view, limited the number of competing road hauliers on a route rather than affecting road–railway competition.

During the 1950s, growing Swedish living standards enabled the transport sector to increase its share of investment in real terms without imposing absolute cutbacks on other sectors. Traffic increased (Table 7.1) from 26 billion (10^9) passenger plus tonne kilometres in 1950 to 69 billion in 1960 and to 117 billion in 1970. The transport budget rose from 8% of the national budget in 1950 to 9% by 1960. Governments built new roads, raised permissible axle loads, increased expenditure on snow clearance and gradually lifted restrictions on road freight transport.

The view that transport services should each be competitive and cover their full economic costs steadily gained ground in Sweden during the 1950s. A Royal Commission (SOU, 1961) suggested that a significant part of Swedish traffic was not using the transport mode which returned the lowest

Table 7.1 *The growth of traffic in Sweden 1950–87.*

	billion (10^9)				
	1950	1960	1970	1980	1987
Passenger km	12.2	45.6	69.9	85.5	100.1
car	5.6	33.2	56.3	67.3	80.1
bus				7.3	9.0
railway	6.6	5.2	4.7	8.5	7.9
air		0.2	0.6	1.4	2.9
Tonne km	13.3	23.4	47.4	50.7	73.7
road	2.7	6.8	21.0	23.0	26.2
railway	8.6	10.9	17.3	16.5	17.8

Sources: NKTF (1980); Nordic Statistical Secretariat (1989)

economic cost to the community and recommended a liberalization of the regulations governing hire and reward traffic rather than legislative curbs on long-distance road transport. The Commission also recommended the removal of restrictions on farmers', foresters' and consumer co-operatives' traffic and suggested that counties should regulate road freight up to 150 km (93 miles) beyond their borders.

The 1963 Transport Act established the principle of free consumer choice amongst the transport modes with modal competition on as near equal terms as feasible on those routes with sufficient demand to support competitive services. Each transport service should recoup its costs by taxes and charges on its own customers. Recommended changes were made in three stages (1964, 1966 and 1968). Government cash inputs continued to ensure the provision of basic transport in thinly populated areas where the maintenance of road and rail traffic was a desirable prerequisite for further economic development but uneconomic for the operators.

There was a progressive relaxation of the need test for road haulage licensing between 1964 and 1968 and a considerable increase in the total permitted carrying capacity of the road haulage fleet. The rate of growth of the carrying capacity of the road haulage industry which had been 12% per annum during the regulated period 1954–64 rose to 16% per annum after the 1964 liberalization but later fell to 8% per annum between 1966 and 1968 and 6% per annum between 1966 and 1972. At the same time the larger firms were increasing their share of the market and hire-and-reward road transport increased its share at the expense of own-firm transport from 60% of the tonne miles in 1961 to 80% in 1974. The vehicle taxation system was revised in 1968 as were the regulations concerning speeds and drivers' hours and carrying capacity. The need test was repealed and regulations which had prevented the joint use of cars for journeys to work and school were rescinded.

In 1968 deregulation of road haulage was halted in the face of falling demand for long-distance haulage due to economic recession and an increasing public concern with road congestion and environmental issues.

In the early 1960s the railways asked for substantial new investment in order to fight road competition. The 1963 Act led to a clearer identification of traffic and facilities and substantial rationalization of finances. The railway investment programme continued to be regulated through the national budget but the Act made a clear distinction between short-term production plans and the long-term development plan, which was to be realized through a five-year rolling investment programme.

The 1963 Act removed SJ's common carrier obligations and split SJ into 'business' and 'social' networks. The business network of 4400 track km (2700 miles) which comprised the main railway lines plus some major cross country routes and branches (Price, 1968), carried 90% of the traffic and produced 81% of revenue (49% freight plus 32% passenger). Released from the burden of cross-subsidizing thinly trafficked routes, the business network was now in a better position to compete with road traffic over the longer distances. Profits from business network lines could be used to cross-subsidize other business services whose income covered only variable costs. On the business network as a whole, annual revenues were intended to cover annual costs of operation (including depreciation at a rate fixed by government but depending on economic conditions) and the repayment of government loans over a five-year period. Loans for rolling stock and ferries were to be repaid out of revenue at full commercial rates. Infrastructure and traffic were separately costed. The business network was expected to make enough profit from traffic movements in good years to carry it through any subsequent lean years but the state was prepared to take responsibility for interest payments on loans for infrastructural investment.

In 1966 SJ was freed from the requirement to treat all customers equally, to publish contract rates for individual customers and from other restrictions on price setting. A new fare structure and passenger timetable was introduced in 1968 providing more and faster intercity trains which stopped at fewer stations. Railhead passenger services were co-ordinated with feeder buses. The two remaining major private railways were integrated into SJ.

Income failed to cover variable costs on the 'social network' of branch and secondary lines (carrying about 10% of the traffic). The network was operated by SJ on behalf of the Swedish government which paid a so-called 'collective ticket' for the services rendered and covered maintenance sufficient to allow trains to run at a safe speed of at least 90 kph (56 mph). Fares and charges were normally the same as on the business network. The government guaranteed the operation of passenger services on 3300 km (2000 miles) of the social network for the foreseeable future. The future of the remaining 2800 km (1740 miles) which carried only 1% of the passenger traffic, was to be discussed every five years.

There was a very cautious attitude to domestic air transport subsidy since post-war governments were concerned to retain as much business as possible for their state railways. However, there was a gradual development of 'secondary' domestic links during the 1960s.

The Royal Commission (SOU, 1961) had argued that the losses on many rural services were due to the provision of a standard of transport above the minimum necessary and recommended the reduction of services along the progression standard railway–railbus–road bus–rationalized bus–subsidized bus–taxi. At each stage mode, frequency and price of the service should be reconsidered, since there was no advantage in raising fares unless increases produced a more economic operation. The minimum transport standard was defined as the level of passenger service which, if further reduced, would give rise to adverse social consequences such as increased local unemployment or the encouragement of outmigration. Although standards of service vary considerably from region to region, it was agreed that a food shop, pharmacy, post office, doctor, dentist and comprehensive school should be accessible for most dwellings within 30–40 minutes and department stores, lawyers, hospital and high school within two hours' travelling time by public transport. The subsidy given in order to maintain a minimum transport standard should be in reasonable proportion to the number of people using the service.

7.3 The second stage of deregulation

Between the full implementation of the Transport Act of 1963 and the next major Transport Act in 1979 the Swedish economy faltered in the after-effects of a rapid increase in the price of oil and there was little growth in GNP for several years. The demand for transport grew from 117 billion traffic units in 1970 to 166 billion in 1980.

Attitudes to transport policy changed. Enthusiasm for an intercity transport market in which free competition would create an efficient transport system gave way to a greater concern for the contribution transport might make to wider objectives such as raising the quality of life, retaining the settlement pattern, protecting employment in all parts of the country and limiting environmental damage which might be caused by traffic (SOU, 1975, 1978).

The most compelling reason for reconsidering transport policy, however, lay in the growing gap between the two major planks of Swedish social democracy – freedom of consumer choice and the maintenance of a high standard of welfare and opportunity for all citizens. Governments were reluctant to curb the development of private transport in order that public transport might be brought nearer to viability or to impose a permanent share-out of the transport market between the modes. The pursuit of equality of opportunity committed governments to minimum standards of transport provision but resulted in increased wages for public transport employees in line with inflation to a point where even a minimum transport service became quite expensive to operate. Freedom of consumer choice resulted in the continued growth of private transport, a consequent decline in public transport patronage and a rapidly growing imbalance between public transport income and expenditure. Subsidies covered 20% of public transport costs during the early 1970s but rose to 50–60% by 1982 (Ministry of Transport, 1984).

In 1972 more stringent quality controls were imposed on new entrants to the road haulage business and on their 'economic suitability'. A transport policy review (SOU, 1975) proposed that all remaining capacity controls be abolished and territorial restrictions removed. Licences should be granted to individual hauliers and corporate bodies on equal terms. Licensing was held to increase the cost of road haulage insofar as the restrictions prevented lorries from picking up back loads or part-loads. There was a shift from fixed to movement-related taxes and charges on road traffic in order to reflect the full socio-economic costs they were thought to impose on the community. It was argued that the more a traffic mode is relieved of fixed costs, the easier it will be for it to compete. If some transport modes have to cover their fixed costs and other do not, there is not an optimal market.

Although tax revenues from road users were bringing in two billion SEK more than was being spent on road improvement and traffic safety, the Transport Ministry emphasized the overcapacity of empty seats in private cars, made substantial cutbacks in the Swedish road programme in 1981 and reduced the budget for snow clearing and winter road maintenance. Only 70 km (43 miles) of motorway were promised for the 1980s, (although in fact 190 km (118 miles) were actually built up to 1988. The distribution of investment funds, which had been 70% on national trunk roads and 30% for county roads was changed to 50% for each.

The groundwork for further reform of public transport services was prepared by cost benefit analyses of individual transport services. A reorganization of local government strengthened the counties and created subordinate districts of sufficient size to support qualified administrators.

The 1979 Transport Act, introduced by a non-socialist coalition government, emphasized the role of transport in evening out the social and economic differences between people and regions. In contrast to the 1963 Act, which had tried to ensure that transport services accepted full cost responsibility for their operations, the 1979 Act required them to take all the social and economic costs attributable to their activities into account. The same principles of full socio-economic costing were to apply to all traffic modes and all would be required gradually to introduce new patterns of charging.

Behind the 1979 Act lay an attempt to distinguish charges which financed the operation of transport services from charges levied to influence the behaviour of consumers. It was realized that some investments that were socially and economically desirable were not being made because cost responsibility financing required a level of charges which might fail to encourage the effective use of a facility. There was now less concern for the relative economic advantages and disadvantages of each mode of transport than for the extra costs which each individual trip imposes upon the community (including the external effects such as noise pollution, congestion and accidents). Transport operators should be encouraged to set prices which would reflect short-term marginal costs to the community, appreciating that exact marginal cost pricing could not be achieved at all times and in all places.

In moving away from commercial criteria to much less well-defined concepts of total social and economic costs and benefits, the 1979 Act gave much more latitude to transport planners and their political masters. An explanatory paper, published much later (Ministry of Transport, 1984) argued that concepts of 'the interest of society' were much too vague and that rigorous cost benefit analyses of the effects on different groups of people should determine what the total economic and social cost of investments and charges were. Ultimately the weighing of costs and benefits in different areas and to different people becomes a matter of political judgement and the objectives of transport policy become subordinate to the wider goals of society.

The Transport Act of 1979 established a National Transport Advisory Council to oversee the working of the Act and to consider transport aspects of regional policy. The Advisory Council also acts as a court of appeal against railway closure, determines inter-county bus routes and sets general fare levels for buses and taxis within the counties. A body of Traffic Commissioners deals with judicial aspects of the Act.

The 'business' and 'social' railway networks were reorganized. Some of the services of the social railway were added to the business railway to make a 'national network' for which SJ was required to undertake a long-term research and investment programme. The SJ budget was increased by SEK100 million and SEK200 million of capital debts were written off so that SJ would be able to relate passenger fares to marginal costs and to produce a better distribution of traffic in socio-economic terms. SJ was given full commercial freedom to use its grants and subsidies since it was believed that, in competition between transport services, the quality of service was as important as price. Passenger fares (outside peak travel times) were drastically reduced in 1979. Ancilliary services of SJ were hived off and the container business transferred to a company jointly owned by rail and road haulage interests. In 1983 the state began to compensate SJ for rebates for pensioners and students and other state welfare policies.

The new policies, notably the reduction in off-peak fares at a time when the cost of private motoring was growing steeply, at first led to congestion on the railways as passengers returned to a system which had been starved of investment for several years. By the mid 1980s, however, a more commercially directed investment policy had succeeded in broadly matching services to demand.

In 1979 a drastic reduction of tariffs on *Lineflyg*, the domestic airline, doubled its summer traffic and put the firm into profit. Competition between long-distance railway passenger and air services was now established on an essentially commercial basis and there was a considerable rationalization of air services in 1980 to adjust to this new situation. The attempt to relate domestic fares to total socio-economic community costs has led to the imposition of fixed charges for airport use and rather low movement charges related to the number of passengers carried.

Competition between air and railway services is not wholly determined by strictly economic considerations. Time elasticity appears to be much greater than price elasticity, especially among business travellers. The growth of air transport has made investment in fast intercity trains less attractive but they were introduced from the beginning of 1990 between Stockholm and the main provincial cities at hourly intervals. Both air and inter-city railway services generally charge fares which cover their variable costs and contribute to fixed costs but air fares contribute more to fixed costs than railway fares.

Responsibility for local public transport was devolved from state to counties and districts. Swedish county transport funds are derived from local taxes and from an earmarked proportion of their block grant from the state. The size of the block grant is determined by a complex formula in which population size, density, economic and other special circumstances are the main elements. The proportion of public transport costs covered by subsidies ranged from 34% in Uppsala county to 41% in Norrbotten (the most sparsely populated county) and 63% in the Stockholm area.

Devolution in Sweden does not enable a local authority to pursue transport objectives different from those of the national government, as has happened in Britain. Political parties and interest organizations are represented on committees, commissions and administrative boards at all levels. The powers of elected county councils have been recently increased but county administrative boards still provide an important element of national administration at county level. Technically qualified administrators, such as highway engineers may be responsible both to the county council and to the state. County administrative boards survey the transport facilities and traffic generating factors within their jurisdiction and prepare county plans for passenger and freight traffic, taking into account present and anticipated economic developments and population movements. The national government can use its ultimate control of finance to provide a strong incentive for the local administration to rationalize its transport services.

Counties are responsible for ensuring public discussion of major transport policy proposals. Transport planning involves a high degree of co-ordination of investment and operations since population densities are seldom high enough away from the major cities to justify modal competition. County Transport Authorities (CTAs) were established, consisting of nominated representatives of county and district councils. The Gothenburg and Malmö Transport Authorities extend across county boundaries. CTAs determine priorities in the building, maintenance and snow-clearing of county roads and apportion their transport budget between roads and public transport services. The state subsidizes up to 70% of the cost of private roads which are considered to be significant to the population of an area.

Having taken over the issuing of franchises to local bus operators (which implied acceptance of the principle of cross-subsidy by the franchisee), CTAs were later empowered to undertake a total reorganization of public transport in their areas and to negotiate short-term contracts for bus, social railway, taxi, ferry and local air traffic services to mountain areas. Public transport licences are held by county councils or their nominees and transport operators work to contracts on a cost-plus basis. CTAs determine fares and timetables on stage and supplementary bus services and may appoint SJ as a subcontractor to keep railway lines and stations open. Alternatively local passenger trains may be replaced by a stage bus service. Supplementary services link smaller settlements off the main roads to local shopping centres or to stage bus routes. Most settlements lying over 2 km from a stage route have a supplementary service allowing several hours in town once or twice a week. CTAs also administer the transport grants available under regional development policy within rules laid down by the state. Monthly season tickets are normally available on all public transport services in the county. Concessionary season tickets at reduced rates are available to children and pensioners.

The 1979 Act abandoned the search for a national uniform minimum transport standard and required county and district planners to establish satisfactory standards for their areas, accepting that circumstances and therefore the minimum standard would change in the future. Local transport is the responsibility of the district councils which also contribute to public transport subsidies in proportion to their share of the traffic generated. District councils contract out school transport, which forms the basic public transport service in many really isolated areas, also dial-a-bus, minibus and taxi services. The state contributes one third of the operating costs of dial-a-bus and archipelagic traffic and similarly subsidizes air transport to settlements in the northern fells which cannot be reached by road in summer.

Transport subsidies to regionally Assisted Areas were introduced in 1971 and increased in 1974 in the belief that regional exports could be stimulated by a wider distribution of regionally produced goods and that both the export of finished goods and the import of their components should be subsidized. However, the export of raw materials and the import of finished products were not subsidized in order to preserve the protection of distance for local producers. Subsidies were granted to railways and to road transport firms (but not to lorries owned by the purchaser of the transport service) and consisted of payment in arrears of a proportion of the actual transport expenditure incurred ranging from 10% in southern Norrland (and on distances elsewhere of less than 400 km) to 50% on goods travelling over 700 km to or from Lapland and the Finnish border area. A subsidy to traffic with the island of Götland is built into ferry and air freight charges. The system was therefore simple and discriminatory. There was a minimum distance of 300 km/186 miles (later 250 km/155 miles), a minimum cargo of 500 (later 300) kg and a minimum turnover of subsidized transport of SEK3000 per annum.

State subsidies to passenger and freight movements within the Assisted Areas amounted to about 11% of all regional aid to these areas in the mid-1980s. In the view of the Commission (SOU, 1984: 74), the transport subsidy had a positive effect in influencing labour intensive firms to locate in Assisted Areas; firms with high transport costs however, would continue to locate in more central areas of the economy. There are also subsidies for unremunerative bus services covering up to 50% of the deficit on local transport services in the Inner Aid Area (providing that fares cover at least 50% of actual expenditure). In 1973 inland air fares and telephone charges on long distance routes were heavily reduced.

7.4 Further deregulation in the 1980s

As a result of devaluation, a rationalization of manufacturing industry and improvements in the terms of trade, the Swedish economy revived in the mid-1980s. Traffic rose from 136 billion vehicle journeys in 1980 to 174 billion in 1987 and the government embarked upon a major investment programme which included road building and the upgrading of sections of the railways. Nevertheless the share of transport in the national budget had fallen to 4.8% by 1980 and to 3.5% by 1986.

A further stage of deregulation took place in July 1988. All parties now supported the view that a road transport model should be used for future railway investment and that road and rail should be put on an equal footing and take social, regional and environmental costs and benefits into account when considering future investment. The three largest political parties supported the alignment of Swedish transport policy with European Community transport policies as far as is possible without lowering Swedish standards on pollution, health and safety. Regional policy will be given great weight in deciding between alternative road investment proposals and in the selective upgrading of roads to take heavier vehicles. Future legislation will enable the construction of toll roads with the help of local authority and private capital (Riksdagen, 1987–88).

The national government renounced the power to veto well-founded private and local authority investment programmes. The National Roads Authority will only concern itself with trunk roads after 1991, devolving responsibility for all other roads to the CTAs.

The Act provided for further lifting of regulations on commercial traffic and bus transport. Coaches, whether long-distance, private hire or tourist, were freed from state regulation of charges and timetables. In new road construction priority will be given to the trunk road system and to bypasses. Transport funds given to CTAs were substantially increased so that as many investment decisions as possible should be taken locally. Revisions of county transport plans will only be made at ten-year intervals in order to give security to local transport operations.

Railway freight tonne-km had been rising steadily since the 1950s but passenger km showed no long-term growth trend. The Transport Committee came to the view that although almost all the investment going into SJ was directed to its most competitive services, SJ, saddled with a network which did not conform to twentieth century geography, was unlikely to be able to fight off the competition of road and air transport in the 1990s without further substantial tranches of investment. SJ asked for SEK9 billion (about £900 million, at 1987 prices) to be spent between 1988 and 1997 just to keep the railway in its existing shape.

A National Rail Infrastructure Authority was therefore established to take over railway tracks, signalling, safety, electric traction equipment, marshalling yards and passenger platforms. While most of the budget of the Infrastructure Authority is concerned with maintenance of the track and power supply, it has a rolling ten-year infrastructure investment programme, of the order of SEK10 billion (£1 billion, at 1987 prices). Private firms, SJ and the CTAs are free to share investment costs with the Infrastructure Authority. The proposed new Mälar Express railways, linking Stockholm with the major towns of East-Central Sweden will, for instance, involve five CTAs.

There will be a two-part tariff for the use of the railway infrastructure – a movement charge (set at the estimated short-term marginal cost of the traffic) which will be negotiated annually between the Infrastructure Authority and the government and will vary among the different classes of traffic, and a fixed charge, corresponding to heavy goods vehicle licence charges on the roads, to be paid for every wagon.

The government proposed that payment to the Infrastructure Authority for the use of the track should, in line with road licensing, vary with the amount of wear and tear imposed. This policy would have set charges for running trains on the lighter tracks of lines in thinly populated areas at a higher level than on the more robust main lines and would thus have run counter to regional development policy. Parliament insisted on lower charges for the lighter tracks and transferred monies from other railway development funds to subsidize these charges.

SJ runs the locomotives and rolling stock, workshops, passenger and freight terminal and transfer services and private sidings. Some workshops may be operated jointly with the private firm ABB (Asea-Brown-Boveri). SJ has been reorganized into four operating divisions – passenger, freight, maintenance, buildings – each with separate accounting. SJ pays the Infrastructure Authority for the use of the track and stations at rates which are related to the road taxes paid by cars and commercial goods vehicles. Extra charges are levied for the upgrading of track to allow a superior service to be offered, for example new alignments to allow new ABB tilting trains to come into operation on inter-city routes from 1990. While remaining a state agency, SJ is not required to make a profit and has been finally freed of social obligations. It may close unprofitable services, accept subsidies from the local CTAs to cover the difference between income and operating costs or hand them over to CTA management. It is free to sell its property, borrow and invest on the commercial market and has greater freedom to negotiate market wages. It can choose which services to provide as long as revenues cover costs in the long term.

The railway network was again divided into main lines (6180 km) – a somewhat enlarged version of the business railway of 1963, county railways (3600 km, of which 500 km are freight only), the Inland Railway and the Iron Ore Railway (Jackson, 1989). On the county railways, CTAs have the sole right to operate railway passenger services, either under their own management or contracted out to SJ. They must either have taken full responsibility for these services by July 1990 or replaced them with buses. SJ has the right to run freight trains over the whole railway network.

Although SJ may close unprofitable services and suggested some very unpopular withdrawals of service in autumn 1988, the national government pledged itself, in the 1988 Act, to maintain some passenger services on the main lines through northern Sweden and to pay SJ for operating sleeping cars to the far North. The government had promised in 1985 to retain the northern section of the Inland Railway from Dalarna to Lapland, built during the 1930s as a last attempt to settle more farmers in the remote interior and to provide an alternative route in case the single track northern main line was put out of action in a future war. There is little through traffic on this line and the southern section from Dalarna to Lake Väner has lost its passenger service. In future the line will operate as a separate division of SJ and it is hoped to attract private and perhaps local authority investment in connection with local tourist developments. In fact track and station facilities may be given to anyone who will make an equivalent investment and guarantee to operate traffic on a section of the line. Meanwhile the state will buy some traffic on the line while further negotiations about its long-term future take place. The Iron Ore Railway, built largely by British interests at the beginning of this century to bring ore from Lapland to the ports of Narvik and Luleå, and still carrying 23% of all Swedish freight tonne-mileage, will also be treated as a separate division. Its eventual future will be decided by a joint Swedish–Norwegian Committee for the rationalization and co-ordination of traffic on the line.

A new law on air traffic is promised which will establish extra environmental charges for domestic flights and will progressively reduce the subsidies paid to airports with between 100,000 and 200,000 domestic passengers. Airports in the forested northern counties, on the other hand, will receive extra investment and a new airport will be built at Ardvisjaur, on the Inland Railway in Lapland.

Deregulation of competition is however confined to national services. The implementation of devolution and rationalization after 1979 led to a considerable increase in local and regional bus traffic (Table 7.1), which was largely attributed to the simplification of fare structures and lowering of fares. Although this rate of growth was not maintained in subsequent years, the increase in demand led to more economical operation of public transport services at higher load factors.

Devolution and rationalization did not solve all the transport problems of thinly populated areas and cuts in services eventually took place. By 1986, the Norrbotten CTA was refusing to subsidize routes where fares brought in less than 20% of revenue and sought to hand over responsibility for some school and post buses to the county and postal authorities respectively. Many stage bus routes were converted to supplementary taxi or minibus operation and there was a redistribution of subsidies towards the more heavily used routes (Zetterberg, 1986). The devolution of responsibility can thus lead to a greater application of market principles in the most thinly populated areas and to a slow, staged withdrawal of public transport in areas of outmigration.

Buses and trains under the control of CTAs are still protected from competition since most public transport cannot cover costs through charges. Where CTAs decide to replace railway services by buses, they will continue to receive railway operating subsidies from the state for the first five years of bus operation in order to pay for the development of an acceptable new service.

The Infrastructure Authority is responsible for the track on branch lines where the CTA undertakes to operate five return services per day. Where the traffic does not justify a service at this level, SJ has insignificant freight traffic, and no private interest is prepared to assist with investment, the Infrastructure Authority can withdraw from its responsibilities and the line will close after three years.

Taxis were deregulated but must have meters which issue printed tickets and receipts. Swedish taxis, usually minibuses, play a very important role in urban and rural local transport, contract for much of the transport needed by the health and education services and replace buses on thinly used rural routes. Half the income of taxis is derived from contract work for local authorities. County taxi authorities will ensure that socially necessary services are maintained.

7.5 Opposition to further deregulation

It is difficult to see how further deregulation of transport would provide a politically acceptable contribution to the solution of the social and economic problems of contemporary Sweden. The new Green party, which won 20 seats in the 1988 election, regard themselves as outside the left–right (Communist to Conservative) spectrum of the other five parties and do not favour economic growth, free trade, closer association with the European Community or nuclear power. They appeal to the suspicions of many Swedes that the pursuit of high living standards by means of an expanding, export-oriented economy will threaten distinctive Swedish cultural values and ways of life. In this context several 'Green' policies are also supported by the Centre and Communist parties including the development of railway and other tracked transport rather than building motorways or constructing road bridges to Denmark.

Within two months of entering Parliament at the general election of September 1988, the Greens had initiated a major transport debate and had rallied the Centre and Communist parties in support of many of their transport proposals (Riksdagen, 1988–89). The threat of their continued growth, whether substantiated in the event or not, is likely to strengthen those members of the ruling Social Democratic party who incline to increased regulation on environmental grounds. The Liberals, while favouring individual choice between transport modes, support economic guidance and administrative restrictions designed to reduce the adverse environmental side-effects of road traffic and would allow local authorities as well as the national government to impose such controls. The Conservative party is becoming increasingly isolated in its support for parallel transport policies to those of the European Community and for the interests of private motorists and road transport in general. All parties favour the further development of road and rail container traffic and faster passenger trains between the major cities.

There is a growing commitment to the restoration of a cleaner environment. It is strongest among the Green, Centre and Communist parties but supported by many Social Democrats. Relevant transport policies include tighter controls on road transport, further attempts to legislate for some transference of long-distance traffic from road and air to railways and measures to expand the role of public transport in the three large cities. In Stockholm, in particular, increased charges on cars entering and parking in the city are being contemplated at the same time as public transport fares are reduced in the hope of cutting back the morning inflow of commuter traffic by 20%.

The objectives of Swedish regional policy, set out in 1970 and reiterated in a later policy document (SOU, 1984: 74), are to combine the efficient use of resources to produce economic growth in the medium and long term with an improved geographical balance in the development of economic activity. Regional policies should also provide security for the individual during periods of structural change. The existing pattern of population is therefore to be protected (without rigidly supporting every existing settlement) and a reasonable equality of access to job opportunities and social welfare is to be maintained. Transport policies should contribute to the equalization of regional economic opportunity and the reduction of disparities in living standards. Both capital investment in transport links and transport subsidies to or within problem regions are widely believed to be necessary but not sufficient to support economic development but their effectiveness is very difficult to measure.

Swedish investment plans for roads until the year 2000 are clearly related to transport and regional policies since the three counties which include the big cities, which have 37% of the total population are only allocated 29% of the road budget. On the other hand the Stockholm area will receive a substantial part of the railway investment. The counties surrounding the big city areas (with relatively few commuters to those cities) and the forested counties of northern Sweden, with 42% of the total population will be allocated 52% of road investment. Railway freight will be geared to the needs of SJ's best 200 customers, with container traffic planned to amount to one-third of the freight volume (apart from iron ore).

Sweden's Scandinavian neighbours have followed rather similar paths towards transport deregulation and devolution but their geography has determined a different balance between transport modes with a much larger role for coastal shipping. A succession of minority governments in recent years has made radical changes more difficult to achieve. All three countries have devolved decisions on local transport to their county authorities but the Danish Ministry of Transport had to intervene in 1974 to rein in heavy county spending on secondary roads. The national railways of Denmark and Norway have not been subdivided and have a much closer relationship to their Ministries of Transport than SJ has. There have been widespread closures of local railways and branch lines in Denmark but not in Norway, where there is very strong political support for their retention. Counties subsidize branch line services in both countries. Norwegian rural bus services are operated by regulated private companies rather than by CTAs.

The return to power of the Swedish Social Democratic party after the election of 1982 and the recent growth in influence of the Greens have set clear limits to the further pursuit of deregulation in Sweden. The 1988

Transport Act achieved more deregulation of the commercially viable parts of the transport system but the basic geography of the country and its population distribution determine that deregulation beyond this would only increase the cost of provision of the social transport service and thereby exacerbate the regional differentiation of wealth and opportunity which the majority of voters are determined to avoid. There is little scope for further devolution of transport policy to county level in order to increase the flexibility and efficiency of the large subsidized sector.

References

Jackson, C. (1989) Sweden's track authority sparks a quiet revolution. *Railway Gazette International* 249–52.

Kritz, L. (1976) *Transportpolitiken och lastbilarna* Stockholm.

NKTF (Nordisk Kommité for Transportøkonomisk Forskning) (1980) *Transportarbedet i Norden, 1960–1990*. Copenhagen.

Nordic Statistical Secretariat (1989) *Yearbook of Nordic Statistics, 1988*. Copenhagen.

Price, E. (1968) Reshaping the railways of Sweden. *Railway Gazette International* 255–7 London.

Riksdagen, (1987–88) *Årsbok* Stockholm, pp. 165–74.

Riksdagen, (1988–89) *Protokoll* Debatt om trafikpolitiks miljökonsekvenser, 23 November 1988, Stockholm, p. 30.

SOU (Sveriges Offentliga Utredningar), 1961 *Svensk Trafikpolitik*, p. 23.

SOU, (1975) *Trafikpolitik – behov och möligheter*, p. 66.

SOU, (1978) *Trafikipolitik – kostnadsansvar och avgifter*, p. 31.

SOU, (1984) *Regional utveckling och mellomregional utjämning*, p. 74.

Ministry of Transport, (1984) *Busslinjetrafiken – forslag till ändringar i lagstiftningen*, Stockholm.

Zetterberg, J. (1986) Norrbotten remodler busstrafiken *Svensk lokaltrafik* (Stockholm) **5/86**, 7–9.

CHAPTER 8

Transport deregulation in advanced capitalist nations – the case of the USA *

Kenneth Button

8.1 Introduction

Transport regulation can never be viewed in isolation. Attitudes and policies are influenced by a wide variety of factors many of which appear somewhat distant to transport itself. This is to be expected if one considers the role transport can play in such things as: helping to improve the geographical cohesion of a country; stimulating economic activities; and lubricating the wheels of commerce. Equally, but less often considered, the transport sector is a major component of most developed economies and, therefore, in its own right may exert influences over such macroeconomic matters as levels of inflation and the balance of payments. All this needs bearing in mind when reviewing recent events in the USA.

The changes which have occurred in transport regulation in the USA are also only part of a larger trend. Indeed, the late 1970s and early 1980s witnessed a general liberalization of regulation in a wide range of markets (McKie, 1989). The term 'deregulation' is often coined to describe these changes but some care must be taken in interpreting the events which have occurred.

The US regulatory system can essentially be divided into three broad forms of control. There is 'economic regulation', which places constraints

*The author would like to acknowledge the funding he has received over the past five years from the Chartered Institute of Transport, the Embassy of the United States in London and the Economic and Science Research Council (Grants DO232224 and R 000 22 1010). This has enabled him to study various aspects of transport regulation in the United States.

141

over such things as charges, number of suppliers, output levels, etc, and certainly there has been liberalization in many sectors with respect to such regulation. In contrast there is also 'social regulation', governing such things as safety standards, consumer protection, qualifications of suppliers, etc, and here there has been no discernible abatement in regulation. Finally, there is 'anti-trust' policy which is aimed at controlling monopoly power, mergers, etc, and here while there have been few legal changes there has been some *de facto* liberalization in the way policy has been implemented.

To further complicate matters, there are two important levels at which regulations may be imposed – the individual state and the federal levels. Movements towards liberalization of, say, economic regulation at one level may be in conflict with moves towards greater regulation at the other level. Differences between the views of some states and the federal position on regulatory strategies have been common for many years with regard to transport activities.

It is against this wider background of change within the US that this chapter should be set. In terms of organization, the chapter sets out initially to provide a very brief background to the system of transport regulation which developed from the late eighteenth century in the United States. It then moves on to consider why quite dramatic changes to the regulatory regime were set in motion in the 1970s and what these changes mean in terms of the current regulatory system. Consideration is then given to the consequences for the US transport sector of the reforms and, from a longer-term perspective, what the outstanding issues are.

It should be pointed out that our discussions are not intended to be all-embracing. Space constraints limit the amount of detail which can be provided but in addition to this, the focus is on US domestic transport and, primarily, on federal regulation. International transport is a subject in its own right and is, save for one or two instances where it seriously affects the domestic scene, largely ignored here. But even with regard to domestic transport there are caveats. For example, inland waterways and pipelines are, because of space constraints, excluded. The nature of highways policy and the greater use of private funding is another area omitted. Equally, the various controls exercised by the fifty states of the US and hundreds of major cities over transport internal to their boundaries is given only cursory treatment.

8.2 The development of regulation

As in many countries, the modern phase of transport regulation in the USA came about because of fears over the potential monopoly power of railroads. Indeed, the Interstate Commerce Commission (ICC), formed in 1887 under the Act to Regulate Commerce, was the first federal regulatory commission of any kind in the country. The federal legislation, however, actually followed earlier regulatory statutes in a number of states.

The ICC was given powers to control railway rates and entry and exit into and out of the industry. Rates were required to be reasonable and just and had to be published. Prohibitions were placed on such activities as charging higher rates on shorter hauls than longer if the former formed a component of the longer haul. The powers of the ICC over these matters were gradually refined and extended around the turn of the century (e.g. the Elkins Act of 1903 with regard to rate rebates and the Hepburn Act of 1906 with regard to the specification of maximum rates).

As technological change progressed the ICC was given additional responsibilities. In particular, the 1935 Motor Carriers Act brought both trucking (road haulage) and inter-state busing within the ambit of ICC control. In the case of trucking, the ICC had powers to control market entry to routes (although 'grandfather rights' were afforded incumbent carriers already in the market in 1935) and to establish maximum and minimum rates. It largely gave this latter responsibility over to regional rate bureaux of established truckers which jointly determined the rates which were then simply filed with the ICC. Entry to the inter-state bus market was similarly regulated as were fares.

The rationale for regulation of trucking and bus services was somewhat different to that of the railroads. There were, as with the railroads, a range of social arguments for regulation concerning such things as safe operations and the need for adequate services. Further, in the context of bus operations there was a particular desire to develop effective competition to counteract the dominant position enjoyed by Greyhound while at the same time ensuring a full network of services was being supplied (Button, 1987). In addition, however, questions of market stability (especially at a time of serious economic depression) and equality of competition with the railroads were important motivation factors. Within the trucking industry in particular there were also established, incumbent operators seeking protection from the rigours of competition from new entrants.

Interstate US aviation came under the regulatory umbrella of the Civil Aeronautics Authority – later the Civil Aeronautics Board (CAB) – in 1938. The legislation was initially passed to ensure efficiency in the provision of mail services, to foster safety and to introduce greater stability to the industry. In particular, the industry was seen as prone to suffer from excessive competition. There was thus both a public interest motivation and a private interest element (in that incumbents favoured protection from potential competition) underlying the policy. The CAB exercised controls over market entry and fares and also, until the Federation Aviation Administration took over responsibility in 1958, concerned itself with matters directly related to safety.

8.3 The forces for change

While detailed changes to the regulatory system took place in the three decades immediately after World War II, the regime of transport regulation which had grown up in the nineteenth century, and was substantially extended in the 1930s, continued to exercise control over much of the transport industry in the USA. There were critics of the system who pointed to potential inefficiencies – e.g. Jeyes (1951) with respect to aviation and Nelson (1959) more generally – but their voices carried little weight at a time of national economic expansion when concerns over costs minimization seemed somewhat academic.

A large number of economists argued, almost from the outset, that many of the regulations over transport would not achieve their stated objectives and may actually prove counter-productive. This was particularly true, for instance, after 1935 when there were continuing assertions that modes such as trucking are inherently competitive and economic regulation, therefore, unnecessary. Hard evidence about the impacts of regulation of road and air transport was, though, only slowly accumulated.

By the mid-1970s the regulatory system which evolved in the USA was, however, beginning to show signs of strain. Part of the pressure continued to come from the academic world where studies were appearing pointing to the high 'costs' of regulation. In particular, a series of studies of US domestic aviation compared the fares and services on unregulated, intra-state routes within California and Texas with comparable inter-state, CAB regulated services and found the latter lacking (Button, 1989a). This type of empirical evidence of itself was not sufficient to bring about change, and, even if it were, the exact nature of the reform could have taken many different shapes.

Ideas were also important in the package of influences leading to liberalization in the 1970s. Changes in ideology and developments in economic theory took place. Regulation had grown up in the belief that it served the public interest. The so-called 'Chicago School' however took a somewhat different view and this contributed to the new climate of opinion which emerged in the 1960s and 1970s. It argued that regulation tended to be captured either by those whose behaviour it was intended to control or by the regulators themselves who are more interested in pursuing their own self interests than meeting social criteria. Markets, according to this school of thought, often suffer from imperfections but these represent the lesser of two evils when contrasted to the imperfections of regulation.

This rather pessimistic view of markets and regulation was supplemented by the more optimistic message that by creating 'contestable markets' one could achieve both economic efficiency and avoid the problems of regulatory capture. Provided markets are so free that entry and exist is costless then there is no scope for exploitation and consumers cannot be exploited. The fear that new entrants will begin providing transport services at a lower price will deter incumbents from setting fares or rates above cost. This is true irrespective of the number of suppliers and, indeed, where there are economies of scale or scope (where costs are reduced by producing a range of services) it is quite possible that a single supplier will meet all the market's demand. Of course, this does not preclude the need for intervention for safety reasons or to supply socially important services.

More practical considerations were also instrumental in bringing about change and macroeconomic pressures were possibly of at least, if not more, importance as changes in economic thinking. The combination of inflation and economic depression – the so-called 'stagflation' problem – was a major issue for the Ford and Carter administrations in the early 1970s. Lack of economic incentives coupled with cost-push effects were seen as a significant underlying cause. Regulation was seen by many as both stifling initiative and contributing to high prices so arguments developed for reducing the potency of such regulations. In reality the argument seems flawed, at least for the 1970s, and empirical evidence suggests that transport rate increases were actually tracking general price rises at some distance rather than leading them (MacAvoy, 1979). Perceptions, however, often exercise more sway than fact.

Finally, there were demonstration effects. Overseas, for instance, the UK had deregulated its road haulage in 1968 with no disastrous consequences but even within the US there was evidence from intra-state transport that liberalization could increase efficiency. This came, for example, from Florida where inter-city bus services were unregulated, from Texas and California where inter-state aviation was unregulated, from New Jersey where trucking was unregulated, from Maryland where household goods transport was unregulated, etc.

8.4 The 'deregulation'

In many ways the first of the recent major measures of regulatory reform came about in one of the least expected modes – the railroads (see Table 8.1 for a listing of the main legislative reforms). The early reforms in this industry should perhaps, therefore, be treated as something of a special case and, indeed, the railroads had to wait until 1980 for their most important reforms.

The US railroads had been encountering increasing financial difficulties and, under the near century-old regulatory system, lacked room to

Table 8.1 *Major pieces of transport legislation in the USA (1970–89).*

1970	Rail Passenger Act – created National Railroad Passenger Corporation to form Amtrack.
1973	Regional Rail Reorganization Act – created the US Railways Association to set up Conrail.
1976	Railroad Revitalization and Regulatory Reform Act – removed many regulations over rate setting.
1977	Air Cargo Deregulation Act – initiated free competition for air cargoes.
1978	Airline Deregulation Act – initiated a phased removal of fare setting and market entry controls.
1980	Staggers Rail Act – removed many regulations over line abandonment and gave further freedom in rate setting.
1980	Motor Carriers Reform Act – increased entry and rate setting freedom and reduced the role of rate fixing bureaus.
1980	Households Goods Transportation Act – deregulated households goods transport.
1981	Northeast Rail Service Act – enable Conrail to abandon little-used lines.
1982	Bus Regulatory Reform Act – eased conditions of market entry and exit and phased in relaxation of rate controls.

manoeuvre to improve their position. Initially, the policy had essentially been one of fire fighting with the Rail Passenger Act of 1970 setting out to introduce subsidies to support unprofitable passenger services and to develop partnership arrangements within Amtrack. By 1973, however, the bankruptcy of eight major railroads in the north-east resulted in the Regional Rail Reorganization Act aimed at refinancing and restructuring (within Conrail) part of the system. The established system of controls remained however, until the Railroad Revitalization and Reform Act 1976 increased the rate setting freedom of the railroads in addition to injecting $6.5 billion of investment funds and loans into them. It also facilitated easier mergers and the abandonment of unprofitable routes which the regulatory system had retained and financed through a system of cross-subsidization. The Staggers Act of 1980 continued this process by further increasing rate setting freedom leaving only about a third of maximum rates controlled – and allowing the railroads to abandon more unprofitable lines. Controls, however, have been retained to ensure that shippers captive to the railways are not exploited. The aim is to protect producers of low value bulk commodities, such as coal and ores, where motor transport is not a viable mode and no waterway competition exists, but even here there were subsequent relaxations as with export coal rates in 1983.

Reform of controls over other modes, although possibly more dramatic in their ultimate impact, did not come about through crisis management. Aviation had been under review for some time and the Ford administration began pressing for reform in 1975. Besides academic evidence that the regulatory system was pushing up fare levels there was also mounting pressure for change from several airlines (e.g. United and Pan American) which saw regulation as an impediment to dealing with the high fuel prices and depressed markets which accompanied the Arab oil embargo of 1973. In fact, *de facto* change began in 1976 when the CAB began to loosen existing statutes and gathered pace after the appointment of the economist Alfred Kahn to its chairmanship in 1977. The Airline Deregulation Act 1978 initiated a phased removal of fare and entry controls with a 'sunset clause' resulting in the abolition of the CAB in 1985. Direct subsidies were introduced at the same time under the Essential Air Service (EAS) Program to finance continued air services to small communities until at least 1988.

Reforms in the trucking industry mainly relate to entry conditions and legislation, and as with the airlines followed considerable *de facto* liberalization. From 1977 the ICC, especially under the Commissionership of Daniel O'Neal, had been adopting a more liberal policy towards market entry by using powers set down under the original 1935 Act (Pustay, 1989). For example, the burden of proof switched after 1978 from the applicant having to demonstrate his route authority was in the public interest to the objector showing it was not. Again from 1978, private truckers were enabled to compete with for-hire carriers in certain circumstances. The Motor Carrier Reform Act 1980 ratified such policies. In effect there was an expansion in the types of services which are totally exempt from entry controls other than that the applicant is fit, able and willing and that a useful public service is served. Entry to other services was also made considerably easier. Additionally, with regard to rates, wide zones of freedom were introduced which essentially took control out of the hands of the ICC when rates were set by individuals. To control collective rate making anti-trust immunity was substantially reduced.

In 1982 the Bus Regulatory Reform Act (BRRA) essentially applied the philosophy of the Motor Carrier Reform Act to inter-state bus services (Button, 1987). Initially zones of fare flexibility were introduced but these widened and ceased entirely after three years. Barriers to entry and exit to the industry were removed and the ICC was given greater powers to override restrictive intra-state regulations.

8.5 The consequences of liberalization

Clearly the impact of regulatory reform has both differed in its nature and its intensity across the various transport modes. The exact nature of the changes pertaining to each mode and their timing have obviously influenced events but there have also been other factors at work. Assessment of the various effects is, for instance, compounded by variations in the external market conditions confronting the different transport sectors. In the context of domestic aviation, for example, the 1978 Act was immediately followed by a period of severe national economic depression which, in turn, gave way to an extended period of economic growth. The industry was also hit by the air traffic controllers' strike of 1981. The interactive effects between modes are also influential. Trucking clearly competes with rail freight but equally one can point to competition in the early 1980s between low-cost airlines (such as People Express) and inter-state bus and passenger rail services. Further, many of the reforms are, in the context of the industries involved, comparatively recent and the complete long-term consequences are unlikely to have emerged as of yet.

To isolate the specific consequences of each reform on the associated mode is, therefore, almost impossible. Some broad indications of the effects of the reforms can, however, be established. These are perhaps most usefully reviewed by looking at a number of the broad themes.

One of the primary objects of deregulation was to contain transport costs. Without knowing exactly what would have happened without liberalization, though, it is difficult to say exactly what the effects of reform have been on fares and freight rates. Some indication can be gleaned by simply looking at trends in charges. In terms of aviation there is, for example, evidence that substantially more discount fares became available and that generally discounts have become deeper (see Table 8.2). Some 90% of travellers were estimated by the Air Transport Association to be flying on discounted tickets in 1986 with the average discount some 61% below the coach fare (i.e. the normal economy fare). Further, comparisons between 1976 and 1984 reveal that the coach fares themselves had fallen by about 7%. Not all air travellers benefited, however; the largest fare reductions have come in the 50 markets

148

Table 8.2 *Availability and scope of discount air fares in 1976 and 1984.*

Market rank	Percentage of market with discount fares		Average discount fare as percentage of coach fare	
	1976	1984	1976	1984
Top 50	69	96	78	61
51–100	60	90	80	63
101–150	36	84	80	72
151–200	39	80	80	77
Smaller markets	30	72	80	76

Source: Meyer and Oster, 1987

where competition is most severe and in many small and medium markets coach fare rises have been recorded.

Freight transport rates have also been affected by liberalization. In the case of trucking, there has been a shift away from the rate bureaux and towards independent filings by truckers with 95% of the latter filing for rate reductions. Discounting has increased and by 1981 about a quarter of inter-state freight moved by road was charged at a discount rate. A new dimension to rate setting since reform has been the ability to offer contract rates and many carriers now do this. Overall, there is evidence that truck load rates fell by about 25% between 1977 and 1982 and that less-than-truck rates fell by about 16% (Moore, 1983). A similar picture emerges with respect to the railroads. Surveys indicate that rates paid by major shippers fell some 9% between 1978 and 1982 while overall, revenue per ton-mile (a proxy for rates) fell some 7.5%. Some of this reduction is associated with the increased use of contract rates (with some 5000 filed with the ICC by 1983) and by 1986 more than 62% of coal and 57% of grain were carried under such rates.

Rate and fare reductions have been brought about both by direct cost savings and through innovations in the types of service offered.

Perhaps the greatest direct cost savings have come from lower labour costs but many of these have only been achieved after severe industrial strife. In the bus industry, for example, Greyhound obtained a 15% wage cut from the Amalgamated Transit Union in 1983 but only after a seven-week strike, and shed 1500 workers two years later. Aviation offers a mixed picture both in terms of the airlines considered and the types of jobs involved. In real terms, the annual labour expenditure per employee at, for example, Continental fell by 41% between 1978 and 1985, at Republic by 16% and at Western by over 22% but equally it rose by over 8% at Delta and by nearly 7% at TWA during the same period. To reduce costs some airlines introduced two-tier pay structures with new employees joining on a lower scale while many increased the productivity of labour by, for instance, increasing flying times of aircrew. Even within this framework different categories of labour have enjoyed diverse experiences. Between 1975 and 1984, for instance, the real income of pilots fell by about 1% but that of mechanics rose by 1% and that of flight assistants by 14%.

Liberalization has also brought about changes in the structure of the US transport industries. Relaxation on entry, in particular, has led to innovations in the way services are provided. Perhaps the most pronounced change in this respect has occurred in the aviation industry. Under the CAB, inter-state air services had grown up in a haphazard way with a small number of long-established carriers dominating the jet service market. Deregulation brought in new, low cost operators such as People Express, New York Air, etc, but more importantly perhaps it resulted in a major change in the structure of services. Airlines rapidly realized the benefits of hub-and-spoke operations whereby their flights hub in on a limited number of airports offering the customer a wide range of linking services. The higher load factors which result keep operating costs (and fares) down but does mean, for the passenger, that most flights involve a change of aircraft and, therefore, incur longer door-to-door times. However, taking these conflicting effects into account, Morrison and Winston (1986) still estimated that the 1978 reforms benefit travellers by about $5.7 billion annually (in 1977 prices).

Innovation in other sectors has also resulted in changes in the types of service offered. In the context of inter-city bus operations, the long-term, gradual decline of the industry has continued in the liberalized era (passengers carried falling from 170 million in 1981 to 148 million in 1984 and bus miles of service fell from 1134 million (1824 million km) to 1098 million (1766 million km) over the same period) although this seems to have been more the result of deregulation of other sectors than of the BRRA itself. Innovation has not, however, been absent. Greyhound, for instance, after changes in ownership, has engaged in greater vertical integration by purchasing General Motors' transit bus manufacturing division to achieve economies of scale in its vehicle production activities. It has also divested itself of high cost routes and adopted franchising arrangements where local independent carriers can offer such services at lower cost. Equally, many older, downtown terminals have been sold to streamline operations and to locate facilities at growth points in the company's network. At the same time as scheduled services declined there was a growth in charter and special-service applications mainly serving the inclusive tour market.

Innovation on the railroads has also been pronounced although mainly in terms of the flexibility of services that are part of contract rate agreements – these now frequently cover such things as: delivery times; quantities carried; furnishing of equipment used; dependability guarantees; etc. Innovation, however, also embraces changes in the trailer-on-flatcar and container (piggyback) services which are on offer. Mainly as the result of the complete deregulation of such services in 1981, the number of carloadings of such traffic grew by nearly 60% between 1980 and 1984 by which time they accounted for over 13% of class I carloadings. Trucking firms have responded with overnight delivery services, pickup services at night and at weekends, computer linkages with customers, additional services for new commodities and increased participation in trailer-on-flatcar service.

One of the motivating forces behind much of the original regulation of US transport was the fear of market domination. In the short term, we have seen that liberalization has generally reduced rates on the railroads and thus such fears may appear unfounded. In fact, in many major markets more than one railroad competes for business and does so against inter-modal competition from trucking, pipelines and barges. Indeed, one of the biggest effects of railroad liberalization is that it has taken traffic from the roads – especially through greater use of piggyback services. Indeed, it seems strange in retrospect that one of Congress' reasons for regulating trucking in the 1930s was to protect railroads from unfair competition. As it transpires, it seems the Motor Carrier Act may actually have protected truckers' profits at the expense of the railroads.

The enhanced competition which was expected in some other sectors also materialized rapidly. In the trucking industry, for example, the number of applicants for new authorities grew considerably from the *de facto* liberalization of the mid-1970s to the passing of the 1980 Reform Act and expanded more rapidly thereafter (see Table 8.3). At the same time there was an upsurge of exits from the industry with more than 4000 trucking companies, both local and inter-city, ceasing operations between 1980 and 1984. Much of this latter effect can be explained in terms of a general reorganization of the industry with more efficient carriers replacing the less efficient, but it also partly reflects the poor economic climate prevailing in the early 1980s and the competition being offered by railroads.

Table 8.3 *Entry into the trucking industry, 1975–82.*

Year	Licence applications*		Percentage granted		Number of new and existing firms* (year-end)
	Existing firms	New firms	Existing firms	New firms	
1975	2.8	0.3	55	61	16.0
1976	6.4	0.6	61	62	16.5
1977	8.6	0.6	65	72	16.6
1978	13.0	0.7	69	78	16.8
1979	20.7	1.0	69	80	17.1
1980	18.8	1.5	73	86	18.1
1981	19.1	4.6	88	85	22.3
1982	9.2	4.9	84	55	25.7

* thousands
Source: Moore, 1983

Following liberalized entry, there was also a sudden increase in airline operations and by 1983 there were 22 new jet carriers in the inter-state markets – many like Piedmont, Republic and Frontier being former local operators. Similar trends were exhibited in the inter-city bus industry with the 1470 carriers operating in 1981 rising to some 3000 carriers by 1984.

The longer-term effect may, however, prove to be somewhat different. Trucking has remained broadly competitive but domestic aviation has experienced greater concentration of control. In the two and a half years after 1985 there were 24 acquisitions or mergers in the industry compared with only 15 in the 40 years between 1938 and 1978. Hence while concentration declined in the market in the period immediately following deregulation this trend was reversed from the mid-1980s (see Table 8.4). Whether this means actual competition on individual routes has declined is a more debatable point. The hub-and-spoke system frequently means that travellers now actually have a greater choice of route and airline between their origin and destination (Meyer & Oster, 1987). In some cases, however, mergers have resulted in airlines gaining almost monopoly control over airports (e.g. TWA at St Louis and Northeastern at Minneapolis–St Paul). Further, control over computer reservation systems (CRSs) through which bookings are made and the use of loyalty payments to regular travellers (e.g. 'frequent flier programs') now make it almost impossible for new entrants to penetrate the market (Button, 1989b).

Table 8.4 *Domestic aviation market concentration ratios expressed as percentage of revenue passenger miles.*

Twelve months ending September 30	Top four carriers	Top eight carriers
1977	56.8	81.7
1979	56.6	80.7
1981	54.2	74.5
1983	54.8	74.5
1985	51.7	70.7
1986	65.5	88.7

Source: *Air Carrier Statistics*, various issues

Regulations were originally not only initiated to contain the economic power of transport firms but were often seen as an integral component of wider social policy. In particular, they were often seen as important in ensuring safety criteria were met. Additionally, they were frequently introduced for regional planning reasons and to ensure adequate levels of transport provision were available to those living in remote areas or in small communities.

In terms of safety, the social regulations have not been liberalized as part of the recent trend in regulatory reform – indeed, in some instances they have been tightened. Free market advocates also point to the loss of reputation and business which can accompany undertakings with a poor safety record. In empirical terms it is difficult to find evidence that safety has suffered as a result of deregulation. In most transport industries there has been a long-term record of improvement in accident rates due to technical developments in the equipment used and the infrastructure available. While short-term effects can be misleading, the available data from, for example, the trucking and domestic airline industries suggests that this trend has at least been maintained (e.g. see Table 8.5).

The continuation of essentially social transport services which had

Table 8.5 *Index of fatalities per truck mile and air passenger mile (1974 = 100).*

Year	Truck mile	Air passenger mile
1969		38.3
1970		0.5
1971		50.3
1972		42.0
1973		48.7
1974	100.0	100.0
1975	85.4	27.5
1976	87.2	7.8
1977	89.9	12.4
1978	84.0	25.4
1979	82.7	52.3
1980	68.3	0
1981	74.9	0.2
1982	64.2	37.3
1983	61.9	1.6
1984	60.9	0
1985	57.2	23.8

Sources: derived from Daicoff, 1988 and Jordan, 1986

formerly been funded under the various regulatory regimes by systems of cross-subsidies were felt to be in danger with liberalization. (Indeed, the EAS was designed specifically to meet this problem in the context of air services.) In some cases demonstrable decline has taken place with, for example, reductions in bus services, especially those provided by Greyhound and Trailways, to many small communities but, in general this simply reflects a trend which had been apparent prior to regulatory change (Button, 1987). Further, some small communities, some 95 between 1978 and 1983, have completely lost their air services although this seems to be due more to high fuel prices and interest rates and the general state of the macroeconomy than deregulation (Morrison, 1989). In other cases, the nature of air services have changed. Many small communities have found that the capacity (in terms of seats available) of services has been reduced but at the same time there are more aircraft departures (Meyer & Oster, 1987). Essentially, the airlines have substituted smaller, more suitable aircraft for the work at hand.

Freight services to small communities also seem to have been little affected by liberalization of the trucking industry; indeed, reform may have benefited small communities in that rate reductions seem to be slightly greater for them than for larger community shippers (Pustay, 1989). ICC studies also indicate that there was no significant diminution of services provided to the small communities.

8.6 The outstanding issues

The reforms of the past fifteen years or so in the USA have not been trouble-free. Some of the consequences were foreseen but others have been unexpected. Equally, some of the changes have led, it is generally agreed, to higher benefits than had been anticipated but there are also instances where the reverse could be said to have occurred. In many instances it is difficult to draw even the most general of conclusions because the long-term implications of liberalization have yet to manifest themselves in full.

Even given this high degree of uncertainty, it is unlikely that the current regime of liberal regulation which was developed over the past 15 or so years will go unaltered. Policy makers find it difficult to resist tinkering with regulations and controls. Additionally some outstanding issues remain. In very general terms these relate to: the degree to which further liberalization is desirable and likely to be practicable; the extent to which there is a need for some fine tuning of recent legislation; the need for additional reforms in related areas of economic and social policy (including anti-trust policy); and the degree, if any, to which there should be reregulation in some areas.

While deregulation of domestic civil aviation in the USA has been thorough there still remain residual controls in sectors such as trucking. The ICC, for example, while having much diminished powers, still retains some authority over rates, and market entry and exit. Equally, there are anomalies in that rate bureaux retain anti-trust immunity and can, therefore, still exercise some influence over rate setting. Such residual controls are gradually likely to disappear in the future. Linked with this is the possible extension of liberalization to state controls over intra-state transport. The 1982 BRRA has already essentially given the ICC powers to pre-empt state regulatory commissions' decisions relating to bus transport but such powers do not extend to trucking. The ICC, by reinterpreting the distinction between intra-state and inter-state freight traffic have reduced the influence of state commissions. Given the reluctance of state authorities to relinquish their own powers, it seems unlikely, however, that any further significant liberalization of state regulations will occur without federal action.

The spate of changes which occurred between the mid-1970s and the 1980s has still left much residual regulation and inevitably this will be modified over time both in response to changing external conditions but also as the effects of deregulation elsewhere exercise knock-on effects. The relationship between road and rail freight transport is a case in point where many railroads rates are still regulated. As the relative performance of road and rail change over time so fine tuning of the degree of such regulation will inevitably have to be undertaken.

Deregulation has, as may have been anticipated, brought forth reaction from transport suppliers trying to protect their positions. In some instances actions have already been taken to contain such activities and to protect consumers. A case in point is the code of conduct which has been drawn up to ensure that airlines with their own CRS systems do not exploit the market power this confers on them. Information has to be displayed in an impartial manner rather than to the advantage of any particular airline. Anti-trust policy in contrast, has always been relatively lax with regard to US transport industries on the basis that economic regulation effectively removes the need for it. With deregulation, and in particular the increasing concentration being experienced in aviation, the case for firmer anti-trust policies is being voiced and is likely to draw forth a legislative response in the future.

There are also complementary activities to transport which have been affected by deregulation. Infrastructure (e.g. roads, airports, etc) is the most obvious example. Freeing transport from economic regulation has substantially increased the actual amount of transport undertaken and this in turn has put pressure on the available infrastructure. A logical concomitant of deregulation is a similar deregulation of infrastructure supply or at least public policies with regard to infrastructure which are broadly in line with how a deregulated market would function. This means, for example, making road users more directly aware of the full costs (including that of congestion) of making each trip and airline operators of making each flight. Attempts to do this in the context of airport charges at major airports being related to the actual costs of take-offs and landings have met with legal problems in the US but with little new airport capacity becoming available legislative changes may be inevitable. In the case of roads, tolled facilities are becoming more common and, indeed, some states are paying off debts to the federal government so that they may toll sections of the inter-state system. One can anticipate more of this type of action.

Finally, there is developing a minor backlash and arguments for a degree of reregulation are being voiced (Tolchin & Tolchin, 1983). The arguments often relate to problems of monopoly power beginning to emerge in some sectors and to market instability in others. But there is also concern about the social consequences of deregulation and over perceptions that corruption has grown. Some reregulation, it is argued, could also ensure confidence is retained in the transport industry when recession comes. Many of the arguments for reregulation involve comparisons of an ideal regulatory system with what has happened since deregulation of transport services. The counter view is that, first, regulations are never perfect and, in fact, tend to be more harmful than the disease they are meant to be treating and, second, where regulations need to be introduced they should be directed at specific problems (e.g. monopoly power, consumer protection, etc) rather than be economic regulations over market entry and prices. While it is difficult, and perhaps dangerous, to forecast exactly how legislators are going to react in the long term, it seems unlikely that there will be a large scale reversion to quantity and price controls in the foreseeable future.

8.7 Conclusions

Transport liberalization was introduced over a comparatively short period in the USA. The main legal reforms came about between 1978 and 1982 while broadly similar changes in the UK spanned the years between the Transport Acts of 1968 and 1985. The scale of change, the complexity of interacting effects between modes and the relatively short time period which has elapsed since these reforms makes evaluation difficult. Certainly there have been problems and certainly many of the results have been unexpected but overall the liberalization seems to have produced a more efficient transport system.

Many of the anticipated ill-effects have not materialized and where they have they have been much less severe than had initially been feared. Other problems, such as those of safety, market concentration and reduced social provision, are now recognized as problems that extend beyond the transport sector and can be handled in a more general way through social programmes, anti-trust policy, etc. Transport in this sense is not special and does not need specific and burdensome regulations to control it.

References

Button, K. J. (1987) The effects of regulatory reform on the US inter-city bus industry *Transport Reviews* 7, 145–66.

Button, K. J. (1989a) The deregulation of U.S. interstate aviation: an assessment of causes and consequences, Part I, *Transport Reviews*.

Button, K. J. (1989b) The deregulation of U.S. interstate aviation: an assessment of causes and consequences, Part II, *Transport Reviews*.

Daicoff, D. W. (1988) Deregulation and motor carrier safety *Logistics and Transportation Review* 24, 175–84.

Jordan, W. A. (1986) Economic deregulation and airline safety. In *Proceedings of the 21st Annual Meeting of the Canadian Transportation Research Forum* Vancouver.

Keyes, L. S. (1951) *Federal control of entry into air transport*, Cambridge, Massachusetts: Harvard University Press.

MacAvoy, P. W. (1979) *The regulated industries and the economy*, New York: Norton.

McKie, J. W. (1989) US regulatory policy. In Button, K. J. & Swann, D. (eds) *The age of regulatory reform*, Oxford: Clarendon Press.

Meyer, J. R. and Oster, C. V. (1987) *Deregulation and the future of intercity passenger travel*, Cambridge, Massachusetts: MIT Press.

Moore, T. G. (1983) Rail and truck reform – the record so far *Regulation*, November/December, 33–41.

Morrison, S. A. (1989) US domestic aviation. In Button, K. J. & Swann, D. (eds) *The age of regulatory reform*, Oxford: Clarendon Press.

Morrison, S. A. & Winston, C. (1986) *The economic effects of airline deregulation*, Washington: Brookings Institution.

Nelson, J. C. (1959) *Railroad transportation and public policy*, Washington: Brookings Institution.

Pustay, M. W. (1989) Deregulation and the US trucking industry. In Button, K. J. & Swann, D. (eds) *The age of regulatory reform*, Oxford: Clarendon Press.

Tolchin, S. J. & Tolchin, M. (1983) *Dismantling America – the rush to reregulate*, New York: Houghton Mifflin.

CHAPTER 9

Restructuring transport parastatals: case studies from South-East Asia

Peter J. Rimmer

The activities of the New Right in restructuring transport in Britain are being re-echoed throughout the cities and regions of South-East Asia. Proselytization by missionaries from the World Bank, bolstered by the Asian Development Bank, bilateral aid donors and private bankers, has seen the ideas of the New Right take root. The debate in South-East Asia, however, has been devoid of the usual right wing versus left wing ideology (Rowley, 1985). Basically, recommendations for restructuring state-owned transport enterprises, supplying transport services and infrastructure, are the pragmatic reactions of politicians and bureaucrats to the problems being experienced by state-owned parastatals (Rimmer, 1986; 1988).

As the state-owned transport parastatals account for a substantial part of investment in the main South-East Asian countries – Indonesia, Malaysia, Philippines, Singapore and Thailand (Figure 9.1) – their efficient operation is crucial to sustaining economic growth and improving industrial competitiveness. Management of these parastatals, however, has been perceived as being grossly inefficient, inadequately accountable and a drain on scarce government resources as subsidies, transfers and net lending outstrips revenue. Invariably, their performance is regarded as inferior to private sector counterparts. Hence, the argument that most South-East Asian state-owned transport parastatals should be sold off to private interests. But privatisation is not the only – nor necessarily the most effective – approach for increasing their efficiency. Indeed, rather than apply privatisation as a 'universal fix' we need to assess a range of ownership and management options available to these parastatals to ensure that they operate at maximum efficiency.

156

Figure 9.1 South-East Asia.

Attention, in particular, is focused on examining and evaluating a number of micro-economic approaches that have been used by South-East Asian governments for reshaping and reforming state-owned enterprises and improving their efficiency to achieve better financial results and service delivery. In discussing these approaches a distinction has to be made between:

(a) state-owned transport enterprises operating fleets, such as airlines, ships, trucks and road passenger vehicles in competition with private operators;
(b) state-owned transport infrastructure enterprises operating airports, seaports and road terminals.

Railways do not fit into either category very easily because they operate fleets and provide infrastructure (i.e. track and signalling). Although it is feasible

158

to let out the operation of branch lines at rates to cover costs they soon run down without maintenance or infrastructure. Hence, railways are considered when examining the suppliers of transport infrastructure.

9.1 Fleet operators

Reviews of fleet operators in South-East Asia – their basic structures, incentives and business systems – have revealed rates of return on the large amount of resources invested have been very low. These reviews suggest that much is due to their government's insistence on them undertaking non-economic objectives and to lack of market discipline, incentives and competition. Invariably, these critiques have increased pressure for additional and more onerous controls. This negative approach has encouraged safe rather than enterprising management to the detriment of the overall performance of the fleet operator. A more positive approach, however, would be to promote managerial performance and efficient use of resources allocated to enterprises, to enhance accountability to government and to increase the scope for entrepreneurial initiative. As shown in Figure 9.2, there are three approaches for achieving these objectives:

(a) **The 'in-house' approach,** involving the development of corporate plans that embody both the government's objectives and the para-statal's commercial objectives (i.e. changes in *performance*).

(b) **The introduction of competition** into the activities of parastatals (i.e. changes in *conduct* involving liberalization of regulatory controls).

Figure 9.2 Three approaches to improving the efficiency of state-owned fleet operators.

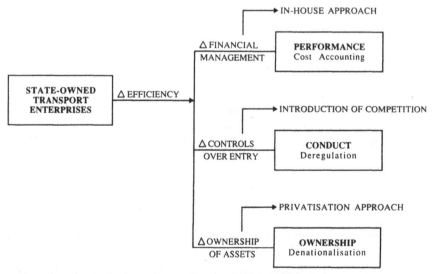

Source: Rimmer with Abdul Rahim Osman & Dick, 1989.

(c) **The privatisation approach** involving the transfer of the ownership from the state to the private sector (i.e. changes in *ownership* or denationalisation).

In-house measures have been pursued in Thailand; the introduction of competition has been followed in Malaysia, Indonesia and Thailand; and privatisation has been considered in Indonesia, Malaysia, Philippines, Singapore and Thailand. Each approach is discussed in turn.

In-house approach

Much could be done to improve the efficient provision of transport services by parastatals without relinquishing state ownership or changing the regulatory conditions under which they operate. This in-house approach based on new planning and accountability mechanisms has been pursued in both India and Pakistan (see Ramanadham, 1984). As it has only been sketched out in general terms in the literature, recourse is made to Australian studies in outlining its key features (Commonwealth of Australia, 1986; 1987; 1988a,b). In particular, attention has to be paid to: the government's relationship with the parastatal (with particular reference to managerial autonomy and financial controls); the need for a disaggregated cost accounting system; corporate planning and the setting of financial and productivity targets; and the provision of non-commercial services. As corporate planning became mandatory for all fifteen state transport enterprises in Thailand in 1984 attention is focused on one of them, the Bangkok Mass Transit Authority, to illustrate the approach.

THE BANGKOK MASS TRANSIT AUTHORITY (BMTA)

Probably the world's largest bus company, the BMTA has incurred substantial losses since its inception (Table 9.1). This is not surprising as BMTA is required by government to charge low fares. There is no way that it can operate over sprawling networks and make money from the rates imposed at below cost. Although the average fare recovery ratio was 78% – high by Western standards – the large volume of traffic at rates below cost has resulted in substantial and continuing losses. The promised economies of scale from amalgamating private bus companies into a single company never came about because the natural state for buses is competitive rather than monopolistic. Not surprisingly, informal minibus systems in Bangkok offer higher-quality services than the parastatal. Although touted as a means of overcoming low accessibility, the BMTA has had less success than a mix of public and private enterprises would have achieved. The prime rationale for subsidizing BMTA, however, is that it benefits the poor, but direct subsidies to raise their real incomes would be more effective.

In a bid to overcome these problems the BMTA, in response to the government's directive, has produced a corporate plan which sets:

(a) the broad goals agreed between the government and the bus company;

Table 9.1 *Bangkok Mass Transit Authority, revenue, expenditure and subsidies, 1977–87.*

Year	Revenue	Subsidies	Expenditures	Deficits
		(million baht)		
1977	622.9	—	870.6	247.7
1978	1,058.2	—	1,438.3	380.1
1979	1,421.3	—	1,898.3	477.0
1980	1,777.4	—	2,523.3	746.0
1981	2,524.5	—	3,344.3	819.8
1982	2,885.2	80.0	3,939.8	974.8
1983	3,017.8	120.0	4,214.2	1,076.5
1984	3.064.2	—	4,303.7	1,239.6
1985	3,447.7	—	4,553.7	1,106.0
1986	3,144.2	—	4,264.0	1,120.5
1987	3,217.5	—	4,138.2	920.7

Source: Krynetr, 1988: 4; BMTA, 1986, 1987a, 1988

(b) the medium-term strategies for major functional areas which incorporate financial targets based on forecasting changes in traffic and anticipated short-term variations in demand;

(c) the programmes to implement policies in each of the functional areas, including the identification of particular performance criteria relating costs to input levels.

As highlighted in Table 9.2 the annual loss of 1000 million baht will be transformed into a surplus from 1988 with a concomitant reduction in accumulated losses. The key to an anticipated boost in revenue is a progressive increase in the flat fare rate for ordinary buses from 2 to 3 baht between 1987 and 1991 and for air-conditioned ones from 5 to 8 baht for the first 8 km and 2 baht for each additional 4 km with the maximum rising from 15 to 24 baht. Even if the government grants these increases much will depend on the production plan being realized. This plans envisages increasing the number of buses running from 3718 in 1987 to 3954 in 1991 based on having 90% of the buses operating on any one day; a rise in the number of bus trips per day; a growth in daily passenger numbers from 1.4 million to 1.6 million in 1991.

The corporate plan, compiled with the assistance of consultants, has become a valuable tool for reforming BMTA's internal management. Since this plan has been in place BMTA's board and management have been expected to:

(a) outline in advance their planned financial and operational goals and ways of measuring them;

(b) work towards pre-set financial targets free of day-to-day operations;

(c) report on success in meeting these targets and other performance indicators.

It has proved less suitable, however, for defining the relationships between

Table 9.2 *Anticipated revenue and expenditure detailed in BMTA's corporate plan, FY 1987–91.*

Item	Actual 1986	1987	1988	Projected 1989	1990	1991
Fares	3017	3045	4350	4570	4994	5508
Other	470	203	596	439	218	283
Revenue	3487	3249	4947	5009	5212	5792
Operations	2112	2126	2369	2626	2691	2804
Maintenance	1003	1099	1166	1113	1216	1298
Administration	475	206	200	219	243	272
Central office	292	257	284	303	331	350
Expenditure	4180	4279	4814	4783	4908	4953
Profit/loss	− 1037	− 1116	45	9	111	807
Accumulated losses	− 8161	− 9278	− 9329	− 9814	− 9202	− 8395

Source: BMTA (1987b)

the government and BMTA. The level of detail is more than the government needs and many actions should be left to management. Nevertheless, the optimistic plan does provide government with: the opportunity to assess conformity of BMTA's mission with its own objectives; quantified targets and performance criteria; a check on assumptions about government actions relating to pricing, equity–debt approval and transfers to covering operating losses.

Attempts by the Thai Government to restructure BMTA – by changing the rules involving managerial responsibility and introducing actions to ensure that pricing covers costs – are instructive to their counterparts in other South-East Asian countries. Implementing the 'in-house' approach has been difficult because corporate planning is detached from day-to-day operations. Fickle governments have been unwilling to introduce cost-based pricing and peak/off peak pricing necessary to overcome congestion. Also, few governments are prepared for the necessary medium-term commitment to planning for fleet operators. Indeed, it may well account for attempts to decouple fleet operators from the state sector through deregulation.

Deregulation

The introduction of new or increased competition into the activities of fleet operators shows that they are subject to varying degrees of competition. Some parastatals, such as domestic airlines and urban bus services, face competition for some, but not all, of their activities; and there is a group of enterprises, such as long-distance trucking services, that operate in a strongly competitive market. Given this array the opportunities for increasing competition can only be discussed in terms of individual parastatals and the principles of contestability, transparency and competitive neutrality (Table 9.3).

Table 9.3 *Concepts used to describe the 'decoupling' of government from state-owned enterprises.*

1.	Contestability	The recognition of a range of possible means to achieve objectives and the adoption of the position that policy should not inhibit bids by competing agencies unless clear benefits can be demonstrated.
2.	Transparency	The principle that if government decides to modify any process for reasons of public policy it will do so by a decision subject to the usual process of political and financial accountability.
3.	Competitive neutrality	Any public institution will, so far as possible, not be advantaged or disadvantaged in its ability to compete by public policy constraints. Where this may become necessary in the public interest (and thus modify competitive neutrality), the policy is applied in accordance with the above principle.

Source: Based on Roberts (1987: 15).

Where barriers for entry are protecting monopoly status, the case for their continued application needs to be reviewed. Any subsequent deregulation does not mean the end of the government's role. An important strategy is to distinguish between those matters best left to the private sector and those best handled by government (Dick, 1987). For example, ship type, routing, scheduling and freight rates in Indonesian inter-island shipping are commercial decisions. Conversely, the government's task is to: ensure easy entry and exit; to intervene in case of 'market failure' to ensure service to peripheral areas; and to provide port infrastructure and navigational aids.

Even if the barriers are not removed the threat of entry can be an incentive to induce contestability and improve efficiency. Considerable care in introducing competition into parastatals is required to prevent the disruption of existing services affecting the quality of service provided to other groups. In particular, care has to be taken to ensure that non-commercial objectives are imposed over all other firms or met by some other methods (e.g. through taxation or welfare policies or environmental protection regulations). Economists urge, for example, that urban bus services should raise revenue from people who benefit. After pricing all unrecoverable costs these should be reimbursed from government revenue provided that the identified and pre-planned social returns have been delivered (Ramanadham, 1987: 171). These issues are discussed with reference to Indonesian inter-island shipping which was deregulated in 1989.

INDONESIAN INTER-ISLAND SHIPPING

The poor performance of the Indonesian inter-island shipping industry, according to Dick (1987), is the outcome of conflicting forces of competition and regulation. As the market is highly contestable, competition has militated against inefficiency. Apart from the large numbers of firms in the industry, new entry has been facilitated by relatively low barriers to entry and a reserve of willing inter-island participants should profitable opportunities increase. Predictably, in the absence of cartels, these structural conditions have given rise to price and non-price competition. Over time, the transfer mechanism has operated so that more efficient firms with lower costs have been able to increase their share of cargo and capacity at the expense of less-efficient firms. Regulation has handicapped rather than facilitated the spontaneous improvement in efficiency brought about by competitive forces. Although couched in terms of efficiency, regulation has weakened the operation of the market as number of firms and entry have been reduced by licensing. Less efficient firms have been encouraged to stay in the industry by retaining control of go-downs and the provision of subsidized investment funds. Thus, regulation has limited competition and circumscribed the spread of efficiency.

Government attempts to consolidate the industry into twelve groups, however, was frustrated by competitive forces. Despite this policy, new entrants found ways to enter the industry without a licence. They have survived by circumventing route controls, ignoring rate schedules and falsely reporting ship's particulars. This avoidance of regulatory sanctions has been attributed partly to the corruption of officials and partly to personal connections. The conflict between competition and regulation, however, has neither been efficient nor equitable. Indeed, the situation could be improved by a good deal of deregulation.

The status quo has been destroyed by the decision to permit Indonesian shippers the right to tranship cargoes in Singapore and foreign flag vessels. As this displaced capacity, Indonesian shipowners were plunged into crisis and sought to change the size, composition and deployment of their fleets but were blocked by regulation. Paradoxically, the Indonesian authorities sought to preserve their regulations because they feared a proliferation of firms; indigenous (*pribumi*) firms would be harmed disproportionately; and outports would lose their liner services. The real problem, however, is that deregulation threatens the vested interests within the bureaucracy as it would involve a reduction in both staff and income. Yet, national development suffers as the inter-island shipping industry is inefficient. In the end the latter argument prevailed and the Indonesian inter-island shipping industry was deregulated on 1 January 1989. This action has not reduced fares but has prompted the restructuring of the industry. Larger operators have containerized and indigenous operators have found attractive market niches (Dick, pers. comm.) As yet, this lead has not been followed by other fleet operators. The trend has been to pursue privatisation without deregulation (Rimmer *et al.*, 1989).

9.2 Privatisation

Privatisation of parastatals, in its narrowest sense, involves the transfer of the *ownership* of assets to the private sector (i.e. denationalisation). This transfer does not affect the *structure* of the industry in terms of the number of firms, degrees of product differentiation, barriers to entry, ease of entry, or degree of contestability. As governments have sought to attract foreign capital, unleash untapped domestic capital sources and to curtail expenditure, the concept of privatisation has swept through South-East Asia. Yet, there have been few asset sales. Although the most cogent argument for privatisation is that parastatals have lost their comparative advantage, the greatest emphasis has been on their poor returns. Private interests have not wanted to purchase parastatals that have made losses on prices that have been deemed fair. Nevertheless, Malaysian Airlines System has become a private corporation and Thailand has sold shares in its national airline. Most activity, however, has been concentrated in Singapore and it is worth discussing the activities of the Public Sector Divestment Committee before examining a specific case study (Singapore Government, 1987).

THE PUBLIC SECTOR DIVESTMENT COMMITTEE (PSDC)

The PSDC in Singapore was appointed by the Minister of Finance to identify state-owned transport enterprises and other government-linked companies for disinvestment. Basically, it sought to extract government from activities which no longer needed to be undertaken by the state and to avoid or reduce competition with the private sector. Also, the Committee was asked to identify opportunities for broadening and deepening the Singapore stock market. The committee focused on the *privatisation of ownership* and distinguished between:

  (a) 'partial privatisation' involving the initial sale of shares to a subsidiary;
  (b) 'further privatisation' involving the sale of shares of a partially privatised company;
  (c) 'effective privatisation' involving sale to the extent of giving up control of a company;
  (d) 'total privatisation' involving complete withdrawal from a company.

Thus our interest is focused on 'effective' or 'total' privatisation ('partial' or 'further' are basically in-house measures). The Committee recommended a policy of total privatisation within a ten-year period where initiative is decentralized and order is maintained through adequate monitoring, control and direction. Among its recommendations were that the Government should reduce its stake in Singapore Airlines Ltd and Neptune Orient Lines Ltd to 30% as its first target; and divest itself of Singapore Airport Bus Services Pte Ltd. It has not only sold shares in its national airline (though 63% is still held by the government's Temasek Holdings) but has privatised the bus system operated by Singapore Bus Service (1978) Ltd by permitting the entry of Trans-Island Bus Services Ltd and is seeking a private company to run the Mass Rapid Transit (MRT) system.

SINGAPORE BUS SERVICES (1978) LTD AND THE MRT

Singapore Bus Services (SBS) provides a good example of a private company operating a successful public service (Singapore Government, 1987). With more than 2400 buses on 219 routes and 7600 workers SBS operates one of the largest bus services in the world. Its quality of service has shown continuous improvement (Table 9.4). Accident rates declined from 3.4/100,000 km in 1978 to 1.0/100,000 km in 1987. Similarly, the number of complaints decreased over the same period from 5.1 to 2.6 per million passengers. When the shares were first offered on the Singapore Stock Exchange in 1978 they were oversubscribed 27 times. This confidence in the private company has been justified by subsequent performance. As a guard against any complacency the Singapore Government authorized the Trans-Island Bus Services Ltd (TIBS) to operate and provide 'healthy' competition to SBS in a bid to enhance the efficiency and performance of the Republic's bus services.

Table 9.4 *Traffic, financial and productivity statistics for Singapore Bus Services (1978) Ltd, 1983–87.*

	1983	1984	1985	1986	1987
Traffic					
Av. daily fleet (no.)	2393	2502	2610	2619	2607
Place km/day (million)	43.4	42.7	47.2	50.1	50.4
Ridership (million)	745.7	771.7	818.6	843.1	880.4
Load (per cent)	29.9	31.3	30.4	29.3	30.4
Financial (S$ million)					
Total revenue	315.5	312.5	328.7	330.1	353.2
Total expenditure	305.8	302.7	314.4	285.9	300.6
Profit after tax	5.8	5.9	9.0	30.1	36.5
Total value added	202.3	203.5	210.6	222.9	246.3
Value added per worker	0.019	0.023	0.025	0.026	0.03
Productivity					
Unit yield per 100 place-km (S$)	1.99	2.00	1.91	1.80	1.90
Unit cost per 100 place-km (S$)	1.93	1.94	1.81	1.57	1.60

Source: SBS (1987)

Properly managed it is expected that the company operating the MRT (Mass Rapid Transit) Corporation will be as equally successful as SBS (and TIBS) in providing Singaporeans with a fast, reliable and comfortable form of public transport. The capital cost of construction of MRT lines and stations was paid by the government, and their maintenance is the responsibility of the MRT Corporation. As fare revenue from MRT operations covers operating costs (including replacement of rolling stock and other equipment) a government company, the MRTC, is running the MRT. Privatising the MRTC is seen as the best guarantee of efficiency because management will be responsible to the changing demands of the public. This arrangement typifies the Singapore Government's overall policy of allowing the private sector to operate in areas where the government's direct participation is not essential.

The appeal of privatisation is that it promises to improve efficiency by: removing government constraints on financial independence; imposing the discipline of the financial markets on transport organizations by forcing them to compete for funds; and developing a more flexible approach to managing resources and service innovation. The extent to which these gains are realized, however, depends on the degree of competition. The critical point is not the transfer of assets from public to private ownership but the retention of monopoly power – an argument evident in discussing infrastructural enterprises.

9.3 Infrastructural enterprises

State governments provide most transport infrastructural services in South-East Asia. A comprehensive list of infrastructural enterprises is not available but those in Thailand are indicative of the organizations involved (Table 9.5). Questions have been raised about the adequacy of infrastructure provided by these organizations and its efficiency in meeting society's goals (economic, social and environmental) at the lowest cost in terms of the nation's total resources. State-owned infrastructural operations, however, cannot be considered in the same terms as private enterprises. Returns may have to be considered over a wider period together with an explicit recognition of social objectives. Not only do profits have to be considered but so do consumer benefits because many infrastructural operations are natural monopolies. Without a recent survey of transport infrastructure in the countries under review pinpointing over- and under-investment in airports, roads, railways and seaports it is not possible to discuss the level and composition of investment by the state or questionable decisions about the location, quality and operations of existing infrastructure (including the failure to use cost–benefit analysis in contemplating new investment). Similarly, there are few records of difficulties over maintenance which have stemmed from non-economic infrastructural extensions and pricing policies. Thus, all that can be highlighted are ways for improving the efficiency with which existing infrastructure is being managed.

Most infrastructure, with the exception of roads, is provided by state enterprises. Not only do they suffer from the same afflictions as fleet operators (operational and strategic constraints and ill-conceived social objectives) but they possess, as instanced by airports, a high degree of monopoly power. This feature makes it difficult to provide incentives for managers and to evaluate performance. As outlined in Table 9.6, a range of options have been listed for improving the performance of parastatals. They include: injecting or bolstering competition to the widest extent possible (an option not available to natural monopolies); permitting a well-motivated management greater autonomy over pricing and purchasing policies;

Table 9.5 *State-owned infrastructural enterprises in Thailand.*

Enterprise	Established date	Government participation %	Employees no.	Stock mmB	Revenue mmB	Assets mmB	Total investment mmB
Port Authority of Thailand	1951	100.0	6,373	2,300	995	2,670	1,183
Airport Authority of Thailand	1979	100.0	2,363	830	692	354	1,445
State Railway of Thailand	1951	100.0	19,988	5,712	3,807	1,157	7,235
Expressway and Rapid Transit Authority of Thailand	1972	100.0	3,128	815	127	3,633	7,441
Bangkok Dock Company	1943	100.0	10	160	151	143	30

Source: Wilson, 1986

Table 9.6 *Possible options for improving the performance of state-owned transport infrastructure organizations.*

Option	Increased flexibility	Commercialization of of public enterprise	Privatisation
1. Introduce or strengthen competition	X	X	X
2. Allow greater operational autonomy	X	X	X
3. Review strategic controls on borrowing	O	X	X
4. Better definitions, targeting and costing of social objectives	X	X	X
5. Monitoring and efficiency audits	X	X	X
6. Financial targets	X	X	X
7. Performance-related and sanction structures	X	X	X
8. Improved consultative arrangements with consumers and employees	X	X	X
9. Private sector participation (e.g. contracting out)	X	X	X

Source: Derived from Commonwealth of Australia, 1988b

reconsidering controls over borrowing; and redefining the targeting and costing of non-economic objectives (e.g. job creation and servicing rural areas) so that parastatals can focus on a few objectives. Another set of options encompasses the institution of regular audits (and current cost accounting of assets); the setting of financial targets (i.e. appropriate rate of return); the creation of performance-related incentives for managers of parastatals; and improved consultation with both workers and consumers. Finally, there is the possibility of increasing private sector participation. Managers could be given the power to contract-out the provision of infrastructural services rather than producing them in-house, enter joint ventures and offer shares in the parastatal. For example, Malaysia's Port of Klang Authority has hived off the management of its container terminal to a private operator, Konnas Terminal Kelang Sdn Bhd (a joint venture between Kontena Nasional and P&O Australia Ltd). Similarly, the International Terminal at Manila's North Port has been let to a consortium headed by E. Razon Inc in association with Sea Land Orient Ltd.

This list of options open to state-owned infrastructure enterprises is distilled into three basic approaches for improving efficiency – the critical issue being the extent to which parastatals can operate at 'arm's length' from government control. As outlined in Figure 9.3, the basic options for improving the performance of parastatals engaged in the provision of infrastructure are:

Figure 9.3 Approaches for improving the efficiency of state-owned infrastructure enterprises.

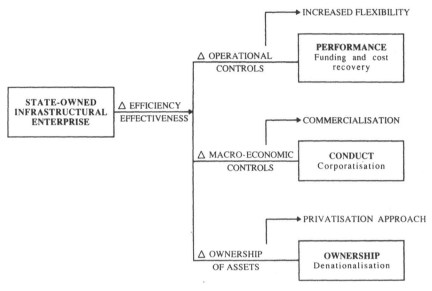

Source: Rimmer with Abdul Rahim Osman & Dick, 1989.

(a) **The increased flexibility approach** which maintains state ownership and macroeconomic controls (i.e. over borrowings) but removes, on a case-by-case basis controls over day-to-day management (e.g. staffing, price-making, investment and asset management).

(b) **The commercialization approach** that maintains state-ownership but removes strategic macroeconomic controls over borrowing.

(c) **The privatisation approach** which involves the sale of the state's assets to the private sector.

A brief discussion is made of their appropriateness by reference to individual case studies.

Increased flexibility

This is appropriate for parastatals that cannot be subject to full competitive disciplines because they operate in markets with an important element of natural monopoly. When implementing this approach enterprises would, on a case-to-case basis, be freed from more detailed controls over personnel and specific investments in return for being required to meet specified financial targets. In addition to their commercial task, they may be still required to meet clearly-defined social objectives. Any subsidies to particular consumers, however, would be 'transparent' in that they are supplied as direct budget grants or shown in published accounts. Besides an increased emphasis on independent reviews of efficiency and performance there should be scope for increased competition at the fringes. Even if the entry of other firms does not come about from the removal of barriers the threat of potential rivals will create a 'contestable market' and encourage competitive behaviour (i.e. by dividing state ownership on a regional rather than a national basis). With a ceiling on foreign borrowing, most parastatals in the countries under review could adopt the increased flexibility approach. It is unclear, however, whether there are parastatals in the countries under review that could meet the demands of full commercialization or operate in a fully competitive environment. Much will hinge, as witnessed by Bangkok's Second Expressway, on the ability of government to inject the efficient management methods of the private sector into the bureaucracy.

BANGKOK'S SECOND EXPRESSWAY

The Thai Government has used the Build Operate Transfer Model to galvanize its transport bureaucracy. The overall aim of adopting this model is to reduce the number of bureaucrats and to stem government spending by limiting any increase in foreign indebtedness. Basically, the seven step Model involves:

(a) the identification of high priority projects through a preliminary in-house study which involves site investigation;
(b) the instigation of a professional study by an internationally-recognized engineering firm to ascertain technical, commercial and financial characteristics and the forecast growth demand statistics before preparing a proposal;
(c) the selection of a financial adviser (usually an international merchant banker) charged with the task of procuring project finance;
(d) the presentation of the proposal to the relevant Thai Government ministries and commencement of detailed negotiations;
(e) the establishment of a Head of Agreement between the Thai Government and the project's sponsors which specifies the basic conditions of the contract and the shareholders arrangements prior to the establishment of the project company;
(f) the negotiation of a list of other contracts (e.g. operating, escrow and construction) based on the Head of Agreement including arrangements with the bank for project finance and the commencement of a detailed design (with project risk being shared among the project operation company, government, financing banks, and institutions and other involved firms); and the implementation of the project following the signing of contracts with the Thai Government.

The Build Operate and Transfer Model has been invoked by the Thai Government in the construction of the US$880 million Second Expressway Project intended to ease Bangkok's chronic congestion (Figure 9.4). The letter of intent for the 30 km expressway was awarded by the Thai

Figure 9.4 Project location map showing Bangkok's Second Expressway System.

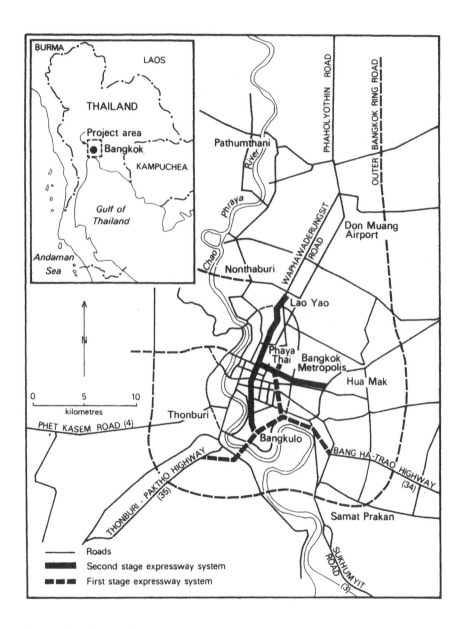

Source: Based on JICA, 1983.

Government through international tender to Japan's Kumagai Gumi Group – a company engaged in similar projects, such as Hong Kong's Eastern Harbour Crossing and Australia's Sydney Harbour tunnel. The letter of intent was signed in 1989. As the baht is relatively stable against the softer currencies all funds for the project are to be procured from the local financial market although 20% of the total finance will be backed by guarantees of foreign banks. (Project finance is difficult to obtain where, as in Turkey, the annual currency devaluation exceeds 10%.) According to an agreed percentage formula all revenue from the Second Expressway will be pooled with the tolls from the existing First Expressway into a Toll Collection Account – the recipients will be the Expressway and Rapid Transit Authority of Thailand and the project company, the Bangkok Expressway Company.

The extension of the Build Operate and Transfer Model in Thailand is problematical. It is being used for major infrastructure projects which normally have been constructed from public funds. Clearly, some infrastructure projects, such as Bangkok's Second Expressway, will generate enough revenue to cover project risks. While these projects will be built using the Build Operate and Transfer Model those with public welfare purposes cannot generate sufficient revenue. In these projects the Thai Government will be required to bear part of the project risk. Although the Thai Government has granted incentives to the private sector engaged in the Build Operate and Transfer Model it is not keen to share the risks. Nevertheless, the Thai Government appreciates that project risk-sharing may be more profitable than if it had been responsible for the whole project. A similar Build Operate and Transfer model has been invoked in Malaysia.

MALAYSIA'S NORTH–SOUTH HIGHWAY

In March 1988, the Malaysian Government awarded a 22-member consortium led by United Engineers (Malaysia) Bhd the contract to complete and operate the country's 904 km North–South Highway from Bukit Kayu Hitam in Perlis to Johor Bahru (a task which also includes the completion of the 42 km North Klang Expressway near Kuala Lumpur and the widening of the congested Federal Highway between Port Klang and the suburbs of Petaling Jaya). Already, 386 km of the North–South Highway has been built for the Malaysian Highway Authority by a South Korean/Japanese joint venture under a straightforward contract (Figure 9.5).

Based on inflation-adjusted tolls over a 25-year concession period, this new privatisation exercise – prompted by a shortfall in government funds – will reduce travel between Alor Star and Johor Bahru from 15 to seven hours (Seaward, 1987a,b; 1988). Over the first five years of the M$3.4 billion (US$1.7 billion) project – later increased to M$4.7 billion – the tolls have been fixed at M¢5 and increments above ¢5 per year are unlikely to be politically acceptable. The Malaysian Government has agreed to provide a supporting loan programme of M$150 million per annum for five years (repayable over a ten-year period). No standby loan facilities were offered, however, as a hedge against external risks, such as fluctuations in foreign

Figure 9.5 Malaysia's North–South Highway.

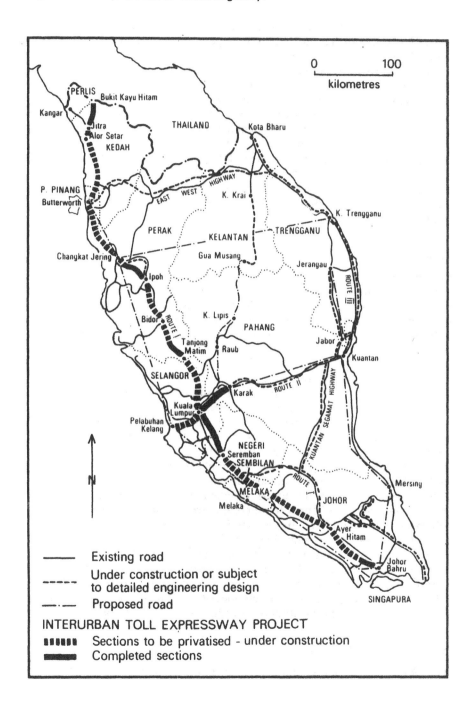

0   100
kilometres

PERLIS   Bukit Kayu Hitam
Kangar
          Jitra   THAILAND   Kota Bharu
          Alor Setar
          KEDAH
P. PINANG   EAST   WEST   HIGHWAY   K. Krai
Butterworth
                                                              K. Trengganu
          PERAK   KELANTAN   TRENGGANU
Changkat Jering   Gua Musang
                    Ipoh   Jerangau   ROUTE III
          Bidor   ROUTE I   K. Lipis
                    Tanjong   PAHANG   Jabor
                    Matim   Raub   Kuantan
          SELANGOR   ROUTE II
                            Karak
          Kuala
          Lumpur
Pelabuhan
Kelang   KUANTAN SEGAMAT HIGHWAY
                    NEGERI
                    Seremban
                    SEMBILAN   Mersing
                                    ROUTE
          MELAKA   JOHOR
          Melaka
                                        Ayer
                                        Hitam
                                                Johor
                                                Bahru
N   SINGAPURA

—————— Existing road
- - - - - Under construction or subject
          to detailed engineering design
—·—·— Proposed road
INTERURBAN TOLL EXPRESSWAY PROJECT
▪▪▪▪▪▪ Sections to be privatised - under construction
▬▬▬▬ Completed sections

currency. The concession holders have also agreed to limit borrowings to M$1 billion of which not more than M$500 million can be borrowed from overseas by the consortium's foreign partners – a Japanese group headed by Mitsui & Co, a French group led by Dragages et Travaux and a British group led by Taylor Woodrow International.

As the agreement represents a renegotiation of an earlier arrangement the construction period has been extended from five years·to seven-and-a-half years. This concession reduces the overall interest as income from constructing the most lucrative stretches of highway will be used for later phases of the project. A critical element has been the calculation of the traffic projections as the contractors have a traffic-volume guarantee. As successive engineering consultants have scaled down this figure the consortium's revenue projections from anticipated toll income have been scaled down. The whole project is a major step in the Malaysian Government's programme leading to commercialization and privatisation of state-owned infrastructure activities.

Commercialization

Commercialization of state-owned activities goes further than the flexible approach through the introduction of competition and an 'arm's length' relationship with the state. It provides for managerial autonomy, including the removal of strategic macroeconomic controls over borrowings, industrial relations co-ordination, executive remuneration and superannuation. As a basic guide for administrative action, commercialization would be apposite for public enterprises which: experienced full and effective competition from all parts of the public sector for their business; operated solely on commercial principles (i.e. state services would be provided on a full cost recovery basis); had an appropriate track record; and were subject to the same capital market disciplines as their private sector counterparts. Parastatals would be stripped of unfair competitive advantages over the private sector, such as subsidized finance or a captive share of the market; they would also be required to pay taxes and dividends like any other commercial enterprise. Any social (and noncommercial) objectives would be specified in a clear contract with the government and would apply to all competitors. It may not be possible for enterprises (particularly, those involved in infrastructural services), however, to meet the commerciality tests in full. Nevertheless, it should be possible, to work towards full commercialization through the measures leading from 'increased flexibility', to efficiency and accountability. In theory, once a parastatal has been commercialized (or corporatized) it is relatively simple to privatise. The activities of the State Railway of Thailand, however, indicate the difficulties of introducing commercialization.[1]

STATE RAILWAY OF THAILAND

The SRT, the greatest loss-maker after the Bangkok Mass Transit Authority, is afflicted by all the problems common to railways: competition from road transport for freight and passengers following the completion of parallel highway facilities; a bloated labour force (reputedly one-third higher than required); government-controlled charges that are below the costs of carrying passengers and most freight; and inability to recover costs from operating services on a large number of low-density routes. Although demand for passenger transport is still growing the SRT requires both operating and capital subsidies. Conversely, the state-owned Transport Company Ltd, operating buses to and from Bangkok in a competitive environment, has broken even by franchising services to private operators.

Following the Transport Company's lead the SRT sought to improve its sales and marketing skills, passenger service and depleted revenues by leasing out its new inter-city trains to private operators through a competitive bidding process. In June 1985, three routes were opened for bidding: Bangkok to Surin; Bangkok to Phitsanulok; and Bangkok to Khon Kaen. Four companies bid for the first route and six each for the second and third routes. Assessments of the companies were made in terms of their qualifications (financial standing, relevance of current business and past experience), rental and other factors (marketing strategies and proposed on-board services shown in Table 9.7). Subsequently, the three contracts were awarded to different companies with the rentals equivalent to 75% or more passenger loading. The leased trains began operation in September 1985.

Table 9.7 *Specifications for operating Thailand's inter-city trains, 1985.*

Route	Distance km	Train make-up type	Trains/day no.	Cars needed no.
Bangkok–Surin	420	1A, 2O	4	2A, 4O
Bangkok–Phitsanulok	387	2A, 2O	6	4A, 4O
Bangkok–Kohn Kaen	450	2A, 2O	6	4A, 4O

Note: A – Airconditioned; O – Ordinary car
Source: State Railway of Thailand (pers. comm.)

Results have varied markedly between routes. As a profitable operator of air-conditioned buses between Bangkok and various provinces in the north-east, the lessee of the Surin route was successful from the outset in running the train. The lessee was able to branch out into running refurbished private coaches attached to the Hat Yai and Ubon Ratchathani rapid trains for a per-kilometre charge for a modest profit. Considerable marketing problems were experienced and initial losses incurred on the Phitsanulok route but satisfactory results were obtained once the company replaced the operating staff with local people and stopped experimenting with the timetable. Conversely, the Khon Kaen operator experienced severe competition from road transport and incurred heavy losses from the outset. As timetable changes, and the extension of the line from Khon Kaen to Udon Thani and a fare reduction failed to remedy the situation, the contract was terminated in August 1986. When the contract was opened for renewed bidding seven companies, including the original operator, applied. A new operator was selected at almost the previous rental. Subsequent operating results have varied markedly though the new company managed to make an overall profit between August 1986 and August 1988. Since then it has only chosen to run the train with just one air-conditioned unit to obtain a commensurate rate reduction.

Surveys by the State Railway of Thailand have shown that the leased trains have been successful in attracting two-thirds of their loadings from buses and private cars; the other third comprised passengers that travelled hitherto by second and third class rail. Yet inclusive fares charged by private operators are slightly higher than those charged by the State Railway of Thailand (though strict comparisons are complicated by differential pricing for morning and afternoon, and weekday and weekend trains). Similarly, the operator of the private coaches charges passengers slightly more than the second class fare on the State Railway of Thailand but, as shown in Table 9.8, they get additional services (video, carpeted floor, free main course, a snack, coffee, soft drink, iced water and cold towel). Unfortunately, these marketing initiatives are threatened by the railway unions who want the services to return to SRT control once the existing contracts are at an end. Such action has prompted other governments in South-East Asia to consider privatisation as a means of freeing themselves of the labour problems that have bedevilled parastatal operations.

Table 9.8 *Specifications for on-board services on Thailand's inter-city services.*

Item	Surin		Phitsanulok		Kohn Kaen	
	1A	2O	2A	2O	2A	2O
Main dish	X		X	X	X	
Coffee & snack	X		X			
Soft drink/iced water	X	X	X	X		
Blanket			X		X	
Cold towel			X	X	X	
Video show			X		X	
Hostesses	2	4	3	3	2	2
Ticket inspector	– – 1 – –		1	1	– – 1 – –	

Note: A – Airconditioned; O – Ordinary car
Source: State Railway of Thailand (pers. comm.)

Privatisation

The transfer of the ownership of infrastructure from state to private hands may not generate any net community gains. Although private monopolies would minimize production costs they would not attain allocative efficiency as they would be inclined to price above, or reduce output, below the desired level. Consequently, prices would have to be regulated thereby removing the incentives for productive efficiency. Besides concerns about service access and affordability for specific groups under private monopolies there would also be concerns about their power. As instanced by the Singapore Port Authority the case for privatisation hinges on: its effect on the competitive environment; whether managerial incentives and capital market pressures outweigh the scrutiny of infrastructural enterprises; whether the long-term gains outweigh short-term costs.

PORT OF SINGAPORE AUTHORITY (PSA)

PSA is a statutory body with a natural monopoly with both capital and reserves, and total assets in excess of $S3 billion. Employing 8357 workers, it is engaged in:

(a) regulatory activities such as the demarcation of anchorages, control of navigation, port clearance, licensing of harbour craft, control of port waters and seaport land within port limits;
(b) infrastructure development including the construction of wharves and warehouses, installation and maintenance of navigational aids, dredging of navigational channels, and hydrographic surveying;
(c) cargo handling;
(d) ancillary support activities such as pilotage services, tug towage, slop reception and ferry services.

Already, the PSA has privatised some parts of cargo handling and ancillary support activities (50% of the berths have been leased to shipping agents). PSA, however, does not intend to privatise crucial services such as pilotage, water supply and port security but would be willing to privatise tug towage, bunkering, slop reception, towage services and exhibition facilities. Technically, like other statutory authorities in Singapore, the PSA could be transferred from the state to the private sector. Any attempt to privatise the Singapore Port Authority, however, raises questions over the conflicts between shareholders and consumers (i.e. good dividend yields as opposed to low tariffs); foreign versus local ownership (the relaxation of the 20% maximum foreign shareholding is suggested); and cross-subsidization (this would have to cease or be replaced by subsidy). It is likely, however, that PSA, at best, would only be partially privatised (though ownership of some services may be sold to the private sector).

This privatisation decision can only be resolved on a case-by-case basis. Where privatisation occurs, the sale of assets through a competitive bidding process should ensure that the sale price reflects future earnings from the asset. Without efficiency gains the state would be better off retaining the enterprise. Conversely, if efficiency gains are realized by privatisation the enterprise, such as the Singapore Port Authority, should be sold.

9.4 Conclusion

Decision-makers in South-East Asia have focused increasingly upon the efficient production of transport services. This interest has highlighted the issue of which state-owned fleet operators and infrastructure should be managed by the state and which by private enterprise. As the study suggests privatisation propagated by the New Right cannot provide a 'universal fix' to the problems afflicting state transport enterprises managing the operations of transport fleets or infrastructure (or in the case of the railways both fleets or infrastructure). Nevertheless, much can be done for the accountability of both types of state-owned transport enterprises through the preparation of corporate plans, establishment of rates-of-return, relaxation of government controls and improved cost accounting of information.

Indeed, in-house improvements may be preferable to the creation of a private transport monopoly (i.e. the degree of competition is more important than ownership). Similarly, increased flexibility and commercialization (or corporatization) may be preferable to a privately-controlled infrastructural organization. These matters, however, can only be resolved on a case-by-case basis that takes into account transport mode, social objectives and current financial position. Clearly, there is now a veritable flood of material from the New Right on how British experience can be transferred to developing countries. As the case studies here demonstrate there is, at least in South-East Asia, a wealth of local information on different approaches to making state-owned transport enterprises more efficient. While foreign advice may provide useful information on how to secure the necessary finance a closer examination of the benefits and pitfalls derived from different case studies may provide a surer guide to decision-makers in South-East Asia.

Note

1. *Corporatization* is a New Zealand variant of commercialization – a process by which governments convert a parastatal 'from a departmental form into a limited liability company, with performance criteria and a financial structure which seek to mirror those of equivalent private sector firms' (McKinlay, 1987: 3). As parastatals are already in the market place they have the necessary precondition for a contestable public monopoly. This situation has led to the proposition that parastatals should be transformed into state corporations run by managers as successful business enterprises. Within the bounds set by government these managers would be responsible for resource use and pricing decisions (Gregory, 1987). Controlled by boards drawn from the private sector, these enterprises will be expected to pay tax and dividends and operate in a normal commercial way (i.e. as a competitive private enterprise). Non-economic functions would be separated from the corporation. Thus, commercialization and corporatization should be considered as approaches in their own right.

References

BMTA, (1986, 1987a, 1988) *Annual reports*, Bangkok: Bangkok Mass Transit Authority.

BMTA (1987b) *Ongkarn konsong monchon krungtep: plan wisah hakij BE2530–2534* [Bangkok Mass Transit Authority: corporate plan, 1987–1991], Bangkok: Bangkok Mass Transit Authority.

Commonwealth of Australia (1986) *Statutory authorities and government business enterprises: proposed policy guidelines – 1986* Canberra: Australian Government Printing Service.

Commonwealth of Australia (1987) *Efficiency in public trading enterprises* Council Paper No. 24, Canberra: Office of Economic Planning Advisory Council.

Commonwealth of Australia (1988a) *Reshaping the transport and communication business enterprises* Canberra: Australian Government Printing Service.

Commonwealth of Australia (1988b) *Economic infrastructure in Australia* Council Paper No. 33, Canberra: Office of Economic Planning Advisory Council.

Dick, H. W. (1987) *The Indonesian interisland shipping industry: an analysis of competition and regulation* Singapore: Institute of Southeast Asian Studies.

Gregory, R. (1987) The reorganization of the public sector: the quest for efficiency. In Boston, J. and Holland, M. *The fourth Labour government* Auckland: Oxford University Press: 111–34.

JICA (1983) *Feasibility study on the second stage expressway system in the Greater Bangkok: Final Report Volume 1: Text* Tokyo: Japan International Cooperation Agency (for Government of the Kingdom of Thailand, Ministry of the Interior and Expressway and Rapid Transit Authority of Thailand).

Krynetr, P. (1988) Bangkok Mass Transit Authority: a case study of monopoly versus competition. Unpublished paper presented at CODATU, Indonesia.

McKinlay, P. (1987) *Corporatisation: The solution for state owned enterprise* Wellington: Victoria University Press for the Institute of Policy Studies.

Ramanadham, V. V. (ed) (1984) *Public enterprise in the developing world* London and Sydney: Croom Helm.

Ramanadham, V. V. (1987) *Public enterprise: from evaluation to privatisation* London: Frank Cass.

Rimmer, P. J. (1986) *Rikisha to rail transit: urban public transport systems and policy in Southeast Asia* Sydney: Pergamon.

Rimmer, P. J. (1988) Buses in Southeast Asian cities: privatisation without deregulation. In Dodgson, J. S. & Topham, N. (eds), *Bus deregulation and privatisation: an international perspective* Aldershot: Avebury: 185–208.

Rimmer, P. J. with Abdul Rahim Osman and Dick, H. W. (1989). Priming the parastatals: improving the efficiency of state-owned transport enterprises. Paper presented at the Asian Transport Policy Seminar sponsored by the

Asian Development Bank and Economic Development Institute of the World Bank, Manila, February 1989.

Roberts, J. (1987) *Politicians, public servants and public enterprise: restructuring the New Zealand government executive* Wellington: Victoria University Press for the Institute of Policy Studies.

Rowley, A. (1985) Private affair in Asia, *Far Eastern Economic Review* 25 July.

SBS (1980–1987) *Singapore Bus Service (1978) Ltd, annual reports* Singapore: Singapore Bus Service Ltd.

Seaward, N. (1987a) Paving the future way, *Far Eastern Economic Review* 15 January 1987.

Seaward, N. (1987b) Delays on the road, *Far Eastern Economic Review* 28 May 1987.

Seaward, N. (1988) On the road at last, *Far Eastern Economic Review* 31 March 1988.

Singapore Government, Ministry of Finance (1987) *Report of the Public Service Divestment Committee* Singapore: Government Printer.

Wilson, G. W. (1986) Privatization in transportation: the case of Thailand. Unpublished paper presented at the World Conference on Transport Research, Vancouver, British Columbia, Canada: May 1986.

PART IV
Conclusions and recommendations

CHAPTER 10

Deregulation: prospects, possibilities and the way ahead

John Hibbs

Experience of deregulation, in various modes and in a number of countries, is sufficient to form the base line for considering the future. In the case of airline deregulation in the United States it is now plain that the modal interface, defined as terminal infrastructure, is a potential cause of distortion. This may be seen to apply equally to the issue of track costs and pricing, currently a renewed topic for debate in the United Kingdom; the present author (Hibbs, 1982) stressed that some form of road-use pricing was a *sine qua non* for the deregulation of urban bus services. The issue thus raised must form the underpinning of any analysis of the prospects for deregulation itself.

More positive inputs come from previous experience of deregulation in the UK. It is germane to record the effect of abolishing price control of railway services in the Transport Act 1962; although it took some years (and a report from the Prices & Incomes Board – PIB, 1968) for the railways to adopt market-based pricing, its beneficial effect on their income cannot be questioned. In 1968 a further Transport Act deregulated road freight transport (despite vehement opposition on the part of the industry), and an analysis of the economic cost of retaining such regulation in Ireland (Barrett, 1982) shows the extent of the gain in the UK.

The unfinished business in the field of transport deregulation today concerns air and bus services. It is clear from the experience of deregulating air services between the UK and the Republic of Ireland that substantial increases in traffic can follow from competitive markets in air transport, and it is also clear that the base line in Europe is not the same as that which applied before airline deregulation in the USA. But however attractive the prognosis for further deregulation of air transport in Europe, the constraints appear to be such as to make one hesitate to explore the issues further. The growing market dominance of the big state-owned airlines suggests a situation not unlike that of bus transport in the UK before 1986, but whereas the government here had the will to break up the state-owned monopoly so as to give deregulation a chance to work, it is questionable whether the same strength of will may exist in Brussels.

The same caveat applies to the railway systems of Europe, although UK experience suggests that the deregulation of their road competitors could do much to concentrate the minds of managers upon the efficiency gains that await them when the financial bottom line becomes a reality. The real problem here, as Kenny (1982) showed, is the cleavage in political economy between the common law tradition and the civil code that governs most countries in continental Europe. This is why, as Yearsley (1986) effectively put it, in Europe there is no deregulation! Where transport is classified as a state responsibility, the private sector can only enter the market as franchisees (whether of the local authority, as in France, or of the state railway, as in West Germany), or as 'tenants' (as in Belgium). In practice, this means that the involvement of the private sector in railways is limited to 'les petites trains touristiques', as in France, or to highly subsidized franchisees, as in Switzerland.

For these reasons, then, the analysis that follows lies in the road passenger transport sector of the UK. (There are lessons to be learned from the Irish dimension, where political economy has evolved away from a common base with that of the UK, to produce the parastatal company.) The course of events in the UK has already been presented in Chapter 2, so that the argument of this concluding analysis commences from the introduction of bus deregulation in 1986.

10.1 Forecasting an uncertain future

Few commentators have questioned the widespread conclusion that the consequences of the Transport Act 1985 cannot be satisfactorily assessed until some ten years have elapsed. So radical was the change, extending beyond deregulation to the restructuring of the industry, that the kind of instant assessment beloved of journalists and politicians could not have any significant value. The initial set of changes in the Transport Act 1980 had themselves far from run their course by 1986; indeed the removal of price control in 1980 has yet to have the invigorating consequences that it had for the railways, some six years after its enactment in 1962. Further, as has been recorded, deregulation has yet to extend to London, and privatisation to Scotland; the expected break-up of market-dominant publicly-owned bus companies in the former metropolitan counties has not been effectively pursued.

For convenience, then, the base line from which this analysis will start may be termed '1986'. The so-called D-day, or 'big bang', while fraught in some cities was a non-event over much of the country, and deregulation did not become a fully effective regime until January 1987. Thus it would seem necessary to wait until 1996 before drawing firm conclusions about the outcome of the legislation. By that time, though, so many exogenous factors will have complicated the situation that statistical and financial comparisons will have little value. If we are to try and penetrate the future now, less than half way through the period of change, we shall need to use a different style of analysis.

In this we can find support from the arguments for the legislation itself, for these, while predicting a net welfare gain (*Buses* White Paper, 1984), did not extend to specific predictions as to how that gain might be achieved. Those who opposed the legislation were obliged to defend the status quo, which they did by making dire predictions as to the expected net welfare loss. These predictions were not infrequently set in apocalyptic language, and illustrated with pungent cartoons, whereas the supporters of the legislation rested their case upon the analysis of the former system, going back to its early days (Chester, 1936), that it 'impoverished the consumer' (Plant, 1932). Therefore, they argued, things could only improve if regulation was removed (or reduced to basic quality control).

The reluctance of the supporters of the legislation to engage in the doubtful art of prophesy was justified by the failure of events to measure up to the catastrophe predicted by its opponents, and it is with this in mind that its further prospects will be assessed. As the popular song has it, 'the future's not ours to see', but as the half-way point is approached, a number of trends can be identified, and perhaps some recommendations may emerge for adjustments to course for the better organization of things in the future.

10.2 Managers and the consumer

Current research by the author, the initial findings of which were reported at the PTRC Summer Annual Meeting in 1989 (Hibbs, 1989), suggests that managers remaining in the UK bus industry since 1986 (it appears that a substantial number left the industry at that time) are experiencing enhanced satisfaction. While press reports indicate that only a minority have made substantial capital gains, it is to be assumed that a substantial element of this satisfaction is job-related. Furthermore, a strong distaste is being registered for the idea of 'competing for the market' (i.e. tendering and franchise), while the Belgian concept of tenancy is seen to be abhorrent. From this it may be deduced that the bus managers of the post-1986 regime value their freedom to take realistic decisions in the market; there is indeed evidence that the transfer of decision-making to the subsidizing authority, characteristic of certain counties before 1986, was resented, as an interference with market satisfaction.

This emerging evidence suggests that prospects for the consumer are advantageous. Herzberg (1966) has stressed the importance of many non-monetary satisfactions as motivators among managers, and one of these must clearly be the freedom to actually manage, to take 'bottom-line' decisions. And since in a competitive market this makes survival dependent, in the long run, upon maximizing consumer satisfaction, it would seem that the underpinning arguments for deregulation were justifiable.

Neither is the shift to a consumer-satisfaction ethos limited to managers. For them it would seem that the product of the industry is taking priority over the admitted fascination of its process (which in the past served without doubt to blind many bus managers to the importance of the product). But the product is only as effective as its delivery, and it appears that this is still appreciated in only a minority of cases. What is meant by this is the importance of point-of-sale staff in ensuring consumer satisfaction.

The exceptions here are interesting, and highly significant for the prospects of the deregulated industry. Highlighted in the trade press has been the public appreciation of improved quality in the delivery of the product where attention has been paid to the point-of-sale. Two examples quoted turn upon co-ownership: the companies are People's Provincial, of Fareham, and Luton & District. In the case of the former improvements were noticed by the public and reported in the press as from the day the company became a full co-operative. Two further examples turn upon re-structuring: one being the former NBC company Go-Ahead Northern based at Gateshead, and the second being the former municipal undertaking at Hull. In these cases (and to a lesser extent elsewhere) the re-structuring has been in the field of rostering, replacing the old pattern where a driver might return to a given route once in six weeks or so with the concept of the 'small rota', and the actual fostering of a team spirit among drivers who come to feel that they 'own' the routes on which they work. (It must be said that the small rota principle had been advocated by managers within the NBC organization, prior to 1986; its introduction was not therefore a direct consequence of deregulation, but rather was facilitated by privatisation.)

A conclusion may thus be foreshadowed that the consequences of bus deregulation, and its concomitant, privatisation (or, better, re-structuring), are working through to the benefit of the consumer by way of the increased freedom of managers to take bottom-line decisions independent of political or administrative edict, and the pressure of the market to see that these decisions are product-related. It must not be expected that such a process can deliver the instant satisfaction that proponents of deregulation are supposed (erroneously) to have expected, but rather that the pressure is on to discover what the market signals as its requirements, and to satisfy them.

10.3 The prospect in view

This moderately optimistic conclusion could form the basis for a rather bullish forecast, were it not for the considerable uncertainties in what is still a very fluid situation. Of these, perhaps the most important, if not the most frequently discussed, is the capitalization of the bus industry.

Quoted shares in UK bus companies have been virtually non-existent since 1968, when the British Electric Traction Company agreed to sell its bus-operating subsidiaries to the then Transport Holding Company. (Not a few of these companies had significant outside shareholdings, and were quoted on the London and provincial stock exchanges.) Even before that, it appears that the capital stock of the erstwhile Tilling Group companies had lost significant market value, which is unsurprising in view of the fact that their shares were all held by the state. What is more, it has been claimed that Sir J. Frederick Heaton's established principle, as chief executive of Thomas Tilling, of keeping the finances of each of his companies entirely independent, had been abandoned under state ownership. Rumours circulated from time to time to the effect that this or that company was in difficulties, but all was smoothed over in the annual report of the group.

Thus the capitalization of the industry had lost any financial rationality long before even the imposition of an arbitrary indebtedness upon the newly-formed National Bus Company in 1969. The problems of setting a market price for shares in newly denationalised companies have been highlighted several times in recent years, and the bus industry differs from the better-known examples only in that its privatisation took place piecemeal. But in the process of selling off the NBC companies, the readiness of the market to invest improved as time went on, so that there is as much likelihood of overcapitalization in some cases as there is of undercapitalization in others. To this must be added the quasi-political decisions as to the selection of management groups as preferred purchasers of the so-called Public Transport Companies in the former metropolitan county areas, and it is clear that a highly artificial situation exists in the capital structure of the bus industry in England and Wales, and, potentially, in Scotland too.

With such distortions, it is impossible for the capital market to function normally, and, as a consequence, many board-room decisions must take on a shade of unreality. This, as much as anything else, gives an air of irrationality to some of the strategic decisions that are currently being made, as well as to the emergence of certain ownership groups throughout the United Kingdom. In a deregulated industry the emergence of ownership groups need not be a clog on competition, provided that adequate anti-trust regulations are enforced, but instability due to the artificial capital situation is probably a more serious problem. What is more, it is commonly assumed that it will be some ten years before a process of profit-taking, and some insolvencies, can lead to a more stable and rational situation.

The uncertainties arising from this analysis must act as a barrier to any attempt to project the future consequences of deregulation as such. In addition, there is some evidence that managers in some companies are still unsure as to their mission. Few textbooks in the area of strategic decision-taking have used case studies from the bus industry! Competition is still seen by many as on-the-road confrontation, rather than as a process in which the company strives to offer the mix of price and quality of service best matched to customer demand. (It must seem strange that the latter definition is to be found in Ponsonby's analysis (Ponsonby, 1969), and was what he was teaching his students in the 1950s.)

It seems that some delay in the benefits of deregulation reaching the consumer was inevitable. There may be a kind of inertia, of a behavioural kind, that can perhaps be accounted for by the scale and impact of change, after 50 years of regulation and quantity control, with its attendant protection. No doubt we should be grateful that there was not the sudden total collapse into chaos that the prophets of doom forecast, with a vehemence that indicates their fear of change. But the interim conclusion remains, that the forces of the market will continue to move the industry away from its product-driven past to a market-led future, since in anything but the short run this is the only way to survive.

We may add in passing that such a process must involve the evolution of a more sophisticated approach to costing than the industry tolerated in its protectionist years, and (as has been suggested) a complementary shift away from cost-plus pricing. There are signs that this evolution is already taking place. What is a more open question is the significance of market domination.

Expectations that the Transport Act 1980 would produce a competitive pattern in long-distance coach operation were quickly disappointed, as National Express used its strong route cover and its hegemony of the High Street booking agencies and the coach terminals to see off the initial attempt at competition by the Consortium (Douglas, 1987). Even so, Douglas concluded that there had been a net welfare gain. Currently we have seen an increase of competition on the Anglo–Scottish routes, where National Express has challenged the incumbent, while at the same time coming under criticism in the media as to the quality of its own services. From this scenario it is possible to conclude, provisionally at least, that market dominance is a relatively short-run clog on pressures towards consumer satisfaction.

One criticism of the dispensation prior to 1986 was the manifest examples of diseconomies of scale, due to the remoteness of management in the larger bus companies. The evidence suggests that decentralization of management decision-making has been pursued, though to different degrees in different companies. In an industry where there is general agreement that true economies of scale are limited, span of control becomes a key measure, and the author's current research suggests that there is general awareness of this. For consumer satisfaction, and hence the continued financial health of bus companies, it is thus essential that the contestability of the market be maximized; a subject to which we shall return.

If the pressure of the market is thus to discourage market domination, and to undermine the viability of firms whose dominance is unduly effective, the emergence of a series of ownership groups would not seem to herald the 'return to the 30s' that some pessimists have forecast. The dominance of the Tilling & British combine, and that of SMT in Scotland, was after all a consequence of the protection afforded by the Road Traffic Act 1930, and the 'establishment' of the industry, along with the railway companies, had undoubtedly foreseen the stability that the Act would afford them. That this stability would in due course decay into complacency, and that in the 1960s and after managers would be accused, with good grounds, of abusing the monopoly that the Act gave them, was not foreseen by its proponents. In today's dispensation the penalties for abuse of the quasi-monopoly of market dominance are more readily apparent.

There are however forces making for distortion in the market, which must be examined before we leave the prospects for the consumer. The possibility of political change, as a general election approaches, must be reckoned part of the problem of inertia that has been discussed, if it were to be true that a hankering remains for a more dirigiste system, such as the opposition parties would seem to favour. Such a system would, it appears, transfer decision-making to the local authorities, working through a tendering process such as exists today for 'socially necessary' services. To comment on this is to enter a grey area, for there is little work on the consequences of the existing system.

Observation however suggests that the extent, though not the effectiveness of tendering depends strongly upon the political will of the local authority concerned. Heroic attempts seem to have been made to arrive at an objective definition of what is 'socially necessary', but these, at least from the perspective of New Right theorists (including the neo-Austrian school of scholars such as Hayek) must lean more to ingenuity than to rigour, in the face of the subjectivity of the market. Nevertheless it must be observed that a prima facie case could be made out for recognizing the tendering system as a clog on the working out of market forces: the tendering authority is, by definition, a purchaser, equipped with a more or less deep purse, but lacking in the ability to assess subjectively the value of what is being bought.

Paradoxically, the tendering system can also be seen as aiding the pressure of competition to satisfy the consumer, by favouring the entry of new suppliers to the market. Widespread evidence from the trade press suggests that small traders have moved from the charter sector to line-haul operation by way of experience of running tendered services. It is not easy at present to strike a balance of cost and benefit in this matter, where data is still largely anecdotal; there is an urgent need for research.

Perhaps equally problematic is the impact of the UK anti-monopoly legislation. As has been seen, there appears little need for concern about market dominance so long as the market is contestable, and so long as the 'patchwork quilt' of ownership groups remains in place. There seems to be a consensus that the Office of Fair Trading has been less than effective in maintaining standards, but here again the evidence is scattered, and no systematic work has yet been done to analyse it. The work of the Traffic Commissioners, on the other hand, in enforcing the quality control aspect of the 1985 Act, seems to have been above reproach, reinforced as it is by extensive reports of their decisions in the trade papers, *pour encourager les autres*.

The foregoing discussion may be summed up by reference to the extent of contestability, which must be the touchstone against which the prospects for the consumer and the industry are judged. Here we must remember that Baumol (1982) postulated the opportunity for speedy entry and exit of firms into the transport industry, 'hit-and-run competition', as the key to effective contestability. That possibility is still significantly limited.

Here the most obvious constraint is the so-called 42-days rule, whereby notice has to be given of any new initiative, and of exit from the market. As early as 1963 the present author advocated some such brake upon the speed of change after deregulation (Hibbs, 1963), but only for an interim period, since the subsequent perturbations could not be forecast. The need to give such notice has proved redundant, but for the immediate future its effect is plainly to rule out hit-and-run by requiring the trader concerned to show his hand. (The 42-days *exit* rule may be a greater constraint, but an alternative exists, to which we shall return.)

The most problematic area is perhaps the embargo upon co-ordination that has proved so difficult for the Office of Fair Trading to enforce. Ostensibly, any market-sharing agreement between two or more traders can be a barrier to the entry of new competition, yet to take this to the extent of outlawing co-ordinated headways or interavailability of return and period tickets must work to the consumers' disadvantage. In any case, gentlemen's agreements in smoke-filled rooms well distanced from the territory of any of the traders concerned can never be adequately policed. (Word has it that these are not unknown.) Part of the problem here is that, while economic theory would predict that new competition should occupy the vacant slots in a given headway of journeys, the whole history of the industry shows a tendency for competing services all to leave at the same time; only a theory of management behaviour can account for this, but such a theory is still lacking.

Even more difficult, and probably even more of a barrier to contestability, is the issue of predatory pricing. Although the industry has so far fought shy of price wars, there have been a number of reported cases where a large firm has been able to use its resources to undermine the competition of a new entrant by keeping fares low. In some cases it has been claimed that the fares concerned have involved the larger firm in a net loss at the margin. Reaction time for policing such situations may be so slow as to be overtaken by the demise of the competition, thus bringing the fair trading laws into disrepute. It may be that awareness of the risk of predation is the greatest disincentive to potential competitors from the coaching sector, with its characteristic small-trader background.

Before we turn to the possibilities for improvement of the prospect, there is one remaining issue to be faced, which is the argument that the market is itself in decline. Figure 10.1 suggests that this may be the case, but also indicates the point of impact at which this decline might be halted. That impact must be a more sophisticated and hard-hitting marketing effort than the bus industry has ever known, and while there is evidence that some firms are aware of both the need and the relevant techniques, the scale of effort required may not be fully recognized. For the conventional wisdom is still that 95% of passengers travel regularly on one or at most two services, and can be expected to continue to do so.

Even if true, this neglects the 5% who may be impulse buyers, as well as the need to ensure repeat purchases from the rest. (Marketing language like this being still foreign to most of the industry.) Still more, it neglects the essential need for promoting sales in new market segments. Positive, aggressive marketing is essential for the prospects of the industry; deregulation makes it possible, but it is not yet too much in evidence.

Figure 10.1 Public transport – the cycle of decay (with acknowledgement to Professor K. M. Gwilliam)

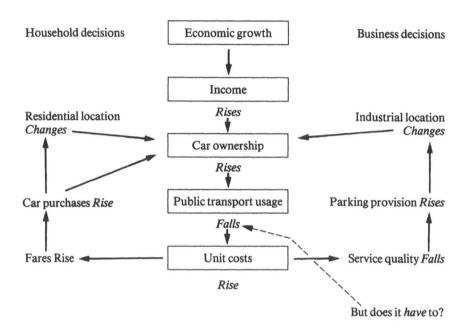

10.4 Possibilities for the way ahead

The intellectual baggage inherited from 50 years of protectionism is still holding back the UK bus industry and inhibiting its ability to exploit deregulation to the advantage of the consumer. No prescription can be made to overcome this problem, and only time and experience will release the energies locked up in the situation. The process of capital readjustment must take its course, and the optimization of fleet size must equally follow from market pressures, which will not move fast. (The opportunity seems to have been lost to ensure the break-up of the market dominating 'public transport companies' in the former metropolitan counties, thereby delaying still further the emergence of market-led managerial ethos at or near the point of sale.)

There is much truth in the adage that you can't make people righteous by Act of Parliament, but there are a few adjustments to the statutory framework that could encourage the bus managers to be more market responsive. The requirement to register a local service has very little significance beyond the effect of the 42-days rule. (It does not even produce meaningful data for research, so skimpy is the information published in the regional *Notices & Proceedings* of the Traffic Commissioners.) Given that a strong case can be made for abandoning the requirement to give 42 days' notice of a new service or a substantial change, in order to improve contestability, the registration requirement itself could well be done away with. There would remain a case for retaining the exit requirement of 42 days' notice, if tendering authorities are to be informed of cases where a replacement might be justified on grounds of social need; but this could be equally well achieved by requiring all operators of regular services (appropriately defined) to give such notice in at least one local newspaper.

Though apparently small, this would be a benefit to all operators, by reducing the volume of paperwork that the present system requires. Inspection of *Notices & Proceedings* discloses an atavistic habit of listing the 'grant' of registration (which is in fact mandatory), so a certain symbolic value, of significance to the minds of civil servants, might also be obtained. In any case, by pure Benthamite standards, it is desirable to dismantle any bureaucratic structure that cannot be shown to have a welfare benefit.

More controversial must be the function and consequences of the residual powers of local authorities (including the Passenger Transport Executives) through the tendering system. It must be concluded for the time being that the effect of the system in terms of contestability is open to question. More work and informed debate is needed here, but the defence of the system has to meet the criticism from New Right thinking that it tends to override the subjectivity of the market. In this context the more pro-active local authorities, some of whom seem to be setting up as vicarious bus operators, would seem the first target for investigation.

Finally there is the position of the Office of Fair Trading. With its remit to investigate anti-competitive behaviour, and in the face of market dominance as a clog on the processes of consumer satisfaction, it should have a creative part to play; yet the industry is less than enthusiastic. Managers divide themselves into those who see it as an irrelevant burden and those who actively distrust it. Perhaps a big step forward would be for a more open debate, with the officials themselves involved, as to its future function.

The way ahead, in this author's view, remains promising. To revert to older pattern of constraint and protectionism would be to abandon the UK bus industry to a depressing function of administering charity to the car-less poor. No manager worthy of the name would stay long in that atmosphere. Let the market remain, therefore, to challenge managers to work harder so as to find and satisfy what the consumer wants, at prices the consumer is prepared to pay.

References

Barrett, S. D. (1982) *Transport policy in Ireland* Dublin: Irish Management Institute.
Baumol, W. J. (1982) Contestable markets – an uprising in the theory of industry structure *American Economic Review* 7, 1.
Buses (White Paper), 1984, London: HMSO.

Chester, D. N. (1936) *Public control of road passenger transport* Manchester: Manchester University Press.

Douglas, N. J. (1987) *A Welfare assessment of transport deregulation: the case of the express coach market in 1980* Aldershot: Gower.

Herzberg, F. (1966) *Work and the nature of man* London: Staples Press.

Hibbs, J. (1963) *Transport for passengers* London: Institute of Economic Affairs.

Hibbs, J. (1982) *Transport without politics...?* London: Institute of Economic Affairs.

Hibbs, J. (1989) *Evidence for and against a paradigm shift among bus managers in the United Kingdom since 1985*, PTRC, Proceedings of Summer Annual Meeting, Seminar B.

Kenny, M. (1982) Le droit comparé des transports en commun en France et aux Isles Britanniques. Unpublished PhD thesis, Université Jean Moulin, Lyon.

Plant, A. (1932) Co-ordination and competition in transport *Journal of the Institute of Transport* **13**, 3.

Ponsonby, G. J. (1969) *Transport policy: co-ordination through competition* London: Institute of Economic Affairs.

PIB (1968) *Proposed increases by the British Railways Board in certain country-wide fares and charges* National Board for Prices & Incomes, Cmnd. 3656 of 1968, London: HMSO.

Yearsley, I. (1986) *Abroad there is no D-Day*. Frederick Speight Lecture to the Chartered Institute of Transport (unpublished). Delivered at Lougborough, 28 October.

CHAPTER 11

Deregulation: problems, warnings and a continuing case for regulation

Philip Bell and Paul Cloke

11.1 The grounds for evaluating policy

Not all of the arguments against privatisation and deregulation in the transport sector stem from staunch defenders of the status quo making dire predictions in apocalyptic language, as John Hibbs seems to suggest in Chapter 10. It is true that those espousing New Right concepts have tended to claim both the 'moral' and the 'radical' high ground over the last decade, thereby casting anyone who disagrees as conservative, inflexible and anachronistic. It seems equally valid to suggest that the language and politics of economic efficiency have assumed greater legitimization over this period, challenging wider ranging notions of cost and benefit and replacing them with rather narrower economic concepts. Acceptance of these changes can make any critic of New Right policies appear rather like a dinosaur enjoying a wilderness experience! Before examining the evidence of the effects of privatisation and deregulation that has been presented in this book, however, we think it opportune to question some of the broader-brush assumptions made by supporters of these measures.

Several previous chapters have stressed that privatisation should not be analysed in isolation of the wider political circumstances in which it was born. Evaluation of whether policy measures are good or bad, beneficial or detrimental, and so on will therefore very much depend on an assumed analysis of these wider circumstances. We use the term 'assumed' analysis because very rarely are commentaries of specific policy measures such as those discussed in this book accompanied by an explicit framework of analysis of the wider political scene. Sometimes, as with many of the chapters here, the constraint on space means that such matters have to be suppressed to an implicit level. On other occasions, however, there is an unwillingness to accept that economic analysis cannot be objective, apolitical or neutral. Rather, discussion of policy assumes that decisions are matters of technical unbiased arbitration, and that criticism of different policy regimes such as regulation and deregulation can be accepted at face value without reference to underlying frames of political analysis.

We believe that policy studies are inherently political, both because policy is an apparatus of the state which in turn is driven by highly politicized social relations, and because policy students bring their own political proclivities to their studies (see Cloke & Little, 1990). We further believe that the political and economic backcloth to the policy trends of privatisation and deregulation is an essential prerequisite to the understanding of specific changes in transport policy (Bell & Cloke, 1989).

In illustration of these contentions it is useful to review the widely agreed list of factors which have been used in favour of regulation and deregulation of transport. Regulation is thereby supported in terms of:

(a) facilitating comprehensive transport networks, including those which are unremunerative;
(b) thereby, providing access to non-mobile social groups;
(c) ensuring safety of operation;
(d) protecting infrastructure on the grounds of national security;
(e) creating order out of potential chaos.

All of these reasons can be viewed in a technical sense as legitimate grounds for policies of regulation. Equally, deregulation has strong supporting arguments:

(a) it allows a clearer distinction between those parts of the transport system which serve the market economy;
(b) it provides incentives for operators to perform efficiently;
(c) it permits efficient operators to seek a share in, or greater share in the market.

These arguments collectively also represent a seemingly legitimate reason for undertaking a particular form of policy activity. How, then, if both sets of supportive arguments are valid, is the decision made as to which to pursue? Is it currently merely a question of the advantages of deregulation outweighing the disadvantages of deregulation, or alternatively the inefficiencies of the market being less than those of the state sector? Such a weighing up of 'advantage' and 'efficiency' raises immediate definitional questions relating to who decides what is efficient or advantageous, and which social groups bear the brunt of disadvantage and inefficiency. Either there is some form of automatic higher order economic truth about efficiency (of the kind currently being exercised in arguments that higher unemployment is required so as to depress wage rises so as to lower inflation) which transcends issues of disadvantage, or we must look deeper into prevailing political economic circumstances to discover why one policy is favoured over another.

Chapters 1 and 8, dealing with Britain and the USA respectively, have presented clear indications of the circumstances which have favoured the introduction of privatisation and deregulation policies. Kenneth Button has demonstrated that deregulation in the USA was at least partially linked with both a rejection of the regulatory mechanisms in place at the time and with an ideological switch itself associated with prevailing economic conditions and ideas. Regulation was judged to be both of high cost, and prone to capture either by transport industries or the regulators themselves, with these organizations seeking to perpetuate themselves regardless of their actual achievements. During a period of economic stagnation and inflation – stagflation – popular ideology began to adopt ideas from the economic theories of the Chicago School, and wider matters of public expenditure, economic efficiency and the freedom of markets were subsumed into policies for specific sectors such as transport. Thus 'technical' matters of transport are subjugated to wider ideologies of the relationship between the private and public sectors.

In Britain there was a similar context for policy change. Chapter 1 highlights key ideological goals of the Thatcher administration – for example to reduce the power of trade unions, to change the nature of local authority activity, and to reduce local public spending – which when combined with significant doses of political pragmatism led to a programme of privatisation and deregulation. We also point out in that chapter that the objectives of different parts of that programme have not been mutually consistent, and that policies for any particular sector, such as transport, have encapsulated a range of political and economic goals which render the evaluation of 'success' extremely problematic.

Deregulation, then, is a response to previous political and economic policies, and has been promoted in particular circumstances at particular times in different nations. It has a strong ideological component, and seems to be influenced by 'demonstration effects' presented by the implementation of similar policies elsewhere. All of these factors are politically charged, and therefore analysis of them is similarly politically charged. The decisions of governments are bound up with the power that is generated from prevailing social relations within the wider order and purpose of the state.

Most theorists of state purpose and function (see Dunleavy & O'Leary, 1987, for a summary) suggest that particular groups in society – often classified as class or capital fractions – are able to dominate social relations to the extent that they derive consistent beneficial bias from state activities. Major changes in the direction of government policy may therefore be considered in the light of the changing needs of these powerful groups. For example, it might be argued that key fractions of capital found it profitable to operate within a regulated market in the 1960s and early 1970s, but that their opportunities for capital accumulation became restricted at the end of that period and a deregulatory phase was required in order to create new opportunities for profit. At the same time, the necessity to assemble and mollify large place-based workforces can be linked with policies of collective consumption such as the state provision of housing and transport. However, with the greater flexibility of the location and size of labour requirements in the late 1970s and early 1980s, the necessity for collective consumption dwindled and public sector functions could be handed over to the private sector.

These ideas have been woven together in the concept of a changeover from Fordist to post-Fordist relations in economy, society, politics and culture (see, for example, Harvey, 1989 and Martin, 1989). Space does not permit a full treatment of the complex debates surrounding these concepts, but very simply it has been proposed that particular economic regimes of capital accumulation have been accompanied by 'ensembles' of relations which have been broadly beneficial to the implementation of the regime concerned. Thus, 'Fordist' accumulation based on specialist large-scale forms of production was linked in Britain with a strong patriarchal welfare state, set procedures for labour representation, and some devolution of policy-making to local governments. It is argued, somewhat contentiously, that a new – post-Fordist – regime of production, based on flexible forms of capital accumulation, has been associated with a rather different ensemble of social–cultural relations including the privatisation of welfare, a promotion of acquisitive sectional interest, and an 'enterprise' culture. Strong local government and trade unions would be barriers to this accumulation regime and have therefore been the subject of social and political conflict. Seen in this light, the debate over regulation and deregulation represents a small facet of a much wider search to understand societal change in developed nations.

The chapters in this book by Brian Fullerton, Kenneth Button and Peter Rimmer serve not only as excellent sources for comparative ideas relating to the detailed planning of transport systems in different nations, but also as a strong reminder that these changing public–private sector relations are a crucial backcloth to policy change in a range of different nation-states. Equally they demonstrate that there is no 'universal' or 'automatic' post-Fordist response in any one nation. Compare, for example, the very high and consistent priority given to social welfare in Sweden with that in the USA, and the different levels of unionization and local government power in South-East Asian nations compared with those in Fordist Britain.

The grounds for evaluating transport policies, therefore, are wide-ranging and complex, and belie any easy or trite summaries of policy success or prognosis. It is, however, important that specific policy measures are located fully within this wider political–economic framework and that links are drawn between structural issues and particular policy events. We now turn, therefore, to a discussion of the impacts of the 1985 Transport Act in Britain. This presents a useful specific illustration of the implementation of a multi-faceted policy of privatisation and deregulation. It also presents a worldwide demonstration effect which, as Peter Rimmer acknowledges in Chapter 9, is likely to be readily copied in some of the South-East Asian nations, and indeed will form part of the broad New Right package currently being grasped at by Eastern European nations wishing to borrow the perceived successes of the West.

11.2 Deregulation of public transport in Britain

Given the potential framework for evaluation presented above, it is important to avoid two significant pitfalls.

(a) Being overimpressed by propaganda evaluations of policy inspired by a government which will naturally be seeking to legitimize its own actions.

(b) Being overzealous in searching out hidden agendas and deterministic outcomes of either theory or ideology since we have acknowledged in previous chapters that economic and social structures are worked out differently through particular agencies in particular localities, and that ideology has been intermixed with political pragmatism in the implementation of policy.

Such avoidance is perhaps more easily suggested than performed. Assessments of the impact of post-1985 transport systems in Britain run into immediate difficulties regarding different perceptions of what is a 'proper' time-span over which developments should be charted. Thus in Chapter 3 Martin Higginson stresses that while it is the essence of a deregulated environment that no stable outcome is reached, it is expected that there will be an initial burst of activity followed by a slower rate of change once the most pressing adjustments have been made. What we have already seen in the first four or five years of deregulation, then, might be thought of as formative in this sense. Conversely, John Hibbs in Chapter 10 suggests that a decade needs to elapse before the 1985 changes can be assessed satisfactorily. Instant judgement will thus not have any significant value, and Hibbs' own analysis is carefully couched in terms of 'emerging prospects'.

Both of these views are appropriate. It would be foolish to make definitive snap judgements on the evidence to date, particularly as government sweeteners - for example, the transitional grants and innovation grants in rural areas (see Chapter 6) - have operated over this initial period. Evidence presented in this book suggests that in coming years both the likelihood of powerful operators to exploit the new conditions, and the ability of local authorities to continue subsidies at current levels are likely to change significantly. However, it is also the case that these initial five years after the Act are sufficient to detect the nature of Higginson's 'initial burst of activity'. Changes in operator and local authority behaviour can at least be understood against this new backcloth.

Empirical evidence of the impacts of the Act is equally prone to very different emphases of analysis. Chapters 4, 5 and 6 present accounts of research in three different locality types. Each account offers a range of indicators which can be used to indicate success or failure, depending on the required meaning to be attached to these labels. In the metropolitan regions, for example, revenue support has been decreased (by an average of some 20%), network penetration has been slightly increased, and service frequencies have been increased during most time periods, while there are less early morning and Sunday services, fares have increased by an average of 27.5% in real terms over the first two years, patronage of services has fallen by some 16.2% on average – with greater decreases in areas where expenditure limits have been imposed on local authorities – and wage rates for workers in the bus industry have fallen. For Hibbs (Chapter 10), the consequences of deregulation are working through to the benefit of the consumer because managers have increased freedom to take decisions. For Banister and Pickup (Chapter 4), the savings to payers of taxes, rates and the community charge, are being passed on to a reduced band of travellers through higher fares. For the government, a 20% saving in public expenditure has been achieved at no cost in terms of service levels. Yet it could (and in our view should) be argued that the inability of deregulation to halt the decrease in general bus use, and in particular the reduction in bus use by non-mobile low income groups, is a very significant disbenefit of the policy. Such an outcome is unsurprising, though, given the expectations of the reduced role for collection consumption, including public transport, in the post-Fordist ensemble of social and economic relations.

In the outer metropolitan areas, the picture is slightly less conclusive, but Stanley points to some important factors which make future prospects quite gloomy. Initially in these areas levels of commercial registrations were high, leading to considerable savings in local authority subsidy. Non-peak (Sundays and early mornings) and low-load (often rural) services were replaced through local authority tenders, and although there were few examples of sustained competition between operators, fare levels were reasonably stable in real terms. However, this pattern of operations has been disrupted by dramatic levels of deregistration of commercial routes. Having pre-empted potential competitors, the large and entrenched operators are able to deregister in the expectation that they will win routes back with local authority subsidy. This appears to be a wilful strategy by managers who have increased freedom to take such decisions. As Stanley notes in his example of Bee Line services in Berkshire, the routes which were deregistered were selected less because of their poor financial importance and more because of a perception that the county council would be forced to reinstate them. In the event this perception was remarkably accurate. Deregistrations in a context of low rates of local competition have increased the number and cost of local authority contracts and any initial savings have been quickly eroded.

If the post-deregulation picture in metropolitan areas suffers by comparison with the previous political commitment to inexpensive mass-use systems, the outer metropolitan areas 'benefit' because of a lower level of pre-deregulation use of buses. Patronage reductions are therefore not as significant as in the metropolitan areas, but as Stanley indicates, fares increases are now becoming sustained, at least in part because bus companies are having to pay higher wages again in order to attract sufficient staff, a particular problem in the South-East. Certainly most passengers in these areas have not experienced any great benefit from on-the-road competition. Indeed, it seems increasingly to be the case that established operators consider the buying up of smaller potential competitors as the most efficient method of dealing with their new decision-making arena. Thus competition is being reduced not increased in the restructuring of the industry into ever larger units. We return to this point later in the chapter.

In the outer rural areas (Chapter 6) we presented evidence from a study in rural Wales where pre-deregulation levels of bus use were comparatively low. Here, aside from the more densely populated urban corridors, local authorities had to issue contracts for most routes and the low level of competition for tenders led to no significant savings being made in these areas. Moreover, the largest entrenched operator in the area, Crosville Wales, had begun to adopt a management strategy of not bothering with any route that would not return a reasonable profit, and several routes were thereby relinquished to private operators who at the stage of the next tender will be able to bid at a more realistically profitable (and therefore expensive) level. Again, the signs are that local authorities will face increasingly higher bills for socially necessary services in future years. In some senses, the impact of deregulation in rural areas such as those discussed in Chapter 6 is certainly not as catastrophic as some commentators predicted prior to the legislation (Bell & Cloke, 1990). Currently, the pre-deregulation networks are still largely in place and the rural non-mobile still receive roughly the same (poor) levels of service as before. Deregulation has not, however, increased opportunities in these areas. The theory that deregulation would sponsor competitive services resulting in higher frequencies and lower fares has been a mirage. If the fears for the future are confirmed, and local authority spending restrictions have the impact of being able to support fewer subsidized services in rural areas, deregulation – far from detaching rural services from the dead welfare hand of the public sector – will actually have heightened operator perceptions of the poor economic returns to be made from many rural bus services. It will actually be more of a case of 'subsidize or bust' than it was before. In these locales at least, John Higgs' exhortation in Chapter 10 to let the market remain in order to satisfy what the consumer wants at prices the consumer is prepared to pay will be falling on empty bus-shelters.

11.3 Deregulation, privatisation and social necessity

Evidence from these specific studies of bus deregulation permits some further discussion of the broader components of policy available to current and future governments. As Peter Rimmer has suggested in Chapter 9, there are a series of combinations of reform with which to change existing public sector transport systems. In Britain the particular mix of privatisation, deregulation and contracting out seems to have permitted managers to adjust their networks of provision, but has largely failed to stimulate the promotion of new competitive ventures (see Chapter 5). In Peter Stanley's words, the market for local bus services is 'ultimately not worth contesting' certainly within the current arena of competition.

It could be argued, therefore, that the current policy programme is experiencing internal conflicts of objectives. There is neither a sufficiently free marked in which to stimulate full competition and the benefits that are thought to accrue from such competition, nor sufficient willingness to regard public transport as a collective welfare necessity. The particular form of 'half market, half social necessity' which is currently in place satisfies neither objective, although it has achieved (at least in the short-term) the goals of diminishing trade union power and reducing public expenditure on subsidies. Many of the fears of opponents of the measures have not been fully realized precisely because competition has been relatively muted. It might then be relatively pointless to switch to one of the alternative systems described in Chapter 2, which would permit some competitive edge, but allow more co-ordination in the network. Greater acceptance of regulation would also allow some measures to be taken against the emergence of powerful regional monopolies. Evidence presented in this book suggests that both the ability of transport workers to bargain for higher wages and the numbers and costs of subsidized services will increase again over the medium and long term.

These apparently conflicting objectives point to a more detailed examination of the ideas of competition and social necessity which are central to any privatisation and deregulation programmes.

Competition

Several of the previous chapters have highlighted the concept of *contestability* as the key factor in the evaluation of competitive regimes. If contestability is achieved, then the prospects both for the transport industry and for the transport consumer are held to be good by supporters of deregulation. Although there are a number of different levels of contestability (see Dodgson & Katsoulacos, 1989), perhaps the most commonly identified threshold of effective competition is the presence of hit-and-run competition. Thus the provision of a transport service can only be effectively competitive if the circumstances governing contestability permit the free entry and exit of operators on any route in any area.

There is almost universal agreement that this level of contestability has been limited in the case of post-deregulation bus service provision in Britain. Evidence in Chapters 4 and 5 suggests that in the more highly populated areas, which in theory represent reasonable arenas of competition, fewer, larger operators tend to run most of the services, with smaller firms often limited to tendered work under the 'socially necessary' schemes. Peter Stanley stresses the point, for example, that the only two cases of on-the-road competition have occurred in the outer metropolitan areas of his study. Elsewhere, actual or threatened competition by smaller firms against larger firms has been met either by the bludgeoning tactics of short-term saturation services so as to run the competitor off the road, or by the buying out of the smaller by the larger firm as the quickest method of preventing competition. In the remoter rural areas, which arguably represent less promising arenas of competition, there are far fewer commercial registrations, and therefore far less opportunity for on-the-road commercial competition.

Privatisation and deregulation of buses in Britain appear quite quickly to have produced a competitive market in which conditions are ripe for the emergence (or indeed re-establishment) of an oligopolistic operation.

Although the emergence of government statistics on this point is being delayed, it seems clear that some early purchasers of denationalised bus companies have pursued a quick realization of assets by selling off key property (notably bus stations and offices) in high-value urban locations. Fast profits have led to the capitalization of some companies which has permitted further acquisitions of bus companies. With so many management buy-outs being favoured by government as a legitimation both specifically of denationalisation and of the wider ideology of the enterprise culture, large highly capitalized operators were presented with fairly easy pickings from new owners to whom a fast profitable resale would often be most attractive. As Peter Stanley suggests in Chapter 5 there could soon be five or six companies controlling the whole bus industry. Early sales permitted by the taking of quick profits are now being replaced by further purchases by bus companies who see acquisition as a route to seeing off potential competition and gaining valuable production resources such as experienced drivers and town centre bus stations.

These conditions during the slide towards oligopoly have certainly presented managers with more freedom of decision-making. This freedom has, however, been inevitably geared towards profitability and corporate success rather than consumer services. Naturally it can be argued that success and service go hand-in-hand, but evidence thus far permits a gloomier interpretation. Innovation, such as the introduction of minibuses, has been undertaken with a multiplicity of objectives in mind, and high on the list have been the reduction of drivers' wages and the forestalling of potential or actual competition. Conditions are now changing, however, with the onset of increasing oligopoly. Drivers are able to bargain for higher pay rates again, and these additional staff costs will inevitably be passed through to the consumer or the local authority tender. With less competitors around, these cost increases will be less challenged even under a supposedly competitive system. Contestability will therefore decrease, not increase over time, and consumers will have their willingness to pay stretched to the limit, while local authorities will have their ability to pay similarly stretched.

One possible evaluation of this particular deregulatory programme is that further steps should be taken to free the market and improve contestability. John Hibbs in Chapter 10 argues that some delay is inevitable in the benefits of deregulation reaching the consumer, but the only way forward is to permit a more market-led future in which current barriers to contestability are broken down. These barriers include:

(a) the 42-days rule, which refers to the current notice required for any entry or exit to the market, and which is seen as a significant barrier to hit-and-run competition.
(b) the embargo on co-ordinated workings and inter-related ticketing by different operators. This embargo is enshrined in the legislation and policed by the Office of Fair Trading.
(c) predatory pricing, whereby a highly capitalized existing operator can undermine a new competing operator by keeping fares artificially low.

Before this situation can be policed as an unfair trading practice, the competitor may have gone under.

(d) local authority tendering is seen to override the subjectivity of the market, and some local authorities are criticized for establishing themselves as 'vicarious bus operators'.

It is interesting to take a consumer-eye view of what might happen if these barriers were to be removed, and indeed a more conceptual view of the degree to which such changes would be mutually consistent. Removal of the 42-days rule might encourage hit-and-run competition, but would lead to chaos for customers. The confusion over who was running what service, when and where which was apparent on Deregulation Day, could be replicated in smaller measure *ad infinitum* unless some notice is served of entry and exit. Moreover notice of exit permits the local authority concerned to replace the service with a socially necessary tender if no other operator is running the route. The notion of 'fast buck' operators switching on and off routes willy nilly, with no sense of commitment to their consumers appears to belie the argument that what is good for the operator is good for the consumer. Removal of the requirement to give notice of entry and exit would be to remove a sensible safeguard for the travelling public.

Permission for different firms to run co-ordinated working and inter-related ticketing schemes would be more beneficial to bus travellers. After all, some routes operated under socially necessary tenders are worked by different operators at some times of the day or days of the week different to the commercial operator on the route. The public are therefore now used to this form of co-ordination. Equally, interchangeability of ticketing only mirrors the customer loyalty policies of the larger concerns who offer reductions on return or period tickets. It is more arguable, however, whether these measures would encourage and sustain attempts by small firms to enter into the competition. Given the current predilection for the capitalization of the industry into bigger blocks, it seems likely that these attempts to co-ordinate – which tend to happen informally at present anyway – would fuel the process of the agglomeration of ever-larger bus companies.

The arguments against predatory pricing appear incongruous alongside calls for the market to have its way. Undermining a competitor through a policy of artificially low fares will perhaps benefit the bus user in the short term, but presumably in the longer term predatory pricing can be replaced by monopolistic pricing within the area concerned to the detriment of the consumer. This particular barrier to contestability begs *additional* regulation in order to protect the new entrant firm – a move not only conflicting with the further deregulation required to lift the barriers already mentioned, but also conflicting with the notion of more free competition generally. The tortuous internal logic, which identifies the risk of predation as a major disincentive to competition yet argues that the free market should remain to challenge managers to serve consumers, will defeat many an analyst of wider deregulation issues in the transport field.

The final barrier – that of local authority involvement in tendering – is fundamental to the conflict between competition and social necessity. Local authorities are seen to lack the ability to assess subjectively the value of the tendered services they have purchased. Such tendering is therefore a constraint on market forces, despite being a mechanism which has achieved initial savings for the public purse and which has permitted the entry of new firms into the stage carriage market. Presumably the removal of this subjectivity would require the cessation of any direct decision-making responsibility from local authorities, thus further distancing important issues of local political representation, and co-ordinative planning, which many commentators including ourselves believe to be important. This point is central to the issue of social necessity which is discussed below.

Far from being under-contestable, we regard the current mix of competition and social necessity to have moved too far away from a planned and regulated oligopoly towards an untrammelled private-sector oligopoly. The example of London demonstrates that *competitive regulation* can achieve a different balance of public and private sector responsibility which (setting aside at this point the fares increases compared with previous fares underpinned by Greater London Council subsidies) can reap considerable benefits for the bus traveller. Tenders to run services have introduced scope for economy and innovation, but the contracting out of particular services within a centrally planned and co-ordinated network has retained the co-ordination of fares and ticketing and full control over the quality and quantity of services. This model may be a more suitable basis for wider reform of bus transport than that of a further headlong rush towards market forces. It would also be more progressive to ensure that gains in efficiency are genuinely that; not merely a case of asset and labour shedding and wage reductions. It is hard to see many bus workers as particularly well paid, and although in areas of labour shortage the market is redressing the balance to some extent, this is not the case elsewhere. Minimum wages and conditions would seem to be a prerequisite for this to occcur.

Social necessity

The deregulation project has further served to beg important questions about why transport should be *public* at all. Market-led transport services will inevitably be driven by a profit motive which will in turn require either the provision of attractive services at the right price (to attract consumers away from alternative suppliers or transport modes) or the exploitation of a dominant market position to structure services and fares towards maximum capital accumulation. The imperfections of these requirements are evident. The first is geographical. Kenneth Button in Chapter 8 has shown how deregulation of transport in the USA led to a decline in bus services, and a loss of air services *to small communities*. It would appear, therefore, that some locations are worse arenas of competition than others, and rural areas and smaller, remoter urban centres have been shown to be disadvantaged under deregulation regimes. The commercial registrations in the rural Wales study area, for example, (Chapter 6) covered a very small part of the overall area. Left to its own devices, then, market-driven transport provision will not supply these unprofitable areas.

What then should society's response be to these 'natural' gaps in the profitable network? Of course there are those who would have us believe that there is no such thing as society (Mrs Thatcher, for example, has been reported as saying this about contemporary Britain). However, even in this acquisitive and self-seeking age it does not seem too archaic to suggest that collective forms of transport for the non-mobile should be one of the primary rights of local citizens. Non-mobility is rarely voluntary and should be an essential target for local government activity. Such activity is not charitable, but a basic response to glaring inequality of opportunity. Although the current provision for 'socially necessary' services has permitted local authorities virtually to buy back pre-deregulation networks of services, there are strong signals that they will soon be faced with dual pressures that will necessitate an erosion of service levels: first, the emergent oligopoly of operators are likely to be able to command higher tenders for socially necessary services; and secondly, further central government restrictions on local government spending will reduce the transport budgets of the local authorities concerned. The social role of public transport in these areas is not a question of local authority planners, with rather cavalier definitions of what is socially necessary, dishing out charity to the car-less poor. This is a fundamental welfare right which should be protected from market-place imperfections.

Social necessity does not only arise in poor arenas of competition. The more densely populated areas, which might be considered to be more fruitful competitive territory, also house significant proportions of non-mobile social groups – some of whom might be unable to afford to use a bus even if the service was being provided on a commercial basis. The comparison is graphic between the 'cheap fares' policies of many metropolitan authorities (prior to their abolition) and the post-deregulation regime where a disturbing reduction in bus use by low income groups has been noted. Equally, there are allied issues in these localities of traffic congestion, environmental pollution and parking. Here too, then, there appears to be a very strong case for local government to be fully involved in planning a transport system which places collective concerns above profit for its own sake. The deregulated system does not permit local authorities the flexibility of effective subsidy through lower fares, and the result has been that the resurgence of public transport under the former metropolitan authorities has given way to reduced patronage and heavier traffic pressures and pollution.

11.4 Looking ahead

Brian Fullerton's account of transport deregulation in Sweden (Chapter 7) has clearly pointed to the conflicts between deregulation and the objectives of a welfare state: it threatens the viability of public transport services in some localities; it restricts the accessibility of non-mobile groups, and it exacerbates the regional differentiation of wealth and opportunity. Sweden is a nation where the majority of voters still appear determined to maintain collective welfare provision. Social aspects of public transport policy are being bolstered by the rising star of Green politics, wherein the development of collective transportation networks is viewed as greatly more environmentally friendly than the proliferation of private vehicles and the roads to drive them on.

In Peter Rimmer's analysis of the restructuring of transport in South-East Asia (Chapter 9) he stresses that increased flexibility and commercialization of transport networks controlled by the public sector may be preferable to an infrastructural organization controlled by the private sector. The privatisation ideologies of the New Right do not constitute a 'universal fix' to the problems of state-sector transport.

In the USA, there are now some pressures for *reregulation* of various kinds, so as to deal with the problems of emergent monopoly power, and to counteract some of the social consequences of deregulation.

Maybe – just maybe – the tide is turning again. The often blind and sometimes unthinking adherence to New Right ideologies of privatisation, when coupled with some very pragmatic implementation in particular sectors such as transport, have highlighted starkly the conflicts between market-led, profit-motivated systems, and the need for collective welfare provision for groups such as the non-mobile. The welfare state in Britain has not been rolled back significantly, it has merely been privatised. There are now signs in public opinion that this process has gone too far. Reform of deregulation to the extent that local authorities resume greater decision-making by operating some form of competitive regulation along the lines of the London model would at least be a start towards redressing the balance. It would certainly have the effect of taking accountability out of the board room (where it can conveniently be forgotten) and putting it back in the realms of local political democracy where it belongs.

References

Bell, P. & Cloke, P. (1989) The changing relationship between the public and private sectors: privatisation and rural Britain, *Journal of Rural Studies* **5**, 1–15.

Bell, P. & Cloke, P. (1990) Deregulation and rural bus services: a study in rural Wales, *Environment and Planning* **A 22**.

Cloke, P. & Little, J. (1990) *The rural state?* Oxford: Oxford University Press.

Dodgson, J. & Katsoulacos, Y. (1989) *Competition, contestability and predation: the economics of competition in deregulated bus markets.* Liverpool Studies on Bus Deregulation WP 6, University of Liverpool.

Dunleavy, P. & O'Leary, B. (1987) *Theories of the state: the politics of liberal democracy.* London: Macmillan.

Harvey, D. (1989) *The condition of postmodernity.* Oxford: Blackwell.

Martin, R. (1989) Industrial capitalism in transition: the contemporary reorganisation of the British space-economy. In Massey, D. & Allen, J. (eds) *Uneven re-development: cities and regions in transition.* London: Hodder & Stoughton.

Index

For Product Safety Concerns and Information please contact our EU
representative GPSR@taylorandfrancis.com Taylor & Francis Verlag GmbH,
Kaufingerstraße 24, 80331 München, Germany

Printed and bound by CPI Group (UK) Ltd, Croydon, CR0 4YY
08/05/2025
01864476-0001